sophie grigson's country kitchen

sophie, grigson's country kitchen

120 seasonal recipes

Sophie Grigson

With photographs by William Shaw

headline

Also by Sophie Grigson:
Eat Your Greens
Sophie Grigson's Meat Course
Sophie Grigson's Taste of the Times
Sophie Grigson's Herbs
Sophie Grigson's Feasts for a Fiver
Sophie Grigson's Sunshine Food

With William Black:
Fish
Organic

First published in 2003 by
HEADLINE BOOK PUBLISHING

10 9 8 7 6 5 4 3 2

Cataloguing in Publication Data is available from the British Library

ISBN 0 7553 1054 3

Typeset in Helvetica Neue and Fineprint by **Fiona Pike**
Designed by **Fiona Pike**
Home Economist **Annabel Ford** and **Kate Fry**
Stylist **Roisin Nield**

Colour reproduction by **Spectrum Colour, Ipswich**
Printed and bound in France by **Imprimerie Pollina s.a.** - L 97003A

Headline Book Publishing
A division of Hodder Headline
338 Euston Road
London NW1 3BH

www.headline.co.uk
www.hodderheadline.com

contents

dedication

This book is dedicated to all those intrepid and determined small producers whose hard work brings so many good things to our tables. May you thrive and multiply.

acknowledgements

First and foremost I would like to thank the amazing team at Headline for all they do to turn my words into real books. In particular, I am phenomenally grateful for the patience of Heather Holden-Brown and Jo Roberts-Miller, who have put up with the most piecemeal and delayed delivery. You girls are saints! Bryone, Wendy and all the rest of you there, thanks for sorting everything out with such grace.

Mr William Shaw, photographer extraordinaire, has been an inspiration, putting heart and soul into making his remarkable record of a year in the countryside. It was sometimes hard to keep up, but always worth it, and William, please don't ever mention ants to me again. The food photographs owe their handsome good looks not only to him, but also to the nimble fingers of Kate Fry and Annabel Ford, and to Fiona Pike who designed the whole book, brave woman.

At home, Sarah Widdicombe and Jennine Hughes have oiled the domestic wheels and kept things ship-shape, as well as being increasingly valued friends. Tall, dark and handsome, Ralph makes sure that raspberries, strawberries and the rest of the fruit flourish, much to our delight. Florence and Sidney have tasted and commented with enthusiasm (usually) and occasional disarming honesty. Mr & Mrs R., next door, have welcomed me in for endless cups of coffee and glasses of wine whenever I've needed to escape, as well as providing recipes, eggs, parsley, runner beans, dogs for walking, and great company. Thank you one and all.

cook's notes

Just in case you are wondering about those little details that never get mentioned in recipes, I am going to tell you about a few of my essential kitchen standards. Most of this will seem obvious to a seasoned cook, but I urge you to read it anyway as it will only take a couple of minutes, and there may be one or two notes that are of use when using this book.

I nearly always use fresh herbs because they give a vigour to a dish that dried can rarely replicate. When I have to buy herbs, I steer clear of those over-crowded supermarket pots of weak-leaved, spindly stemmed 'growing herbs' – they are too immature and sickly to carry any worthwhile flavour. I do use dried bay leaves occasionally, and dried oregano which is so much more intensely aromatic than fresh. Pepper and nutmeg are always freshly ground/grated to capture their true spirit. Ready-ground pepper and nutmeg soon lose their oomph, and are really not worth wasting money on.

All recipes are tested using large, free-range eggs, unless otherwise stated. I use unsalted butter for baking and cooking, though I prefer salted butter on my toast! I employ extra virgin olive oil with considerable abandon: a blended one for cooking proper, and a fancier single estate one for salads and as a condiment added at the end of cooking. If I want a blander oil, I use either sunflower or grapeseed oil. Whatever you choose, don't keep it hanging around out in the light for too long. Oils keep best in a cool dark cupboard, but even there they will turn rancid within six months to a year. You can usually tell by the smell, so check regularly and chuck out oils that have lingered beyond their best.

In the majority of recipes it doesn't matter that much if you swing from metric measurements to imperial. Baking is the major exception: with cakes and biscuits you do have to be more self-disciplined. Note that all spoon measurements throughout the book are rounded. I use a 5ml teaspoon and a 15ml tablespoon.

Finally, please don't imagine that the cooking times I suggest are supposed to be followed rigidly. They are merely guidelines, to give you an idea of what to expect. Be guided by your experience and your senses. Smell, sight, touch, taste and even hearing are important when cooking, and will tell you far more than a bald statement like 'cook for 25 minutes'.

introduction

A record of a year's cooking in a country kitchen... Does that sound like an image from *The Country Diary of an Edwardian Lady*, or Granny Stokes' cosy rosy cottage cooking? Well, forget all that. This is the 21st century, not some throwback to the early years of the last. This is about what goes on in my kitchen, which means it is a loosely modern interpretation of country life and country cooking, founded on seasonal produce and dishes I've loved since I was a child.

The village fête, with its cake stalls and cream teas, is still going strong whatever the weather, but these days village pubs are just as likely to peddle Thai food or lasagne as they are shepherd's pie and roast beef. Basil and coriander are no longer alien substances. The going is still tough for farmers, but the positive outcome of years of agricultural crises is that more and more of them are putting their all into producing the finest meat, fruit and vegetables to sell direct to us, the public.

Farmers' markets are on the increase, thank heavens, giving us ever better access to locally produced ingredients. Joy of joys, you can once again track down beautifully flavoured, locally reared beef, and succulent pheasants from a nearby shoot. Pick-your-owns are thriving, giving us the best quality greens and summer fruit at bargain prices. The hedgerows still yield their bounty of wild garlic, elderflowers, damsons and blackberries. These time-honoured, seasonal ingredients remain the backbone of my cooking, though I may supplement them sometimes with exotic interlopers, or cook them in thoroughly Mediterranean style.

I was born and raised in the country, in deepest darkest Wiltshire, so although I've lived a large chunk of my adult life in cities, I can claim country roots. Nine years out of the big smoke, and I have no wish to return. I'd miss the view of the valley from my front door far too much. I still enjoy the occasional meal in a fashionable restaurant, but my heart lies with the simpler places, where food is presented with honesty and lack of fuss. Likewise, when I cook I may sally forth into chicer dishes every now and then, but I return again and again to those never-forgotten treats of an English country childhood, like cinnamon toast and Grasmere gingerbread – but for that recipe you'll have to buy a copy of *English Food* by my mother, Jane Grigson.

The way I cook now (and here I'm talking in particular about the food I cook for my family and friends, not work cooking) is the product of my past and my delight in the gorgeous simplicity of fresh ingredients. I shop at the bevy of farmers' markets around us when I can, at the supermarket, and sometimes straight from the farm or neighbour when they have something good to sell.

When I moved into my house, in mid-2001, I inherited a garden packed with fruit, which is just heaven. Three apple trees, one pear tree, greengages, Victorias and damsons, gooseberries, raspberries, strawberries and more. I'm gradually increasing the herb count (I do like to have all sorts to hand, so that I can use them with unfettered abandon). I will admit to practically ditching vegetables ever since I discovered an exceptional farm shop (well, farm-hut-in-a-field, actually) and pick-your-own a mere brace of miles away. Courgettes are now the lone vegetable in my garden, grown so that we can eat courgette flower fritters and tiny slim new courgettes to our heart's content throughout the summer.

This book is a celebration of the wealth of fine ingredients grown and raised in our own countryside, not just in my patch, but from Land's End to John O'Groats. We should all take more time to enjoy the pleasures of sitting down together, family and friends, around the table sharing food and life in all its diversity. Here's to happy times and happy meals!

spring

Crab *and* Asparagus Soup

I find some of the traditional British crab soups too rich and cloying to do justice to the crab. However, many of the classic seasonings hit the nail on the head – lemon, anchovy essence, cayenne pepper, spring onions and fresh herbs. In this soup, I've married these with a trio of Asian ingredients to make a soup that is somehow light yet rich, with a fresh and vivid Anglo-eastern flavour. Asparagus add their own vegetable sweetness, but in early summer you could substitute shelled and skinned broad beans or shelled, newly harvested peas, in which case you can reduce the initial cooking to a mere 3 minutes or so.

SERVES 4

1 medium to large **cooked crab**

300ml (½ pint) good **chicken stock**

400ml (14 fl oz) **coconut milk**

250g (9 oz) **asparagus**

cayenne pepper, to taste

2 stems **lemon grass**, bashed flat with a rolling pin

juice of 1–1½ **limes** or 1 small **lemon**

2 tablespoons **anchovy essence**

4 **spring onions**, chopped

½ tablespoon chopped **tarragon**

1½ tablespoons chopped **mint**

½ tablespoon chopped **chives**

• Pick the crab, removing all the flesh and discarding the grey dead man's fingers (see opposite). Keep the brown and the white meats separate. If you have the time, bash up the shell a bit and chuck the pieces into a pan with the stock, adding an extra splash or two of water. Simmer very gently for half an hour, then strain the stock and discard the shell pieces.

• Return the stock to the pan with the coconut milk. Bring up to the boil, then add the asparagus and cayenne pepper. Simmer for about 5–7 minutes until the asparagus is tender. Now stir in all the white crab meat and about half the brown, followed by all the remaining ingredients. Draw off the heat before tasting and fiddling with seasoning. Add more brown crab meat for a stronger crab flavour (especially if you haven't simmered the shell in the stock), more anchovy for saltiness, or lime or lemon juice for sourness. Serve straight away in small bowls. (Save any left over brown meat for a sandwich for your supper.)

Crab

British seaside holidays: water too cold to swim in, deck chairs flapping on the beaches and children oblivious to it all as they drop their lines from the pier in the hope of landing a crab or two to splosh around in their bucket. In April, May and June, the elder, more substantial brethren of those little crabs of holiday fantasy are at their sweet, fullest best before the serious business of sex and breeding reduces their strength. I admit to a predilection for straight dressed crab with home-made lemony mayonnaise, or crab mayonnaise sandwiches on good brown bread with only shredded lettuce and perhaps some sliced cucumber to balance the richness, but no tomato.

HOW TO PICK AND DRESS A CRAB

I have been known to cook crabs myself, but to be honest I can't see why I should make the effort when any fishmonger worth his or her salt can do it so much more easily. The crucial requirement is that the crab should be freshly cooked – i.e. that morning. If I'm offered the choice between a male and female crab, I opt for the male. Some people insist that the hen crab is sweeter, but there is no doubting that the cock is better endowed, with chunkier claws and more capacious body. This makes it easier to pick out the meat, which, given that emptying any crab is necessarily a slow and painstaking job, seems a major advantage to me.

So, once the beast is brought back to your kitchen, here is how to extract the meat.

Begin by twisting off the legs and claws. Crack open the fatter segments of the claws and pick out the white flesh. If you are not the proud owner of a pair of purpose-made lobster crackers and lobster picks, then resort to nutcrackers or a small hammer and a skewer or fine crochet hook. Time and patience will dictate how many of these segments you tackle, but console yourself with the fact that pickings are meagre, to say the least, on the smaller legs.

Now the main body. Turn it on its back and twist off the bony, pointed flap. Push the tip of a knife between the main part of the shell and the bit to which the legs and claws were once attached. Wiggle it around to loosen it, then twist the blade to push it up and remove it. Now you have access to the incredibly rich brown meat that fills the main shell. Scrape it out into its own bowl and keep it separate from the white meat.

Return to the other bit of the body, the bit with all the cavities and little holes. Begin by pulling off the nasty-looking grey gills (the 'dead man's fingers'), which should be binned. Split the body in half. At this stage, a fine crochet hook comes into its own, though a skewer is quite acceptable. Poke it down this hole and that, snaggling out all those sweet, succulent morsels of white flesh to add to the stuff already harvested from the claws and legs. Be patient and thorough, and do your level best not to mix shards of shell in with the meat.

By the time you have finished you should have gathered roughly 220g (8 oz) of brown and white meat from your average crab.

Sorrel Soup

SERVES 4–6

1 **onion**, chopped

30g (1 oz) **butter**

500g (1 lb 2 oz) **floury potatoes**, peeled and cut into chunks

1 litre (1¾ pints) **chicken** or **vegetable stock**

2 really generous handfuls of fresh **sorrel**, roughly shredded

a little **milk**

salt and **pepper**

to serve (optional): a little **double cream**, **fried croutons**

Just the plainest, most basic version of sorrel soup, with no fancy twiddles or deviations. I think it is also the best, in its perfect, tart simplicity. It can be made from late spring right through the summer and on into autumn as your sorrel crop thrusts forward and thrives in full vigour. But, but, but... to me this is essentially a spring soup. The first sorrel soup of the year, with its cleansing sharpness, is one of those small signs that the best, most fecund months sprawl out ahead, and that's something that brings me enormous joy.

If the weather is unexpectedly clement, you can serve sorrel soup chilled, but replace the butter with a tablespoon of sunflower oil.

• Put the onion, butter and potato into a capacious saucepan and place over a gentle heat. Cover tightly and leave to sweat for about 10 minutes, stirring once or twice. Add the stock, salt and pepper and bring up to the boil. Simmer gently for about 15 minutes until the potato is tender.

• Take off the heat, cool for a couple of minutes, then stir in the sorrel. Liquidise in batches. You shouldn't need to sieve it, unless you included a lot of tough stalks. Stir in enough milk to give the consistency of double cream. Taste and adjust seasoning. Reheat just before serving, without boiling.

• Ladle into bowls, and finish with a swirl of double cream and a few crisp croutons, if you wish.

Sorrel

I am writing this at the very beginning of spring. The daffodils are out, the first flowering trees are turning white and the sky is a brilliant blue. From my workroom window I can see birds winging past, twigs in beaks, and if I stand outside the sun is hot enough to warm my back. In short, it is a perfect spring day.

This morning's inspection of the garden revealed that both chives and lovage have already put on an impressive spurt of growth and the fennel is making a shy appearance, but most enthusiastic of all is the sorrel. I've planted sorrel in every garden I've ever had, from the window boxes of my first flat onwards, and it is the one herb that has never let me down.

This particular sorrel is still in its infancy, planted less than a year ago, but grown from one tiny pot's worth to a decent-sized clump. More to the point, there is enough already to provide a bowl of sharp soup for all of us. Once we've moved past that annual staging post, it will again become a regular, if occasional, part of our lunches and dinners right into the late autumn. That's the great thing about sorrel – once established it just keeps right on coming. The one demand is that you cut down the flowering stems that shoot up at an alarming rate in the summer.

You can buy sorrel in supermarkets now and again, but the price is absurd considering its rampant growth pattern. Besides, you never get enough in one small plastic pack to make much of an impression. No, the only answer is to grow your own, just as if you were a wise French housewife.

The lemon-sharp zing of its green leaves makes it an essential herb in France, where it is partnered most famously with fish and eggs. I love a baked egg nestled on a thick puddle of cooked sorrel (shredded and softened in a little butter until it collapses and darkens to a rough purée) mixed with a little double cream, for instance, or a handsome omelette filled with the same mixture, animated perhaps with some scraps of bacon cooked to a crisp. Buttery sorrel purée makes a fabulous accompaniment to rich salmon, or, to turn it into a sauce proper, dilute it with a little fish stock and some cream and season with salt and pepper. I've often used sorrel in stuffings for oily fish – salmon or mackerel perhaps, or indeed, breaking away a little from the French culinary yoke, for pork or goose. The Italian notion of stirring shredded sorrel into a plain risotto (right at the end of the cooking time, along with the Parmesan and butter) is also a good one – no need for white wine as the sorrel provides more than enough sharpness to balance the richness.

As you may have guessed from the above, butter is a better partner for sorrel than oil of any sort, olive or not. I'm all for breaking rules, but this is one I almost never ignore. Raw sorrel provides the one exception – roughly torn up it makes a lively addition to a mixed green salad, as long as it is used in moderation, and then, of course, you will be using best extra virgin olive oil to dress it.

A & M
Leaf Fritters

SERVES 4

a few handfuls of edible leaves,
   such as **comfrey leaves**,
   wild garlic leaves, **large
   lemon balm leaves**, **sorrel
   leaves**
sunflower, **groundnut** or
   vegetable oil for deep-frying

FOR THE TEMPURA BATTER:
100g (3½ oz) **plain flour**
1 **egg yolk**
225ml (8 fl oz) **iced water**
4 **ice cubes**

to serve: **coarse salt, lemon
   wedges**

Ancient and modern: leaf fritters entered my life as a child, when my mother cooked up batches of comfrey-leaf fritters for supper after a walk through the shady, damp lanes where comfrey grows so well. She used a fairly standard European batter, enveloping each leaf in its entirety. Spring walks still mean leaf fritters now that I'm an adult, but since I have finally cracked the secret to a pretty respectable, airily light tempura batter I've followed the Japanese example, producing an occasional treat that smacks of modernity but has its roots settled well into ancient traditions. After all, it was from the Portuguese that the Japanese first learnt the art of deep-frying, though they have taken it further and perfected the most delicate, lacy, crisp and utterly simple batter of all.

Recently I've made these fritters with whatever edible spring leaves I can lay my hands on. The tempura treatment allows the subtle (or in the case of wild garlic, not so subtle) differences in flavour to come through, and I prefer to bring these out with a mere squeeze of lemon and a smattering of salt rather than a more dominant Japanese dipping sauce. I love comfrey and wild garlic, but my children prefer lemon balm and sorrel. Use, then, those leaves that are easily to hand: bounty from a walk, or large-leaved herbs that grow in your garden.

NB Do not use any leaves unless you are absolutely sure that a) you know what they are and b) you know for certain they are edible. Comfrey and wild garlic are pretty distinctive – you can't mistake the pong of wild garlic – but it's not worth taking the risk if you are not entirely certain of what you've got.

TEMPURA TIPS

The **icy chill of the batter** is crucial – the clash of arctic-cold batter and volcanically hot oil is what produces the crispest batter. So the only thing you should do in advance is stand a jug of water in the fridge for a few hours so that it is thoroughly chilled. Don't even think of making the batter until the oil is on the stove and the table is laid and ready.

A few **ice cubes** keep the batter at the right temperature, especially when you are

working in a hot kitchen, or on a hot day. But don't go overboard: too many will eventually make the batter too thin as they melt.

I'd suggest **cooking the wild garlic leaves first** – being very smooth, they work better with a slightly thicker batter that clings more tenaciously (the batter will become a little thinner as the ice cubes melt). If the batter still slips off, try dusting the less glossy side of the leaf with a little flour before dipping it into the batter.

• Rinse and dry the leaves thoroughly. If not using instantly, pop them into a plastic bag, seal and store in the vegetable drawer of the fridge, but only for a matter of hours. Garlic leaves last for a couple of days, but the rest will flop and fade swiftly into uselessness.

• When you are ready to fry, begin by putting the oil on to heat. Remember that this is not the kind of dish that can be kept hanging around once made, so ensure the diners are close to hand and ready to sit at table the minute you call. With the oil beginning to heat up, tip the flour into a bowl (do not sift), make a well in the centre and add the egg yolk. Pour in about a third of the water and start to mix, preferably with a pair of chopsticks or a fork, not an over-efficient whisk. Gradually mix in the rest of the water. The best tempura batter has plenty of little lumps of flour left in it, so whatever you do, don't beat the batter to a state of perfect smoothness. Add the ice cubes.

• To test the oil, drip a drop of batter into it from the tip of a chopstick – it should bob instantly to the surface, fizzing away gaily. Turn the heat down to maintain a constant temperature. One at a time, lay each leaf on the surface of the batter, pressing it down gently so that one side only is coated. Sorrel is the one leaf that does, I find, need to be coated on both sides and, incidentally, it will turn an interesting shade of khaki brown as it cooks. Anyway, once the leaf has its cargo of batter, lay it in the hot oil – don't faff around trying to flatten it if it crumples with the weight of the batter since it will open up again all by itself in the hot oil. Each leaf should take about one minute to cook to a crisp pale ivory with the merest hint of a tan. If they are taking longer, your oil is probably not hot enough, and if they are browning too swiftly then it is over-hot, and in either case your leaf fritters will be less than perfectly crisp.

• As they are cooked, lift them out on to a plate lined with several layers of kitchen paper, let them drain briefly, then serve them up immediately sprinkled with a little salt and accompanied by lemon wedges to squeeze over them.

Warm Salad of Purple Sprouting Broccoli with Anchovy and Orange Dressing

The long stems of sprouting broccoli have a natural affinity with both orange and anchovy. It is a combination of such utter delight that I could make a whole meal of it with little more than some excellent bread to back it up. If that seems too elemental, then at least serve it as a first course so that the flavours are not swamped by other foods.

- Steam or simmer the broccoli until tender. Drain thoroughly.

- While it is cooking, warm the olive oil in a small pan. Add the anchovy and garlic and fry gently, mashing in the anchovy until it has dissolved and the garlic is lightly coloured. Take off the heat and stir in the orange zest and juice and the lemon juice. Season with plenty of pepper, but no salt. Pour it over the hot broccoli, and eat while still warm or at room temperature.

SERVES 4

675g (1½ lb) **purple** or **white sprouting broccoli**

4 tablespoons **extra virgin olive oil**

5 tinned **anchovy fillets**, chopped

2 cloves **garlic**, sliced

finely grated **zest** and **juice** of ½ **orange**

juice of ½ **lemon**

pepper

Purple and White Sprouting Broccoli

It goes with daffodils and the first violets, with early blossom and the first green hawthorn buds. A bit fluffy? Well, I don't care. Purple sprouting broccoli is something worth waxing lyrical about. I get a thrill when I spy those dark green stems and loose leaves entwined, and their dark bruised-purple florets. A big heap of them is a downright gorgeous sight.

When I lay my eyes on a box of white sprouting broccoli down at the market, I reckon I've struck gold. If you live in or around Leicester and a few other blessed spots, you will already know all about it. For a brief period of some three or four weeks round about March, the vegetable stalls in the excellent Leicester central market are piled high with white sprouting broccoli, and it sells like hot cakes. I've watched in amazement as customers fill their carrier bags with the stuff and the piles shrink and shrink in a matter of minutes.

White or purple (there is a slight difference in taste), this stuff puts hefty, brighter green calabrese broccoli in the shade. The flavour is vastly superior, and the balance of leaf, stem and floret just about perfect. To prepare, trim off the thicker stems and remove damaged or extra large leaves. Rinse thoroughly, then either steam or cook in a little salted water until tender. Not *al dente*, mind you – it doesn't suit sprouting broccoli at all. Take care to drain it thoroughly and serve it with a few knobs of butter melting over it or cook for a few minutes more with a drizzle of olive oil, some garlic and a generous few squeezes of lemon juice.

It is good cold, too. Run the cooked stems under cold water as soon as you've drained them to stop them overcooking, then toss in a lemon and olive oil dressing, with a touch of crushed garlic if you wish, and leave to cool. If you chop it up roughly and pile it on to grilled bread that has been drizzled with extra virgin olive oil and rubbed with a cut clove of garlic, then finish it with a few flakes of Parmesan, you have a very presentable and delicious bruschetta.

Warm Chicken Liver and Lardon Salad

SERVES 4

2 good handfuls of fresh salad
  leaves – **watercress**, **young
  dandelions** (spring only),
  cos, **rocket**, **mizuna**,
  nasturtium and so on

3 tablespoons **extra virgin
  olive oil**

60g (2 oz) **lardons of bacon**
  or **pancetta**

220g (8 oz) cleaned **chicken
  livers**, quartered

1 tablespoon **red wine
  vinegar**

1 teaspoon **Dijon mustard**

pinch or two of **sugar**

salt and **pepper**

A French starter, which takes minutes to make,
and has become something of a classic. This is the
bare bones version, but you can play around with
it to your heart's content. Build on the basic by
adding, maybe, a few sliced boiled new potatoes,
some green beans or a handful of cooked and
skinned broad beans, different herbs, a poached
egg, halved cherry tomatoes, or whatever else
comes to hand. Let the season guide your hand.

• Arrange the salad leaves on individual plates, or pile into the salad
bowl. Heat the oil in a wide frying pan and fry the lardons and
chicken livers together until browned on the outside but still pink on
the inside (the chicken livers, that is, not the lardons, which will by
this time be cooked through anyway). Spoon the chicken livers and
lardons over the salad. While the pan is still good and hot, add the
vinegar, mustard, sugar, salt and pepper. Stir around to mix into the
oil and juices, then spoon the dressing over the salad and its cargo
of livers and lardons. Serve immediately.

Asparagus with Mint, Parsley and Honey Vinaigrette

A dish for those first few weeks of the asparagus season when it is still a monumental treat. The freshness of the dressing brings out all that is best in asparagus – and is also very good, as it happens, with cherry tomatoes, or even drizzled over boiled new potatoes.

SERVES 4

at least 250 g (9 oz) fresh British
  asparagus
salt

FOR THE DRESSING:
15g (½ oz) **flat-leaf parsley**
15g (½ oz) **mint**
2 tablespoons **white wine**
  vinegar
1 teaspoon **honey**
150ml (5 fl oz) **groundnut**
  or **sunflower oil**
salt and **pepper**

• To make the dressing, strip the leaves and finer stalks off the thick stems of the herbs. Pile the leaves into a liquidiser and add all the remaining ingredients. Liquidise until you are blessed with a gloriously green, smooth emulsion of a sauce. Taste and adjust the balance of seasonings, then pour into a bowl or a jug.

• Trim the tough lower part of the root from the asparagus. Cook the asparagus in lightly salted water, simmering cosily, for about 5–8 minutes until just tender, but definitely not *al dente*. Drain and run quickly under the cold tap to set the colour and prevent overcooking. Serve the asparagus warm or at room temperature with the mint, parsley and honey dressing.

Grilled Trout with Horseradish, Mint and Lemon Cream

Grilled quickly, trout needs only the simplest of sauces – a perky tomato sauce, perhaps given an extra lift with fresh mint and lime zest stirred into it just before serving, or maybe a vinaigrette laden with finely chopped fresh herbs (chives, parsley, basil, mint and so on, in huge quantity) and finely chopped shallot.

When you see a root of fresh horseradish up for sale, grab it quick to make this richer but no less simple sauce to marry with grilled trout. Quite how much grated fresh horseradish you add is a personal thing. Go lightly at first, then stir in some more if you think the sauce needs more emphatic pungency. Mint, on the other hand, is less of a roof-raiser, even in amplitude, so don't stint. This cream is also delicious with a joint of best roast beef, and there you should let the horseradish have its way – increase the quantity until it bites.

SERVES 4

4 plump **trout**, cleaned
4 strips **lemon zest**
4 sprigs of **mint**
a little **sunflower oil**
salt and **pepper**

to serve: 4 **lemon wedges**

FOR THE CREAM:

fresh **horseradish root**
  (see introduction)
a generous handful of fresh
  mint leaves
1 **sugar cube**
150ml (5 fl oz) best **double
  cream**
finely grated **zest** of ½ **lemon**
lemon juice, to taste
salt

• To make the cream, strip the peel from a knuckle's length of the horseradish root, then grate finely. You will probably weep as it is pungent stuff, but it's worth the few moments of suffering. Strip the mint leaves from their stalks and place with the sugar cube and salt in a mortar. Pound to a paste, then work in the horseradish. Whip the cream until it holds its shape in a very sloppy fashion. Fold in the mint and horseradish mixture, and the lemon zest and a few dashes of lemon juice. Taste and adjust seasoning.

• Pre-heat the grill. Make a couple of slashes diagonally across the thickest part of each fish on both sides so that it cooks evenly. Season inside the stomach cavity, then slip in a piece of lemon zest and a sprig of mint. Brush the outside with a little oil, then grill on both sides until just cooked through. Serve immediately with the horseradish, mint and lemon cream, and lemon wedges.

Spiced Skate with Bacon

Skate is a fish I never tire of. There is something deeply intriguing about the way it pulls away from the central cartilage in long tender ribbons, but it's the taste of the mild, slightly sticky flesh that I really like.

Skate and bacon get on together handsomely – as long as your bacon is the best: not too salty, dry-cured with a sweet, light, clear flavour. I'm fond of crisped bacon so I'd favour two rashers per person, but if you think that might turn out to be a bit too much you won't be judged mean with only one rasher astride each helping of skate.

If you can't get four small skate wings, use two larger wings, each one cut in half.

SERVES 4

4–8 rashers **unsmoked streaky bacon**

4 portions of **skate wing**, weighing about 175–220g (6–8 oz) each

60g (2 oz) **plain flour**

½ teaspoon **cayenne pepper**

½ teaspoon **turmeric**

1 teaspoon **ground cumin**

2 tablespoons **olive oil**

salt

to serve: **lemon wedges**

• Either grill or roast the bacon on a rack in a hot oven until the strips are crisp. Take care not to burn them. Set aside until needed.

• Pat the skate dry with kitchen paper or a clean tea towel. Mix the flour with the spices and salt. Heat the oil in a frying pan large enough to take all the skate, or two frying pans if that makes life easier. Coat the pieces of skate evenly in the seasoned flour, shaking off excess, and lay in the hot fat. Fry for about 3–5 minutes on each side until nicely browned and just cooked through. Drain briefly on kitchen paper. Quickly reheat the bacon for some 30–60 seconds in the frying pan, then serve the skate with the bacon arranged on top and lemon wedges on the side.

Roast Chicken with Asparagus and Cornbread Stuffing

I love roast chicken, no two ways about it. Naturally, the chicken has to be a good free-range animal that has spent its days running around, not huddled in a cage. With that understood, there is little to beat it for a Sunday lunch, especially with a great stuffing. This is one to try in the late spring when the first flush of new season asparagus is over and for a few weeks they are comparatively cheap. Slightly grainy cornbread makes a good base – quite a change from the usual breadcrumb-based stuffings. Remember, though, that the mild sweetness of the cornbread and asparagus means that the stuffing needs plenty of seasoning if it is not to appear bland.

SERVES 4–6

1 large **free-range chicken**
2 tablespoons **olive oil**
½ **lemon**
coarse **salt** and **pepper**

FOR THE STUFFING:

110g (4 oz) **bacon and chive cornbread** (see page 52)
½ **onion**, chopped
1 tablespoon **extra virgin olive oil**, or 15g (½ oz) **butter**
110g (4 oz) lightly cooked **asparagus**, roughly chopped
½ beaten **egg**
salt and **pepper**

• Pre-heat the oven to 220°C/425°F/Gas 7. For the stuffing, first crumble the cornbread. Fry the onion in the oil or butter until tender and translucent, then scrape into the cornbread. Add the asparagus, egg and plenty of salt and pepper. Mix together well. Stuff the cavity of the bird with this mixture.

• Place the chicken in a lightly oiled roasting tin. Squeeze the juice of the lemon half over it, then drizzle with the remaining oil. Sprinkle with coarse salt and pepper. Rub in lightly. Pour a glass of water around the bird, then roast for about 1 hour, basting from time to time and adding a little more water if there is nothing but oil left in the bottom of the tin.

• When the chicken is done, the legs will wobble loosely. Double-check by piercing the thickest part of the meat: between the thigh and the breast. If the juices run pink, return it to the oven for another 10–15 minutes, but if they run clear, then the bird is ready to eat. Yippee.

• Present it proudly at table, not forgetting to dish out the stuffing as you serve up the chicken.

Asparagus

Without any doubt, the most perfect, delectable asparagus I have ever eaten was the one from our own asparagus bed. And one it was, all on its own. Actually, we shouldn't have eaten any, for it was the bed's first year, way too early to be harvesting. My husband, William, just happened to knock it over (he swore blind it was an accident…), so he rushed it into the kitchen and I rushed it into a pot of simmering water. Within half an hour of its demise, it was lying in perfect solo elegance across a large white plate with a little pool of melted butter and a scattering of chopped chives (well – it was our first, so I thought it deserved a touch of glamour). We shared it in the spring sunshine, and it was really and truly the finest-tasting asparagus I have ever eaten. Three months later we moved, waving a sad goodbye to our one-year-old asparagus bed.

We haven't got it together to start one in our new garden, but I have unearthed a fabulous asparagus grower just down the road. The 'shop' is nothing more than a hut in the middle of a field, but the asparagus is always newly picked each morning so I'm not complaining about the décor. And the taste? Well, as long as we eat it straight away, it can almost, very nearly (but not quite) compare with our one home-grown shoot. The moral of this story is, obviously, that you should never leave asparagus lying around in the bottom of the fridge. Whether you grow it, are given it by a green-fingered friend or buy it from farm or shop, cherish it and don't let it linger.

I inherited a proper asparagus steamer from my mother, but admit to rarely using it. Most of the time I simply plunge the asparagus, trimmed of the bottom woody couple of inches of stem, into a pan of lightly salted, simmering water. The pan must be wide enough to accommodate the full length of the asparagus, but that is the only requirement. As long as you take care not to overcook the stems, the tips survive well enough. The only time I excavate the steamer from the back of the cupboard is when I am cooking asparagus for a crowd, which is when it comes into its own.

Not overcooking asparagus is important, but so too is cooking it adequately. *Al dente* asparagus is little short of a crime. It's a habit that had a brief lease of life but I'm glad to say is dying out. It really does nothing for the taste of the asparagus, leaving a sweet, undeveloped metallic tang in the mouth. Asparagus should be tender, with a decent flop of a curve to it when picked up by the base. Substance enough to make it dippable, but not so much that it stays ramrod straight.

Once the first flush is over and home-grown asparagus are plentiful (or with out-of-season imported asparagus), I often roast them in a hot oven: lay the trimmed asparagus in a densely packed single layer in a roasting tin and drizzle with extra virgin olive oil, then season with coarse salt. Turn the asparagus with your hands so they are coated with oil, then roast at around 200°C/400°F/Gas 6 for 15–20 minutes until tender. Serve hot, with shavings of Parmesan softening over them.

Pot-Roast Chicken with Red Onions, Leeks and Spring Herbs

Here, I've employed red onions, carrots and leeks to cradle the chicken: the last of the winter vegetables, still patiently to hand before the late spring and summer vegetables become plentiful.

SERVES 4–6

½ **lemon**

1 large **free-range chicken**

3 **red onions**, each cut into
4–6 wedges

2 large **carrots**, sliced

3 **leeks**, trimmed, thoroughly
cleaned and thickly sliced

4 cloves **garlic**, sliced

a few sprigs of **parsley**

a few sprigs of **sweet cicely**
or **chervil**, if available

a sprig of **lovage**

1 generous glass **dry white
wine**

1 generous glass **apple juice**

to serve: 2 tablespoons snipped
chives
salt and **pepper**

• Squeeze the lemon over the chicken and rub the juice in well. Season with salt and pepper. In a deep heavy-based casserole, just large enough to take the chicken fairly snugly, make a bed of half the onions, carrots and leeks, and all the garlic, parsley, sweet cicely or chervil and lovage. Season lightly. Nestle the chicken, breast-side down, on top of the vegetables and pour over the wine and the apple juice. Cover tightly and place over a moderate heat. As soon as the juices begin to boil, reduce the heat to low and leave to cook gently, without disturbing too often, for 30 minutes. Now carefully turn the chicken breast-side up and tuck the remaining onions, carrots and leeks down around the sides. Cover again tightly and return to a gentle heat. Leave to cook for a further 50 minutes.

• Lift out as many of the second-batch onions, leeks and carrots as you can without injury to yourself or the chicken. Keep them warm. Lift out the chicken, tilt to let the juices that have pooled in the inner cavity flow back out into the pan, then let the bird rest in a warm place for 10 minutes. Tip all the remaining contents of the pan into a sieve over a bowl and press down hard to extract the last of the juices. Stir the contents of the bowl, then taste and adjust seasoning. Reheat if necessary.

• Quickly, cut the chicken up into chunky portions using poultry shears or a large, sharp knife. Arrange the chicken in the centre of the serving plate with the vegetables all around. Drizzle a little of the juices over it, sprinkle with chives and serve immediately with the remaining juices in a separate bowl or jug.

There's something very comforting about a pot roast. It is an endlessly adaptable way of cooking meat, and can be tailored to fit the season by changing the vegetables and herbs you pop in. Very user-friendly. Once the pot is on the stove it needs only the occasional check, and can otherwise be left to simmer away merrily on its own, scenting the house in a most tantalising and appetising way.

Hannah Glasse's Duck Stewed with Green Peas

This eighteenth-century dish deserves to be better known. It is not entirely dissimilar to the better known *petits pois à la française* with its blend of peas and lettuce, but the addition of a plump duck, buried in the centre of the vegetable mass, changes it radically into a richly satisfying, soothing one-pot meal. Save it for that small time when fresh peas are plentiful and lettuces come fresh from the garden. Yes, lettuce, and yes, the much-maligned floppy round-headed lettuce is just the job here. It donates its subtle sweetness to the dish, dissolving as it cooks to amplify the juices.

SERVES 4

1 large, plump **duckling**

1 tablespoon **sunflower oil**

300ml (½ pint) good **poultry stock**, with a rich flavour

a **bouquet garni** of thyme, bay and parsley

450g (1 lb) shelled **fresh peas**

1 large **round lettuce**, shredded

30g (1 oz) **butter**

30g (1 oz) **plain flour**

a small handful of **mint leaves**, shredded

salt, **pepper** and freshly grated **nutmeg**

• Prick the duck skin all over with a fork so the fat can ooze out with ease. Heat the oil in a frying pan and brown the duck all over. Transfer it to a close-fitting casserole, season with salt and pepper, then pour over the stock and tuck in the bouquet garni. Cover tightly and simmer gently for 45 minutes, turning the duck occasionally.

• Now add the peas mixed with the lettuce and season with a touch of nutmeg – do not panic if the casserole seems full to bursting as the ingredients will settle down comfortably under the influence of heat. Cover and simmer for a further 45 minutes or so, again turning once or twice, until the duck is very tender. While it cooks, mash the butter and flour together thoroughly to make a beurre manié.

• Lift the duck out on to a serving plate and keep it warm. Spoon as much of the fat from the surface of the peas as you can – there'll be a fair bit, worth saving to sauté potatoes or fry salmon fillets or something of that nature. Drop dabs of the beurre manié into the peas. Stir and shake the pan to soften the beurre manié into the cooking juices, then cook very gently for about 3–5 minutes until thickened. Using poultry shears or a sharp knife, cut the duck into quarters. Stir the mint into the peas, taste and adjust seasoning. Spoon around the duck and serve.

Sumptuous Cabbage and Potato Tart with Gruyère

SERVES 6–8

450g (1 lb) **shortcrust pastry**

FOR THE FILLING:

1 **pointed spring cabbage**
310g (11 oz) medium **new potatoes**, scrubbed and sliced (no need to peel)
110g (4 oz) **Gruyère**, grated
375ml (12½ fl oz) **single cream**
3 **free-range eggs**
salt, **pepper** and freshly grated **nutmeg**

I should come up with some fancy and intriguing name for this tart to lure you into making it. It is so very much more delicious than you would imagine from a cursory glance at the ingredients list. So, take my word for it, this is a delight of a tart, and you should try it straight away, or at least sometime soon.

The two critical points are firstly that the cabbage should not be overcooked at all, and secondly that you should squeeze it hard to extract as much water as possible to prevent water leaking out into the cream and egg mixture or, worse still, the pastry base.

• Pre-heat the oven to 180°C/350°F/Gas 4. Line a 23–25cm (9–10 in) tart tin, with removable base, with the pastry. Chill for half an hour. Prick the base all over with a fork. Line with greaseproof paper, non-stick baking parchment or foil and weigh down with baking beans. Bake blind for 15 minutes, then remove baking beans and paper or foil. Return the tart tin to the oven for a further 5–10 minutes to dry out, without letting it brown.

• To make the filling, quarter the cabbage lengthways and cut out the hard core. Shred the leaves and blanch them in boiling salted water for 4 minutes, until just tender. Drain and run under the cold tap. Drain again and squeeze as much water as you can out of the cabbage with your hands.

• Cook the potatoes in boiling salted water for about 4–5 minutes until just tender. Drain thoroughly and mix with the cabbage and all but 2 tablespoons of the Gruyère. Beat the cream with the eggs and plenty of salt, pepper and nutmeg. Pile the cabbage and potato mixture into the pastry case and smooth down as best you can. Pour over the cream mixture, and sprinkle the reserved Gruyère over the surface.

• Carefully transfer the tart to the oven and bake for about 35–45 minutes until just set and lightly browned on top. Serve warm or at room temperature.

Eggs

We fantasise about keeping our own chickens. During the day they'd peck about in the garden, popping their heads round the kitchen door to say hello every now and then, and at night we'd tuck them up safely in their own little house, safe from the marauding foxes that trot through the fields. They would regularly lay the most divine eggs just for our breakfast. Every time I find myself leaning too perilously close to making the fantasy concrete, I kick myself sharply. With four cats, nine fish, two gerbils and a snake in the house (not to mention two children), my livestock quota is already exceeded. How would we ever find anyone to look after them all while we went on holiday?

Besides, it is easy to track down proper free-range eggs in the countryside. I mean eggs that come from chickens you can see ranging freely outside in the open air, pecking away busily, having dust baths when the urge takes them and generally getting on with the kind of life that contented chickens relish. A far cry from the lives of caged layers, treated as egg machines rather than sentient beings, crammed into wire cages so restrictive they can't even stretch properly.

The good news is that no one need buy eggs from caged birds any more. Sure, they are still available (though not for much longer, I'm glad to say), but all but the meanest of food shops offer free-range eggs to their public these days. They cost a little more, but the price difference is not so great. By law, producers can only label eggs 'free-range' if they come from chickens that have some access to the great outdoors (though they may spend most of their lives roaming in a pretty crowded barn or shed). So, even if they haven't come from an idyllic farmyard in the depths of rural bliss, they will have had a comparatively decent life.

The one minor inconvenience with absolutely genuine free-range eggs that have come, say, from my next-door neighbour's little brood of chickens if I am particularly lucky, or from the farm down the road, is that you can't be fussy about sizes. This doesn't matter a great deal most of the time, but when it comes to baking, for instance, it can upset the balance of ingredients.

The first thing you need to do is check what size egg you are meant to be using. When you've snipped the recipe from a magazine or newspaper this may not be possible so you'll have to keep your fingers crossed, but most books will tell you somewhere what size eggs have been used when testing the recipes. A 'large' egg weighs in at 63–73g (2.25–2.6 oz). If your egg is heavier still, then you've landed an 'extra large' one, and I hope you feel sorry for the poor hen who had to squeeze that one out. 'Medium' eggs are those that weigh 53–63g (2–2.25 oz) and a 'small' egg is anything weedier than that.

Just in case you are wondering, all the eggs used in the recipes in this book were large ones.

Eggs Florentine

A fine supper dish for the first spinach, showing it off at its best. My one concession to modernity is that I prefer to stir-fry the spinach speedily in a wok. It takes literally seconds and the flavour is so much livelier than when cooked in a saucepan.

SERVES 3 AS A SUPPER DISH, 6 AS A FIRST COURSE

6 very fresh **free-range eggs**
1 tablespoon **vinegar**, if poaching
1 tablespoon **sunflower oil**
675g (1½ lb) **fresh spinach leaves**, rinsed

FOR THE MORNAY SAUCE:
30g (1 oz) **butter**
30g (1 oz) **plain flour**
300ml (½ pint) **milk**
85ml (3 fl oz) **single cream**
30g (1 oz) freshly grated **Parmesan**
30g (1 oz) freshly grated **Gruyère**
salt, **pepper** and freshly grated **nutmeg**

• Pre-heat the oven to 220°C/425°F/Gas 7. If you know your eggs are fresh, poach them, otherwise soft-boil (see below). Heat a wok over a high heat until it smokes. Add half the oil, then pile in half the spinach. Stir-fry swiftly until just wilted, then tip out into a bowl. Repeat with the remaining oil and spinach. Once it is cool enough to handle, squeeze as much water as you can out of the spinach, chop roughly and season with salt, pepper and nutmeg. Spread out thickly in a gratin dish and nestle the eggs on top of it.

• To make the sauce, melt the butter and stir in the flour. Stir for 1 minute, then draw off the heat. Stir in the milk a slurp at a time until the sauce loosens to a cream. Now add the milk in big splurges, mixing it in evenly. Finally pour in the cream. Bring up to the boil and simmer for 5–10 minutes, stirring frequently to prevent catching. Off the heat, stir in two-thirds of the Parmesan and all the Gruyère, and season with salt, pepper and nutmeg. Spoon evenly over the eggs and spinach, then sprinkle the last of the Parmesan over the top. Bake in the oven until golden brown and bubbling. Serve swiftly.

TO POACH EGGS Fill a capacious saucepan to a depth of 7.5cm (3 in) or a touch more with water. Add 1 level teaspoon salt and 1 tablespoon vinegar. Bring up to a gentle simmer, with the surface just rippling. Break an egg carefully into a teacup. Tip neatly into the simmering water, then raise the heat slightly. Poach for 2 minutes. Lift out with a perforated spoon and drain on kitchen paper. Repeat with remaining eggs.

TO SOFT-BOIL EGGS For this dish they need to be just right with runny yolks and barely set whites, so bring a pan of water up to the boil and lower room-temperature eggs gently into the water with a spoon. Boil for 6 minutes. Drain instantly and fill the pan with icy-cold water. Leave until the eggs are cool enough to handle, then crack the shells very carefully and peel off even more carefully.

Lamb

Lamb is really the last of the seasonal domesticated meats. Oh, I know that we can have it all year round, and most of us non-vegetarians do, but its connection with spring and Easter has never been entirely eroded in most people's minds. Does anyone stir at the thought of autumnal pork any more? No, I suspect not. And would anyone care to suggest a specific season for beef? Hardly. But when it comes to lamb, we cling on to old-fashioned certainties. Spring lamb is absolutely where it's at.

Well, who can fail to be heartened by the sight of the first lambs frolicking around the fields in sprightly leaps and gallops, playing tag with each other, butting their poor mothers in search of milk? Not me, that's for sure. I have no qualms about the fact that most of them will end up on the plate – after all, they wouldn't be there otherwise. Indeed, I have been known to whisper 'mint sauce' and 'redcurrant jelly' as I lean over the farmers' pens to admire their curly off-white coats, spindly little legs and mucky buttocks.

Lamb has never attracted the cultural or religious taboos that pork and beef have, and wherever sheep can be successfully raised, lamb or older mutton is consumed with enthusiasm. And wherever it is consumed with enthusiasm, there are favourite flavourings that bring out the best in it: mint and redcurrant jelly here, garlic and rosemary in France, lemon and olive oil in Italy and, to an extent, in Greece, fresh and dried fruit in the Middle East, yoghurt and aromatic spices in India. It is superb cooked medium rare and pink inside, or given long slow braising or roasting until it virtually melts away from the bone. So, when it comes to cooking lamb, there are very few rules to remember, and hardly any to break. Phew. The best advice I can give you is to buy from local producers when you can, or from butchers who source with care and interest. The colour of the meat will depend on age, diet and breed, but it should always be pretty healthy-looking with no greyness, while the fat should be dry, crisp and waxy.

I enjoy spring lamb, and our Easter lunch is nearly always a neat little leg of lamb, roast with this or that, but I prefer more mature lamb. The first lamb of the season is beautifully, occasionally almost disturbingly, tender, sweetly savoury with the delicate nature that comes only of extreme youth. It's a fabulous thing, especially given that you can virtually guarantee that the wee darling has led a merry if brief life. Give it a while longer out in the fields, let it exercise those silly thin legs rather more, and what you end up with on the table is a meat with substance (though hardly ever tough) and certainly greater complexity of flavour.

I guess the important thing here is not that you or I like this one more than that, but that we appreciate the way lamb changes through the seasons. How very pleasing that the chop on our plates does not (or should not) taste exactly the same throughout the year. Down with uniformity! Let's celebrate the small differences, as well as the large.

Lamb Ragout with Sorrel

Though this sounds French, it is based on a recipe given in my antiquated copy of *Cassell Dictionary of Food*. Of course, that doesn't mean it isn't French in origin, but it has certainly had roots in British terra firma for a hundred years or more.

SERVES 3–4

700g (1 lb 9 oz) cubed, trimmed **lamb**

30g (1 oz) **butter**

1 tablespoon **sunflower oil**

1 small **onion**, chopped

1 **carrot**, finely diced

1 tablespoon **plain flour**

generous 300ml (½ pint) **lamb, chicken** or **vegetable stock**

4 tablespoons **double cream**

2 good handfuls of **sorrel**, stems removed, finely shredded

salt and **pepper**

• Sauté the cubes of lamb in 15g (½ oz) butter and the oil until lightly browned. Take out of the pan and reserve. If needed, add the rest of the butter to the pan and, when it has melted, add the onion and carrot. Fry until the onion is tender. Pour off excess fat, return the lamb to the pan with any juices and sprinkle over the flour. Stir so that it is evenly distributed. Pour in the stock and a little salt and pepper, and simmer gently for 30 minutes until the lamb is tender.

• Stir the cream into the pan and bring back to the boil. Add the sorrel and stir until it has wilted down into the sauce. Taste and adjust seasoning, and serve.

Provençal Roast Lamb

SERVES 5–6

1 part-boned and rolled **leg of lamb**, weighing around 1.5kg (3½ lb)

a big handful of **rosemary** sprigs

a smaller handful of **thyme** sprigs (optional, but good)

1 **onion**, sliced

2 tablespoons **extra virgin olive oil**

a generous 150ml (5 fl oz) **chicken** or **lamb stock**

salt and **pepper**

FOR THE PASTE:

3 cloves **garlic**, quartered

finely grated **zest** of 1 large **orange**

4 **anchovy fillets**

1 tablespoon **extra virgin olive oil**

a touch of **salt** and plenty of **black pepper**

Make this when you've trimmed back the rosemary after its first flush of spring growth – you'll need a big handful of the sprigs, as well as a good helping of thyme, to make a comfortable bed for the leg of lamb. Add a paste of garlic, orange and anchovy and you have the best of the big flavours of the southern French countryside, all of which marry very happily with the meat itself.

A part-boned leg of lamb is one where the main bone is taken out, leaving just the knuckle bone as a useful handle to steady the meat when it is carved in luscious, thick slices. Any good butcher will prepare the lamb for you as long as you give a little advance notice.

• Pre-heat the oven to 200°C/400°F/Gas 6. Pat the lamb dry on kitchen paper. Spread the rosemary and thyme out over the bottom of a roasting tin. Scatter the onion over, then spoon over the olive oil. Using your hands, turn the herbs and onion to mix them and coat them in oil. Spread out again. Lay the lamb on top, fat side up.

• To make the paste, crush the garlic, orange zest and anchovy in a mortar, then work in the olive oil, salt and pepper. Smear this mixture all over the lamb. Pour over the stock. Roast for 1 hour (pink), or longer if you like your lamb well done. Every now and then baste the lamb with the stock. When the surface of the lamb is a pleasing mid-brown, cover the joint loosely with foil to prevent burning. Remove the foil 5 minutes or so before the end of the cooking time so the lamb can crisp up a little.

• Let the lamb rest for 20 minutes in a warm place, then transfer it to a warm serving dish. Strain off the pan juices and reheat if necessary. Pour into a gravy boat or small jug (no need to thicken the juices unless you passionately want to as they have such a depth of flavour that they need no help), and serve with the lamb, thickly sliced.

Côtes de Porc à l'Estragon

SERVES 4

4 meaty **pork chops**
a knob of **butter** – about 10g,
  a little less than ½ oz
1 tablespoon **sunflower oil**
2 teaspoons **Dijon mustard**
the leaves of a decent sprig of
  tarragon, chopped roughly
200g (7 oz) **crème fraîche**
salt and **pepper**

This is a dish for a happy occasion but little preparation time. We don't use tarragon half often enough in this country. It adds the kind of fresh green aniseedy flavour that no dried spice can bring. Classically it is married with chicken and eggs, but it is a humdinger with pork, too.

I love pork chops, but then it's easy to get good ones round where I live. By good, I mean free-range – I'd never buy anything else – preferably from a traditional breed so that it is not totally devoid of flavour-imparting fat. Trim some of it off if it seems excessive, but bear in mind that removing too much of the fat removes too much of the flavour.

Ignore any niggling worries that pork chops are pedestrian fare, unsuitable for a special meal. Dressed up with a cream-laden sauce and served with a pile of noodles, or new potatoes, or even tinned flageolet beans (drained and rinsed well) tossed with a hint of butter and loads of parsley, and some stir-fried spinach, they are something to celebrate in themselves.

• Trim the rind from the chops if necessary, and make little nicks around the edge here and there to stop them curling up.

• Heat the butter with the oil in a frying pan just large enough to take the chops. Fry the chops over a moderate heat until lightly browned and just cooked through. Season with salt and pepper, then transfer to a dish and keep warm.

• Add the mustard, tarragon, cream and a little salt and pepper to the pan and stir. Simmer for a minute or two, then taste and adjust seasoning. Return the chops to the pan along with any juices, turn in the sauce, then serve, spooning the sauce over them.

Steak Sandwich with Lime-salted Onions

SERVES 2

1 large **rump steak**, cut about 2.5cm (1 in) thick

4 slices **oats and honey bread** (see page 53) or other sturdy bread

2–3 tablespoons **mayonnaise**

whatever greenery is available, eg, **watercress**, **rocket**, **frisee lettuce**, **little gem**

salt

FOR THE MARINADE:

2 tablespoons **sloe gin** (see page 167) or **port**

juice of 1 **orange**

2 tablespoons **extra virgin olive oil**

4 **juniper berries**, lightly crushed

1 clove **garlic**, crushed

2 sprigs of **thyme**, bruised with the back of a wooden spoon

pepper

FOR THE ONIONS:

1 **red onion**, halved and thinly sliced

½ tablespoon **salt**

½ tablespoon **caster sugar**

juice of 1 **lime**

I seem to be surrounded by suppliers of truly excellent beef in my neck of the woods. The village butcher sells superb free-range beef, and only a little further away are two farm shops where they sell their own, rare-breed beef, beautifully hung to a dark burgundy red, tender and oozing sheer savoury delight. It's not cheap, to be sure, but for an occasional treat there is nothing to beat a really good steak, cooked medium rare. Slicing it thin and clamping it between slices of decent bread makes a handsome meal for two out of one generous slice of rump.

• Mix all the marinade ingredients together and pour them over the steak. Cover and leave to marinate overnight.

• Mix the onions with the salt, sugar and lime juice, then leave for 1 hour. Squeeze and massage for a minute or so with your fingers, then drain off the liquid and keep the onion covered until needed.

• Shortly before you are ready to eat, put the griddle pan over a high heat and leave it to get outrageously hot. Take the steak out of the marinade and griddle for about 3 minutes on each side, keeping the heat high, until done. Season the steak with salt and leave it to rest for around 5 minutes in a warm place. Meanwhile tip the marinade into a small pan and boil down until you have just a couple of tablespoonfuls of syrupy liquid. Toast the bread lightly on one side only and keep warm.

• Now we're on to assembly. Slice the steak thinly. Spread the untoasted sides of the bread with mayonnaise, lay slices of beef over two of them and drizzle with the reduced marinade, then top with greenery and clamp on the other two pieces of bread. Serve straight away, with chips.

Tomato, Potato and Watercress Salad with Gorgonzola Dressing

In the high season of new potatoes, late May and early June, it seems only natural to recourse to frequent potato salads. Everyone loves them, and they work well with all manner of main courses. I'm particularly partial to a combination of tomato and potato – the fresh and juicy against the mealy and starchy. Add peppery watercress and a blue-cheese dressing and you're away. Try it with plain roast chicken, or a barbecued steak.

SERVES 4

60g (2 oz) **watercress**

500g (1 lb 2 oz) **new potatoes**, cooked and sliced

250g (9 oz) **tomatoes**, roughly chopped

1 tablespoon roughly chopped **chives**

FOR THE DRESSING:

45g (1½ oz) derinded **Gorgonzola** or other **blue cheese**

60g (2 oz) **mayonnaise**

30g (1 oz) **yoghurt**

juice of 1 **lemon**

salt and **pepper**

• To make the dressing, mash the Gorgonzola up, then gradually work in the mayonnaise and then the yoghurt. Stir in the lemon juice and season with salt and pepper.

• In a salad bowl, make a bed of the watercress and scatter the potatoes over the top. Strew the tomatoes over the potatoes. Spoon the dressing over the top and sprinkle with chives. Toss at the table, just before eating.

Watercress

To me, watercress always seems peculiarly British. This stems from my childhood when one of the great supper treats was a bowl of soup in the sitting room (watching *The Forsyte Saga*, was it?… or perhaps *Call My Bluff*), followed by a marvellously huge watercress sandwich. Yet, when I reflect upon it, I can think of relatively few traditional ways of using watercress. Tufts of peppery watercress leaves are tucked around roast game birds, we might sip at a watercress soup, and possibly chop it into a sauce, but that's about all I can come up with.

Much as I like the soups and sauces, I have to say that I prefer to bite into raw watercress. I adore the juicy crunch of the stems among the softer, squeakier leaves. But it is the taste above all that does the trick: energising, peppery and pure healthy greenness. The pity of cooking it is that you lose both the texture and the pepper, to end up with an altogether more tame and soothing beast. Don't get me wrong – I love watercress soups and sauces when I'm in the right mood, but it is the jam-packed watercress sandwich that wins every time.

I like it just as much in salads, where it is as good as the more fashionable rocket. In the winter I return again and again to a salad that my mother made frequently, a mixture of watercress, sweet orange and chicory, tossed in a light vinaigrette – it's a combination that lifts the spirits after too much starchy comfort food. There are endless other key combinations – watercress with frizzled bacon and avocado, watercress with strips of grilled skinned red pepper and little croutons of sourdough bread, watercress with shrimps or prawns and chickpeas, and so on and so forth.

To make a watercress dressing for a new potato salad, put a handful of watercress in the liquidiser with white wine vinegar, olive oil, salt and pepper and blitz until smooth. Taste and adjust seasonings, adding a hint of sugar or honey if you wish, then pour over the potatoes. Serve warm or at room temperature.

Parchment-baked Jersey Royals with Lemon Thyme, Olive Oil and Coarse Salt

SERVES 2–4

500g (1 lb 2 oz) small new
  season **Jersey Royals**
4 sprigs of **lemon thyme**,
  or ordinary **thyme** plus
  2 strips **lemon zest**
3 tablespoons **extra virgin
  olive oil**
coarse **salt**

The joy of this method of cooking potatoes, wrapped in neat little parcels of greaseproof paper, is that not an iota of flavour is lost to cooking water. The last thing you want to do is destroy any of that marvellous flavour of the first Jersey Royals, harbingers of spring as surely as daffodils and cuckoos. Once their season is over and done with, replace them with other less exalted new potatoes for a marginally less glorious treat.

Quite how many these quantities serve is a difficult thing to decide. Personally I could wolf down half with no problem if this were part of a simple meal, but if you were cooking the potatoes for a more formal meal with three courses or more, you could squeeze three or even four tiddly portions out of them.

• Pre-heat the oven to 190°C/375°F/Gas 5. Cut out 2 large, heart-shaped pieces of greaseproof paper (about 32cm/13 in across at the widest part and 28cm/11 in long). Lay each one on a baking tray and put half the potatoes on one side of each heart. Divide the lemon thyme sprigs (or thyme and lemon zest) between them, nestling the sprigs down among the potatoes. Drizzle over the olive oil and season with coarse salt. Fold the other half of each heart over to form a skewed semi-circle. Seal the edges, starting at the pointed end, pressing them over and over again and working your way round each package to enclose the potatoes neatly and snugly. Bake for 35 minutes, by which time the potatoes will be tender. Serve immediately in their parcels so that they can be opened at the table.

Slow-braised Purple Sprouting Broccoli with Lemon, Garlic and Olives

The first sighting of purple sprouting broccoli in the spring fills me with delight. It's one of my favourite vegetables – so much more interesting than the lumpen big green calabrese broccoli that has usurped its rightful throne. This slow braising is one of the best ways I know of cooking it, developing its flavour to a deep, mellow nuttiness. When the sprouting broccoli has gone, you can treat ordinary broccoli in much the same way, as long as you cut its hefty form lengthways, from flowering green head down to the base of the stalk, to create more slender pieces. Be warned, though, that ordinary broccoli turns a murky sludge green with this treatment, but it still tastes very good!

SERVES 4

1kg (2 lb 4 oz) **purple sprouting broccoli**

4 tablespoons **olive oil**

juice of ½ **lemon**

6 cloves **garlic**, peeled but left whole

1 **dried red chilli**, snapped in two (optional)

12 **black olives**, pitted and sliced

coarse **salt** and freshly ground **black pepper**

• Trim tough stems and overly ragged leaves from the broccoli. Find a shallow heavy-based wide pan with a close-fitting lid that can take the broccoli in a fairly thin layer (cut the stems if necessary to fit in). Drizzle half the oil over the base, and tip and tilt the pan to distribute it more or less evenly. Tuck the broccoli cosily in the pan, then squeeze over the lemon juice. Season with salt and pepper. Bury the garlic cloves and chilli, if using, right down into the mass of broccoli. Drizzle over the remaining oil and add a small glass of water, too, but no more than that. Place over a low-moderate heat and cover tightly. Leave to cook gently for about 40 minutes, turning once or twice. Add the olives about 5 minutes before the broccoli is done.

• The theory is that by the end of the cooking time most of the liquid should have been absorbed or boiled away, leaving just a thin layer of juice on the base of the pan, so if necessary add a splash or two more water as it cooks, but don't drown the broccoli. If there is too much liquid at the end of this time, remove the lid and let it boil away for a few minutes to reduce. Either way, by the end of the cooking time, the sprouting broccoli should be meltingly tender, and quite divinely delicious.

Broccoli Purée with Crisp Fried Shallots

This is a fabulously smooth and rich purée of vivid green. The fried shallots, appealingly bitter-sweet, serve to emphasise the deliciousness of the purée.

SERVES 4–6

100g (3½ oz) **shallots**, thinly sliced and separated into rings

sunflower or **groundnut** oil for frying

400–450g (14 oz–1 lb) **broccoli**

1 large **baking potato** (around 250g/9 oz), baked or microwaved in its jacket

30g (1 oz) **butter**

100ml (3½ fl oz) **whipping** or **double cream**

salt, **pepper** and freshly grated **nutmeg**

• For the shallots, pour 1cm (½ in) of sunflower or groundnut oil into a small pan and heat up until a cube of bread dropped into it fizzles merrily and browns in 30 seconds. Dry the shallot rings quickly on kitchen paper and fry them in two or three small batches until golden brown. Lift them out swiftly before they turn any darker and drain them on kitchen paper.

• Trim the broccoli and separate florets from stalk. Peel the tough outer layer off the stalk, then slice it. Cook the broccoli in simmering salted water until tender. I do mean tender, not *al dente*, but don't keep on cooking until it is collapsing and rank. Drain well.

• Put the broccoli into the processor with the potato flesh, butter, cream, salt, pepper and a generous helping of nutmeg. Process to a purée, then taste and adjust seasoning, adding a little milk if it is too thick. Scrape back into a clean pan and reheat when needed. Serve scattered thickly with the fried shallots.

Roasted Red Onions with Pine Nuts and Raisins

SERVES 4

3 large **red onions**, peeled
  and quartered
2 tablespoons **extra virgin**
  olive oil
3 tablespoons **red wine**
  vinegar
2 large sprigs of **thyme**
2 tablespoons **caster sugar**
45g (1½ oz) **raisins**, soaked in
  a little water
15g (½ oz) **pine nuts**
1 big tablespoon **capers**
salt and **pepper**

to serve: a little chopped
  parsley

It is so easy to forget that the onion is a proper vegetable, which can be served in its own right. In early spring, however, before warmer weather brings the first of the year's new crop, I turn to it with renewed enthusiasm, thankful for the onion's brilliant keeping qualities. Roasting is a time-honoured method of cooking onions, but the sweet and sour touch is more of an Italian idea. For a dish like this, I prefer capers preserved in vinegar, to provide an extra note of sharpness. Choose the smallest ones you can find, or chop larger capers roughly before adding to the onions.

• Pre-heat the oven to 200°C/400°F/Gas 6. Put the onions into a dish with the olive oil, vinegar and 3 tablespoons water. Add the thyme and sprinkle over the sugar. Season enthusiastically with salt and pepper. Turn the onions a couple of times, then thrust the dish into the oven and roast for 1 hour. Turn the onions every 15 minutes or so and baste with their own juices until they are very tender and browned here and there. Now stir in the drained raisins, pine nuts and capers. Return to the oven for a further 30 minutes, again stirring after about a quarter of an hour. Taste and adjust seasoning, and serve hot or cold with a sprinkling of parsley.

Roast Celeriac

SERVES 4

1 medium-large **celeriac**
a little **sunflower oil**
a knob of **butter**
75ml (5 tablespoons) **sweet**
  Madeira or **Marsala**
salt and **pepper**

If you've never tasted roast celeriac, it is definitely time you gave it a try.

• Pre-heat the oven to 180°C/350°F/Gas 4. Cut the celeriac into 8 wedges and trim off the skin as economically as you can. Toss the wedges in just enough oil to coat. Smear the butter thickly around an ovenproof dish, large enough to take the wedges lying down flat (well, flattish, anyway). Lay them in the dish, season with salt and pepper and pour over the Madeira or Marsala. Roast for about 1 hour, turning the wedges and basting every now and then until they are richly browned all over and very tender. You may have to add a tablespoon or two of water towards the end to prevent burning.

Celeriac

I'd like to fly the flag for celeriac. It is a far more interesting vegetable than its spindly sibling celery. Botanically speaking, the two are extremely closely connected; celeriac is no more than a swollen version of celery, not a root as you might imagine, but a corm or, in other words, the base of the stems.

Appearance may also have something to do with the poor-cousin status of celeriac. It is not exactly a sexy-looking vegetable. Not the kind of thing that is celebrated in paintings. It doesn't often grace the photo pages of glossy magazines or cookbooks, and you rarely see it prettifying the set of a TV cookery programme. But it's what's inside that counts, so don't let poor looks put you off.

Celeriac mash is the obvious place to start mining its treasures. If you want a starchier, milder version, mash the cooked and well-drained celeriac with equal quantities of potato and lots of butter and cream or milk, seasoning it generously with nutmeg (a spice that brings out the best in celeriac). For a purer mash, leave out the potato. The next place to go, for a completely different take, is down the French route, towards *céleri-rave rémoulade*. This is one of the staples of the French *charcuterie* and *traiteur*'s shop, a mustardy celeriac salad. Either grate the celeriac very thickly or cut it into fine batons, blanch for a minute or two in boiling salted water and drain until dry, then turn in mayonnaise sharpened with extra Dijon mustard.

With those two under your belt, you should need little encouragement to move onwards – try celeriac gratin dauphinoise (I usually blanch the slices of celeriac before layering), using either neat celeriac, or a mix of celeriac and potato. Simmered until barely tender, celeriac can be glazed with a little butter, sugar and lemon, or simply tossed with butter and chopped chives or parsley. I add it to vegetable stews, or to big trays of mixed root vegetables, tossed with olive oil, whole cloves of garlic (unpeeled), sprigs of rosemary or thyme and coarse salt, roasted in a hot oven until all are tender. Celeriac makes a good soup, too: gentle, creamy and soothing (see page 182).

CHOOSING AND PREPARING CELERIAC

A medium-sized corm is the thing to go for. Too small and it is a complete pain to peel and prepare. Too large and it becomes spongy – air rather than flesh is eventually what pads them out. Don't be tempted by a celeriac that is anything other than firm. Soft spots and bruises are definite no-nos. Celeriac is meant to be solid and heavy.

Preparation is straightforward. Slice off the tight tangle of roots at the base and trim off any stalks. I find it easiest to slice the celeriac thickly (or cut into wedges if the recipe calls for that) and then to cut off the skin afterwards. As soon as the celeriac is cut, drop it into a bowl of acidulated water (i.e. water with the juice of ½ a lemon or a tablespoon or two of white wine vinegar) to prevent it browning. When blanching or cooking the prepared celeriac, you should again acidulate the water.

Rich and Sinful Baked Bay and Honey Custards

Baked custard falls into two categories, the light and slippery everyday type made with milk and whole eggs, and the irredeemably sinful, rich and dense sort made just for a special occasion with oodles of cream and a vast number of egg yolks. Here we definitely have the latter, for high days and holidays only. Though I am a devotee of real vanilla, I find the almost almondy scent of bay leaves more beguiling here. It harks back to days before the ubiquity of vanilla.

Incidentally, if you don't have the time or inclination to whip the left over egg whites into a batch of meringues, they can be frozen until the mood comes upon you.

SERVES 6

500ml (18 fl oz) **whipping** or **double cream**

3 **bay leaves**

a pinch of **salt**

3 tablespoons **honey**

5 **egg yolks**

1 whole **egg**

to serve: freshly grated **nutmeg**

• Pre-heat the oven to 140°C/275°F/Gas 1. Arrange 6 ramekins or small heatproof coffee cups in a shallow roasting tin.

• Put the cream, bay leaves and salt in a saucepan and bring gently to the boil. Draw to one side, leave to infuse for 5 minutes, then bring back to the boil.

• Meanwhile, bring the kettle to the boil. Stir the honey into the egg yolks and egg until dissolved. Pour in the hot and steamy cream, stirring constantly. Ladle the custard mixture through a sieve into the ramekins, filling them almost to the rim if there is enough to go round. Take the charged roasting tin to the oven and balance it half in the oven while you pour the hot water into the tin around the ramekins. Take the level about halfway up the ramekins and no more, or you risk slopping water into the custards themselves. Gently slide the roasting tin fully into the oven. Bake for about 45 minutes until just set.

• Lift the ramekins out of their hot water bath and leave to cool. Dust lightly with nutmeg before serving.

Serve the custards cold, together with a compote of whatever fresh fruit is around. In early spring it may be blood oranges, but as we march towards summer you may be able to extract the first stems of garden rhubarb to cook down with golden caster sugar, curls of orange zest and the juice of an orange. Later on, try the custards with stewed gooseberries or lightly cooked blackcurrants.

Sweet Cicely

Sweet Cicely ought to be a demurely seductive heroine in a Shakespeare play, a charming virgin whose purity is maligned by a scheming villain who wants to get his wicked way with her. Obviously she emerges whiter than white as the final curtain is about to fall, all ready to espouse her true beloved.

There is a sort of virginal purity about the real sweet cicely, but it has at least one bad habit that would be sorely out of place in our Shakespearean heroine. Let us talk positive to begin with. Sweet cicely, the herb, is not one you will find swinging in a plastic pack from the herb rack in a supermarket. No, unless you can find someone who grows it, you will have to head off to the garden centre to track it down. I would urge you to go as soon as you can, for sweet cicely is a totally charming herb with soft feathery leaves that taste sweetly of aniseed. The white umbelliferous flowers bloom in May, an irresistible lure for the bees of the district.

It takes only a few years for a single small pot of sweet cicely to grow into a sizeable clump, more than you can ever use in one season, but how generous you will feel when you offer all your friends gently scented posies to use in their puddings. This seems as good a point as any to introduce sweet cicely's negative side – it self-seeds with determination. Not as invasively as, say, lemon balm, but in a fairly determined manner. So try to make time to snip off drooping flowerheads and root up plantlets as soon as they are distinguishable.

Sweet cicely's most notable property is that it reduces the need for sugar when cooked with tart fruit such as gooseberries or rhubarb. Drop a few generous sprigs into the pan and you can cut down the sugar by up to a quarter. I can't quite fathom how it works, but for such a delicate flutterer of a herb it really is rather remarkable.

It will also impart a light aniseed flavour that is most pleasing. I've used it with apples, too, in pies and crumbles, and infused it very gently in cream for custards. Traditionally it seems to have been reserved for sweet dishes, but I've found that it also goes exceptionally well with white fish and shellfish. Try adding a few sprigs to fish cooked *en papillote*, that is, in a parcel of foil or greaseproof paper with a knob of butter and shake of white wine, or stir finely chopped sweet cicely into a beurre blanc or hollandaise, or even a seafood risotto.

Custard

SERVES 8

5 **egg yolks**

300ml (½ pint) **milk**

300ml (½ pint) **single cream**

2 tablespoons **caster sugar**

3 sprigs of **sweet cicely**, or
   2 **bay leaves**, a **cinnamon
   stick** or 1 **vanilla pod**, slit
   open

I'm a snob when it comes to custard. I like the real thing, and all else falls short. Instant can't hold a candle to a real eggy custard. If you feel nervous about curdling all those egg yolks, replace one of them with a tablespoon of cornflour. Then it can boil with no danger of curdling. The final custard won't be quite so epically velvety, but I doubt that anyone will complain.

Vanilla is the most obvious flavouring for custard, but for a change try scenting it gently with the light aniseed fragrance of sweet cicely if it grows in your garden, a leaf or two of almondy bay, or a stick of cinnamon.

• Whisk the egg yolks lightly in a bowl. Put the milk and cream into a pan with the sugar and the flavouring. Bring gently up to the boil, then pour on to the egg yolks, whisking constantly. Return to the pan, set over a very gentle heat. Stir constantly until it thickens enough just to coat the back of the spoon and no more. Pull straight off the heat and strain into a cool bowl. Serve hot, warm or cold.

Rhubarb and Honey Compote

SERVES 6–10

1kg (2 lb 4 oz) **rhubarb**,
  trimmed and cut into 2.5–4cm
  (1–1½ in) lengths
4 strips **orange zest**
6 tablespoons **runny honey**
85g (3 oz) **caster sugar**
juice of 1 large **orange**

This is an in-between sort of a time for fruit, when autumnal apples and pears are way past their best, and fragrant, soft summer berries are still on the horizon. Rhubarb steps into the breach. This compote is very good on its own, perhaps with cream or yoghurt, but for a grander pudding serve it with wedges of Daffodil Cake (page 50) and creamy home-made Custard (page 41).

• Pre-heat the oven to 170°C/325°F/Gas 3. Place the rhubarb in a shallow ovenproof dish with the orange zest and drizzle over the honey. Sprinkle with sugar, then pour over the orange juice. Cover with foil. Bake for 25–35 minutes, stirring once in a while, until the rhubarb is tender but not disintegrating. Serve hot, warm or cold.

Rhubarb

Thank heavens for rhubarb, about the only home-grown 'fruit' we've got at this time of year. Of course, it is not actually a fruit, but it is a pudding-provider and that is good enough for me. It is also one of those blessed plants that seems never to give up on even the most distracted gardener. Year in, year out, it thrusts up with fervour, an endless stream of rosy green stems just begging to be snapped off and cooked with enough sugar to take an edge off the sourness.

It is here that I must come clean. I have a garden bereft of rhubarb. I should have invested in a plant last year, but time rushed by and now I am regretting it. I resent buying rhubarb. The price always seems so high in supermarkets considering how difficult it is to stop rhubarb growing at break-neck speed. I shall search out better value at the next farmers' market, but really the only answer is to shove 'buy rhubarb plant' to the top of my to-do list and then head off firmly to the garden centre. Even if it is too late for this year, I should be able to harvest enough to keep us in the occasional crumble by next spring.

If, like me, you are forced to buy your rhubarb, then here is what to look out for: firm stiff stems, not too chunky (say, about the thickness of your big toe at most), preferably with leaves so that you can really assess the freshness. Droopy leaves indicate the rhubarb has been hanging around longer than you would wish. You won't be eating the leaves since they are toxic (due to overconcentration of oxalic acid), but they'll bulk out your compost nicely. Remember not to feed them to the rabbits.

If you grow your own rhubarb, then you will have no concerns over freshness. Towards the end of the season you will have to deal with extra large stems that will almost definitely need to be peeled to remove tough strings on the outside.

Two important things to remember when cooking rhubarb. The first is there is no need to add any liquid (unless perhaps you want it to make, say, a jelly), as it will produce copious quantities of its own. This means that to stand any chance of keeping the pastry crisp in two-crust pies and tarts you will need either to cook and drain the rhubarb before putting it in, or add a protective layer between pastry and rhubarb (say, a mixture of butter, sugar and ground almonds), or toss the rhubarb with cornflour and sugar before piling it in so that the cornflour soaks up and thickens the juices to a gel. The cornflour option is particularly good for two-crust pies, and you might try adding one of the classic flavourings, such as ground ginger, or diced preserved stem ginger, or finely grated orange zest. A little more unusual, but very good indeed, is the addition of a few chopped fresh angelica stems, but that's something you will almost inevitably have to grow for yourself.

Hillside Rhubarb Custard

SERVES 6

220g (8 oz), give or take,
   leftover slightly stale **Victoria
   sponge sandwich**, or other
   plain cake, sliced
350g (12 oz) trimmed **rhubarb**,
   cut into 1cm (½ in) lengths
85g (3 oz) **caster sugar**
a little **butter** for greasing

FOR THE CUSTARD:
900ml (1½ pints) **full-cream
   milk**
1 **vanilla pod**, slit open
   lengthways
3 whole **eggs**
3 **egg yolks**
2 tablespoons **plain flour**
2 tablespoons **caster sugar**

It may not be an everyday occurrence, but once in a while we find ourselves with a chunk of leftover cake. After a birthday party, maybe, or just a sociable afternoon tea. This has become a favourite way to use it up, with the tartness of rhubarb balancing the sweetness of the custard-soaked cake. Any plainish cake will do, with or without filling (a plain buttercream and jam filling gives a particularly delicious richness). You could also use gooseberries, topped and tailed and halved, or sliced cooking apple and, in the winter months, using the year's first delicate, cosseted forced rhubarb will make the pudding a brilliant pink.

• Pre-heat the oven to 190°C/375°F/Gas 5. Grease a 2-litre (3½-pint) soufflé dish, or other fairly deep ovenproof dish. Lay the sponge slices in the bottom. Scatter over the rhubarb, and the 85g (3 oz) caster sugar.

• To make the custard, bring the milk gently up to the boil with the vanilla pod. While it heats up, beat the eggs and yolks with the flour and sugar until pale. Pour on the boiling milk, a splash at a time, whisking it in well. Fish out the vanilla pod and pour the hot custard over the rhubarb and sponge. The rhubarb will float up to the top, which is fine. Stand the dish in a roasting pan and pour enough boiling water around it to come about 2.5cm (1 in) up the sides. Bake for 45–50 minutes until just set. Eat hot or warm. With cream, if you like it.

Jane's Tinned Peach Crumble with Ginger and Pine Nuts

SERVES 6–8

2 x 400g (14 oz) tins **peach slices** in syrup

2 spheres **stem ginger**, chopped (optional)

1½ teaspoons **cornflour** or **arrowroot**

FOR THE CRUMBLE:

220g (8 oz) **plain flour**

¾–1 teaspoon **ground ginger**

pinch of **salt**

110g (4 oz) **caster sugar**

175g (6 oz) **unsalted butter**

30g (1 oz) **pine nuts**

to serve: **cream**

There comes a point mid-spring when fruit is either terminally tedious ('not another orange/apple/banana') or falls into the expensive exotica category. Strawberries and gooseberries and all those juicy sweet summer fruits are still a long way off, and even the garden rhubarb isn't quite up to scratch yet. My mum's solution was to make a tinned peach crumble and I still think it is a brilliant combination. It is the smooth slipperiness of the peaches against the velvety starch of the crumble topping that does it for me every time. For the best result, you need peaches that are tinned in syrup, rather than the more healthy ones that come in light juice.

I've beefed up the crumble mix with a shake of ginger and a scattering of buttery pine nuts. For those of you who really love ginger, a couple of spheres of preserved stem ginger, chopped and muddled in with the peaches, make this even better.

• Pre-heat the oven to 200°C/400°F/Gas 6. Drain the peaches and reserve their juice. Mix the peaches with the stem ginger, if using, in the bottom of a pie dish. For the crumble, sift the flour with the ginger and salt. Stir in the sugar, then rub in the butter until the mixture is a great big mass of buttery crumbs. Sprinkle this evenly and thickly over the peaches. Scatter the pine nuts over the top. Bake for about 20–25 minutes until nicely browned with the juice bubbling through around the sides.

• To make the sauce, mix the cornflour or arrowroot with a tablespoonful of the juice from the peaches. Then stir in another spoonful. Put the rest of the juice in a pan and bring up to the boil. When it is warm, stir one more spoonful in with the cornflour, then tip the whole lot back into the pan and stir. Simmer for 2 minutes or so until thickened. Serve hot with the crumble and lots of cream.

A Spring Ingredient to Avoid

We all make mistakes, and last Easter Monday I made a monster-sized error. I am a great believer in disguise and economy with the truth when something goes wrong in the kitchen, but this was one occasion when I couldn't hide my mistake away, largely because I didn't notice the copious presence of an extra uninvited ingredient in the pudding until it was too late. And the reason I tell you this now is not merely to warn you, but also because William Shaw, who took all the stunning photos for this book, was with us, and I know he will never let me forget it.

I was halfway through serving the baked bay custards with a compote of blood oranges in a rosemary and pepper syrup when my cousin Lucy piped up. 'Sophie,' she said slowly, 'are there meant to be ants in the syrup?' No, no, no, no! I had left the compote out overnight, only loosely covered, and it had been massively invaded. Disgusting. We settled for Easter eggs instead.

Simon Hopkinson's Lemon Posset

SERVES 8–10

1 litre (1¾ pints) **double cream**

275g (10 oz) **caster sugar**

the juice of 4 **lemons**

This elegantly simple, divinely rich pudding comes from Simon Hopkinson's *Gammon & Spinach*, a book which, I am sad to say, disappeared during our last move and is now out of print. If you ever see a copy for sale, snap it up quickly as, unlike so many books written by chefs, Simon's recipes work wonderfully on a domestic level.

I serve this with a fruit compote, maybe some oranges marinated in a little Grand Marnier and icing sugar, with a few crisp biscuits, such as the Orangines on page 238.

• Bring the cream and sugar slowly up to the boil in a large pan, stirring until the sugar has dissolved. The cream will boil up high, so make sure the pan is big enough for its expansion. Let the cream boil for exactly 3 minutes. Draw off the heat and stir in the lemon juice. Strain into a bowl and then pour into 8–10 small ramekins. Leave to cool, then chill for 4 hours before serving.

Frosted Spring Flowers

1 **egg white**

caster sugar

edible flowers – **elderflowers, primroses, violets, heartsease, garden pansies**

Frosting flowers is a frivolous task for a quiet moment. It's the kind of thing that children like to be roped in for, if they don't think it is too namby-pamby. Once frosted and hardened, the flowers will keep for up to 12 hours, possibly even longer. Use them to decorate puddings or cakes.

• Whisk the egg white lightly with a fork to loosen it. Spread the sugar out thickly in a plate. To sugar the elderflowers, dip them head down into the egg white, shake off excess, then dip into the caster sugar. Leave to dry on a baking tray lined with greaseproof paper or non-stick baking parchment, stalks upward. For other flowers, paint the petals sparingly on both sides with egg white, then paint over the green base and a short length of the stalk. Coat in sugar and again leave to dry on baking greaseproof or parchment for 2–3 hours until hard and crisp.

Pithivier
Praliné au Chocolat

This is a devastatingly rich and delicious variation on the classic Pithivier, one of France's very best tarts. Instead of the usual moist almond filling, it has a variegated filling that alternates a densely chocolatey melting cream with a toasted nut and caramel praline filling. It is at its utmost best eaten hot or warm from the oven, slathered in gorgeous unpasteurised Jersey cream.

SERVES 6–8

500g (1 lb 2 oz) **puff pastry**
1 **egg**, lightly beaten
icing sugar

FOR THE PRALINE FILLING:

110g (4 oz) **blanched almonds**
125g (4½ oz) **caster sugar**
2 tablespoons **double cream**
45g (1½ oz) **butter**, melted and
   cooled until tepid
2 **egg yolks**

FOR THE GANACHE:

85ml (3 fl oz) **double cream**
85g (3 oz) plain **chocolate**,
   chopped

• To make the praline, pre-heat the oven to 180°C/350°F/Gas 4. Spread the almonds out on a tray and roast for 6–8 minutes, shaking once or twice, until lightly browned. Meanwhile, set aside 15g (½ oz) of the sugar. Put the remaining sugar into a small heavy-based pan with 2 tablespoons water. Stir over a low to moderate heat without letting the mixture come anywhere near boiling point until the sugar has completely dissolved, and I do mean completely, into a clear syrup. Brush the sides down occasionally with a brush dipped in warm water to remove clinging crystals of sugar. Bring up to the boil and boil hard without stirring at all, just tilting and swirling the pan occasionally, until golden brown. Meanwhile, lightly oil a marble pastry board or a cool baking tin.

• When the sugar has caramelised, tip the almonds into the sugar, stir once, then scrape speedily out on to the oiled surface. Leave to cool and set solid. Break up into pieces with a rolling pin, then grind to a powder in a processor. Add the reserved 15g (½ oz) caster sugar, the 2 tablespoons cream, melted butter and egg yolks. Process again to form a thick paste. Cover and chill until needed.

• Now for the chocolate ganache. Heat the cream to boiling point. Draw off the heat, tip in the chocolate and stir until dissolved. Cool, then chill for at least an hour.

• Divide the pastry in half and roll out the first half. Cut out a 28cm (11 in) circle. Roll out the second half slightly larger, and cut out a 30cm (almost 12 in) circle. Lay the smaller circle of puff pastry on a dampened baking sheet. Spread the praline paste out thickly, mounding it up gently in the centre and leaving a 2cm (just under

1 inch) border around the edge of the pastry. With your finger make a dozen indentations in the paste, spacing them evenly around the circle. Take teaspoonfuls of the chilled ganache, roll into balls and pop one into each indentation. Smooth the edges of the praline paste to meet the balls. Brush the bare pastry border with beaten egg, then carefully lay the larger circle of puff pastry on top. Press the edges firmly together. Make a small hole in the centre, brush all over with beaten egg, then chill the pithivier for at least 20 minutes. Pre-heat the oven to 230°C/450°F/Gas 8.

• Using a sharp knife, make 12 small cuts, evenly spaced, in the edge of the pastry. With fingers, push the pastry on either side of each cut in and up to form a scalloped edge to the tart. Then, using the tip of the knife, score 12 curving lines, each one swishing out from the central hole towards one of the original cuts in the edge. Knock up the edges with the flat of a knife. Bake the pithivier for 10 minutes, then reduce the oven temperature to 190°C/375°F/Gas 5 and cook for a further 20 minutes. Take out and dredge the surface with icing sugar. Return to the oven for a final 10 minutes to finish cooking and glaze. Serve hot or warm.

Daffodil Cake

This is a variation on the classic American Angel-food cake, and earns its floral moniker from the splashes of yellow that mingle with the white of the crumb. It is light and sweet and airy, with a lemony icing to contrast. If you have any home-made elderflower cordial (see page 56), try it with an elderflower icing instead.

SERVES 8–10

150g (5 oz) **plain flour**

9 large **egg whites**

1 teaspoon **cream of tartar**

2 pinches **salt**

250g (9 oz) **caster sugar**

2 teaspoons **vanilla extract**

4 large **egg yolks**

2 teaspoons finely grated
  lemon zest

FOR THE ICING:

sifted **icing sugar**

2 tablespoons freshly squeezed
  lemon juice, or undiluted
  home-made **elderflower
  cordial**

to decorate: a small bunch of
  primroses, or **yellow
  mimosa comfits**, or even
  small **yellow Easter eggs**
  (optional)

• Pre-heat the oven to 190°C/375°F/Gas 5. Sift the flour four times (or even five or six if you wish) to make sure it is as lump-free as possible and well aerated. Put the egg whites into a grease-free dry bowl and sprinkle over the cream of tartar and salt. Whisk until they form soft peaks. Set aside 2 tablespoons of sugar and sprinkle the rest over the whites with the vanilla extract. Whisk in until the mixture is glossy and thick. Fold in the flour in three batches, working quickly and lightly.

• Whisk the egg yolks and reserved sugar until thick and pale yellow. Add the lemon zest and about one-third of the egg white mixture and fold in until evenly blended. Take an ungreased 25cm (10 in) ring mould with removable base and spoon in large dollops of the pure white mixture, alternating here and there with dollops of the pale yellow mixture, until they are both used up. Bake for about 35 minutes until a skewer inserted into the centre of the cake comes out clean.

• Now turn the tin upside down and hoop-la it over a bottle or something similar so that it hangs upside down (or support it at the edges on three tins of equal height). Leave to cool in this peculiar position. When cool, use a fork to loosen the sides, easing them gently away from the tin, until the cake comes free.

• To make the icing, gradually beat the icing sugar into the lemon juice or cordial until you have a thick but still marginally runny icing. Spoon it over the cake, allowing it to drip provocatively down the sides. If using comfits or Easter eggs, press them gently into the icing in a decorative fashion before it has time to set. However, if primroses are your chosen decoration, leave it until just before serving to arrange them around the base of the cake.

I like to serve this as a pudding (forget the icing), in thick wedges, with a fresh fruit compote – rhubarb is the obvious choice in the spring – and home-made custard.

NB Rest assured, primroses are edible, though they should only be picked from your garden, and not from the wild. Cuteness is their only value here as they don't taste of anything much, unless you go to the effort of frosting them (see page 47).

Bacon and Chive Cornbread

SERVES 8

110g (4 oz) **plain flour**

170g (6 oz) **yellow cornmeal**

1 level tablespoon **baking powder**

1 tablespoon **caster sugar**

5 rashers **streaky bacon**, grilled until crisp, very roughly chopped

4 tablespoons chopped **chives**

½ teaspoon **salt**

220ml (8 fl oz) **milk**

2 **free-range eggs**

4 tablespoons **extra virgin olive oil** or **melted butter**

With the sun shining fit to burst, the herbs thrusting forth like there was no tomorrow and a pile of fine old-fashioned dry-cured bacon in the fridge, I returned gleefully to an old favourite of mine – American cornbread, bright and golden like the day, studded with the salt of our own gorgeous bacon and flecked with green spring chives.

Cornbread is a doddle to make; leave it plain if you have nothing worth adding, or jazz it up with crisp bacon or fried onion, chopped sun-dried tomatoes, cubes of Cheddar or Parmesan, chilli and spring onion, or vigorous herbs like thyme or sage. I've made excellent cornbread dotted with crushed peppercorns or charmed with strips of Parma ham.

Cornbread is at its best still warm from the oven, with or without dribbling, melting butter over it, but it remains fine and dandy when cold (and doesn't crumble so much). It's great for a simple lunch, perfect with soup on days when the weather is damp and chill, and what's left over makes the basis for a fabulous stuffing for a chicken (see page 16).

• Pre-heat the oven to 200°C/400°F/Gas 6. Grease a 20 x 20cm (8 x 8 in) shallow tin generously.

• Mix the flour with the cornmeal, baking powder, sugar, bacon, chives and salt. Make a well in the centre and pour in the milk. Add the eggs and oil or melted butter, and stir all the ingredients together until evenly mixed. Pour into the tin and bake for 20–25 minutes until firm to the touch. Double-check by plunging a skewer into the centre – if it comes out clean, the cornbread is done.

• Let it rest in the tin for 5 minutes then turn out. Eat warm or cold, cut into chunky squares.

Oats and Honey Bread

MAKES 1 LOAF

200g (7 oz) **rolled oats**

300ml (½ pint) **milk**

30g (1 oz) **runny honey**

400g (14 oz) **strong white flour**

1 sachet (7g) **easy-blend yeast**

2 teaspoons **salt**

The first time I blended oats and honey was, I think, to make some youthful, all-natural face mask. It was extremely sticky, and no doubt did wonders for my skin. Two decades on and I'm far more likely to bring the two together in the kitchen than the bathroom. This bread is one I make pretty frequently because a) it tastes good and b) the inclusion of oats, milk and honey makes me feel as if I'm giving my children something relatively healthy, while they gleefully believe it is just white bread.

There isn't a great deal of honey in the loaf, so it is not particularly sweet, merely retaining a lingering scent.

• Soak the oats in the milk for 10 minutes in a large bowl. Now add the honey, flour, yeast and salt. Mix to a soft but not sticky dough, adding a splash or two of water if needed. Knead energetically for 5–10 minutes until silky-smooth and elastic. Rinse out the bowl, and return the dough to it. Cover with a damp tea towel and leave in a warm place to rise until doubled in bulk – about 1 hour.

• Punch down the dough, then knead again for another 2 or 3 minutes to smooth out. Shape into a round loaf and sit on an oiled baking tray. Rub a little extra white flour over the top, then, using a very sharp knife, slash a cross in the top. Once again, cover with a damp tea towel and leave in a warm place until doubled in size.

• Pre-heat the oven to 220°C/425°F/Gas 7. Bake the loaf for about 25 minutes, turning once if necessary to ensure even browning. It is done when a tap on the base sounds hollow. Cool on a wire rack.

Sweet Pickled Samphire

If you are lucky enough to find and pick a bag or two of samphire when you are wandering by the seaside, or if you see it going cheap at the fishmonger's, preserve some of it in a sweet, spicy vinegar to make the most delicious pickle. It is excellent with fish, salmon in particular, but it goes just as well with pâtés, cured meats and hard cheeses. It will keep for years if need be – I recently found a forgotten half-used jar at the back of a cupboard; it must have been there for at least three years, and it tasted every bit as good as I remembered.

FILLS A 1–1.5 LITRE (2–2½ PINT) PRESERVING JAR

500g (1 lb 2 oz) **samphire**

FOR THE SWEET SPICED VINEGAR:

1.2 litres (2 pints) **white wine vinegar**

600g (1 lb 5 oz) **caster sugar**

24 **allspice berries**

12 **cloves**

2 **cinnamon sticks**

2 tablespoons **coriander seeds**

20 **black peppercorns**

2 **star anise**

• Put all the ingredients for the vinegar into a saucepan and bring gently up to the boil, stirring until the sugar has dissolved. Draw off the heat, pour into a bowl, then cover and leave to cool and settle for 2–3 hours. Strain out the spices.

• Meanwhile, pick over the samphire, removing roots and damaged parts. Rinse thoroughly and dry. Pack into cold sterilised jar(s), then pour in enough vinegar to cover completely (you probably won't need it all, but the remainder will keep in the fridge until your next batch of pickling). Seal tightly, label and store in a cool dark place for at least 2 weeks, preferably 4, before delving into the jars.

Samphire

There are two kinds of samphire: both grow by the sea but neither are seaweeds, despite being often described thus. The commoner of the two, in this country at least, is marsh samphire, which grows on stretches of open, sandy mud and salt marshes, hence the name. It looks like green coral, with crisp juicy forked stems. The taste is fresh and salty, and very appealing. When it is young, I like to eat it raw, tossed into a salad. It is more usual, however, to eat it lightly cooked as an accompaniment to fish.

The other samphire is rock samphire, which grows on rocky outcrops, again by the sea, thriving in the salty sea air. The leaves are flatter and less juicy than those of marsh samphire and the taste is quite different. It has a distinct tang of iodine, which is not so appealing raw, but lovely when muted by a few minutes' dip in boiling water. Like marsh samphire, it goes extremely well with fish, particularly but not exclusively salmon, and makes a superb pickle (see opposite).

You will be able to buy marsh samphire from May onwards at most good fishmongers', though once it hits July a tough string develops in the centre of the juicy stems, making them too tough to eat raw. I'm not sure that I've ever seen rock samphire for sale, so next time you are heading off for the coast, take your pocket plant book with you and a couple of plastic bags just in case you come across some growing near the salty sea. And do be careful – don't reach too far over the edge, and check assiduously that you've plucked the right plant.

TO COOK FRESH SAMPHIRE

Allow about 110–150g (4–5 oz) per person. Pick over the samphire, removing roots and damaged parts. Rinse thoroughly. Steam or simmer in unsalted water for 2–5 minutes (rock samphire needs more cooking than marsh) until slightly softened. Toss in a little butter and serve.

Elderflower Cordial

MAKES AROUND
1.5 LITRES (2½ PINTS)

20 beautiful, full heads of
  elderflower
1.8kg (4 lb) **granulated** or
  caster sugar
1.2 litres (2 pints) **water**
2 **unwaxed lemons**
75g (2½ oz) **citric acid**

I make several batches of elderflower cordial every May, without fail. It's not just that it tastes so much nicer than most bought cordials, but also that I love the whole process. When the first creamy buds begin to appear on the trees I lay in stocks of citric acid (from most chemists) and granulated sugar. Come the next sunny day when the flowers are in full bloom, I try to make time for a gentle gathering amble through the nearest fields, and half an hour or so in the kitchen.

Cordial made from the earliest blooms is good but less fully flavoured, so be patient for a week or so, then gather the biggest, boldest heads of flowers, creamy in colour (pure white ones are older and have often lost a good deal of their scent) and heady with that strange, unmissable Muscat scent. Pick well away from big roads to minimise pollution, and use them as soon as you get home.

The cordial will last for several months in a cool dark cupboard, but if you want to lay down stocks to take you through the autumn and winter months, use plastic bottles, don't quite fill them, and then freeze them.

• Shake the elderflowers to expel any lingering insects, then place in a large bowl. Put the sugar in a pan with the water and bring up to the boil, stirring until the sugar has completely dissolved.

• While the sugar syrup is heating, pare the zest of the lemons off in wide strips and toss into the bowl with the elderflowers. Slice the lemons, discard the ends and add the slices to the bowl. Pour over the boiling syrup, then stir in the citric acid. Cover with a cloth and then leave at room temperature for 24 hours.

• Next day, strain the cordial through a sieve lined with muslin (or a new J-cloth rinsed out in boiling water) and pour into thoroughly cleaned glass or plastic bottles. Screw on the lids and pop into the cupboard ready to use.

TO SERVE ELDERFLOWER CORDIAL

There is nothing nicer on a warm day than a **tall iced glass of fizzy elderflower**. Dilute the elderflower cordial to taste with fizzy water and serve over ice. A slice or two of lemon or a sprig of mint floating on top is always a bonus.

For something a touch more sprightly, add a shot of gin or vodka to create a **brilliant cocktail**. A lemon slice, in this case, is virtually essential. Or add the cordial to white wine and sparkling water to make an **elderflower spritzer**.

Elderflower cordial is also brilliant in cooking. Adding a good slug or two to a **gooseberry fool** creates the perfect marriage of flavours, and it is worth trying too in a **vinaigrette** – mix with wine vinegar, a touch of mustard, salt, pepper and a light olive oil. Surprisingly good with a **courgette, lettuce and broad bean salad**. You might even try adding it to a **marinade** for **chicken breasts**.

Try elderflower cordial in **sorbets** or **ice creams**, or just spooned over scoops of vanilla ice cream, or use a few spoonfuls to sweeten and flavour the **fruit for a crumble**.

summer

Little Goat's Cheese Soufflés

Based on an old English recipe, these cheese soufflés are thickened with bread (it must be of good quality – a sourdough gives a particularly good flavour), but lightened with a base of diced tomatoes and basil or mint, whichever is closest to hand. I use a (fairly) local goat's cheese with a fine depth of flavour.

SERVES 6

225ml (7½ fl oz) **milk**

60g (2 oz) crust-free **soft white bread** (about 3 thick slices)

150g (5 oz) derinded **goat's cheese**, crumbled

60g (2 oz) **butter**, softened, plus a little extra for greasing

3 **eggs**, separated

200g (7 oz) ripe **tomatoes**, deseeded and finely diced

a couple of pinches of **sugar**

8 fresh **basil** or **mint leaves**, chopped

salt, **pepper** and a touch of freshly grated **nutmeg**

• Pre-heat the oven to 220°C/425°F/Gas 7. Tear the bread up roughly, pour the milk over and leave to soak for 5–10 minutes.

• Put the cheese into a processor with the butter, egg yolks, milk and bread mixture, salt, pepper and nutmeg. Process until smooth.

• Mix the tomatoes with the sugar (if they are absolutely fantastic tomatoes, you can leave this out, but in most cases it will be necessary to heighten the flavour), basil or mint and salt and pepper, and divide between 6 buttered ramekins. Whisk the egg whites until they form stiff peaks and fold into the cheese mixture. Spoon this over the tomatoes, filling each ramekin to within 5mm–1cm (¼–½ in) of its rim. Whip the ramekins straight into the oven. Bake for 10–15 minutes until nicely puffed and browned, and serve hot, hot, hot.

Goat's Cheese

I've had the good fortune to spend many holidays near the Loire valley, home to some of the finest goat's cheeses in the world. When we are there we make a twice-weekly pilgrimage to the local market, with a stop at the cheese stall firmly on the schedule. On the whole we are semi-soft lovers, appreciating our goat's cheese firm enough to slice, but still a little moist and crumbly. We opt one week for a log from Ste Maure, another for a pyramid from Valençay, or a simple round from Selles-sur-Cher. These are just the well-known names, the aristocrats of a formidable crowd of accomplished cheeses.

The creation of goat's cheeses has come late to Britain, but we're making headway. Until recently, I would have said we couldn't compete with the French. I'd yet to taste a goat's cheese with the same depth of flavour, those lemony notes and herby undertones that make good French goat's cheeses so special. That's all changing as small producers of raw goat's milk cheeses are gaining expertise, encouraged, I suspect, by their customers' increasing fondness for their creations.

Whenever I see it, I make a point of buying Cerney cheese, modelled on some of those famous French cheeses, with a creaminess and flavour that can stand comparison with the best of them. It's not a clone – the local pasture gives it individuality – but it is a joy to eat, and to cook with. It's one of a hundred and eleven goat's cheeses made in this country that are listed in the 2002 *British Cheese Directory*. Greedy though I am, I can't claim to have tasted more than a handful of them, so I'm hoping that there are others out there that are also a match for their French cousins.

The major form of goat's cheese, the one that most food writers are referring to in recipes, is the semi-soft type, with an ivory interior, sliceable and still a little moist, but not wet, usually with a natural, soft white rind on the exterior, or sometimes a dusting of black ash. This type of goat's cheese is the king of them all when it comes to cooking (and eating as well), with its own distinct culinary qualities. Taste apart, the most noticeable characteristic is that it does not melt and ooze when heated. It softens a little, it browns, but it more or less holds its shape. It's also worth noting that the uncooked curds are usually soft enough to mash but firm enough to crumble.

You may also come across very fresh, creamy, undrained goat's cheese with the mildest of flavours. In French markets it is often sold mixed with chopped herbs and garlic ready to spread on bread, which is something you can recreate at home. I use this type of cheese, without the herbs and garlic, like ordinary cream cheese – it makes a superb cheesecake, for instance. There are also a few hard goat's cheeses (most of them British), aged to a greater or lesser degree, which can be grated like Cheddar.

Iced Broad Bean, Mint and Yoghurt Soup

This is a fabulous soup for a warm day, with its beautiful pale, pale green colour. Be generous with the mint, use a real chicken stock, and you can't go wrong, even if the weather does.

SERVES 6

450g (1 lb) shelled **broad beans**, thawed if frozen

750ml (1¼ pints) **light chicken** or **vegetable stock**

625g (1 lb 6 oz) **Greek yoghurt**

a handful of **mint leaves**, chopped

8 whole **mint leaves**

4 **spring onions**, finely chopped

salt and **pepper**

• Cook and skin the beans (see page 92). Take about one-quarter of them, chop roughly and set aside. Liquidise the rest with a little of the stock. Beat in the yoghurt, then gradually work in the remaining stock. Stir in the chopped mint leaves, salt and pepper. Chill.

• Just before serving, pour into a tureen, and scatter over the reserved broad beans, the 8 mint leaves, roughly torn up, and the spring onions. If the day is particularly hot, you might also float a few ice cubes in the soup to keep it perfectly cool amid the swelter.

Tarragon

Why, I wonder, has tarragon never featured a great deal in British cooking? Cross the Channel to France and it has a well-earned place in the regular repertoire of herbs. Any French cook knows that it goes well with chicken and eggs, just as well as parsley and chives. It grows well enough here, in my succession of gardens, anyway, sinking down into the ground in the autumn and rising again in the spring. In fact, in my first small city garden it was one of the few herbs (along with horseradish and rosemary) that thrived, with absolutely no encouragement from me. While most people complain of mint over-running their herb patch and beyond, mine never survived more than a month or so, but the tarragon, well, that just went on an on. Looking back, I wonder whether it was simply that all the cats in the neighbourhood made a beeline for the mint, but never showed the slightest interest in tarragon.

Anyway, the point is that this is a herb worth exploiting. It is sold cut in supermarkets and occasionally at choice greengrocer's, farmers' markets and so on, if you are lucky, but frankly it makes more sense to pay a quick visit to the local garden centre and buy a small pot of tarragon to plant in your garden, window-box, or pot by the back door. Just rub a leaf and sniff before you hand over your cash. French tarragon, the one you are after, smells of aniseed, while Russian tarragon smells of nothing at all and is not worth a fig.

Besides adding tarragon to creamy sauces for chicken or snipping into omelettes in the French mode, I partner it often with fish. At the simplest level, just stuff the stomach cavity of sardines or sea bass or trout with tarragon before grilling on the barbecue, or roasting in a hot oven with olive oil and lemon juice. Or you could add it to a stuffing proper, made with breadcrumbs, fried onion and garlic, and, say, some pine nuts and freshly grated lemon zest, bound with a little beaten egg, which would work handsomely with fish or chicken. I pound tarragon with garlic and chilli to form the basis of a marinade, too – more of that on page 74.

One quick and easy supper that is something of a feast is a mound of tagliatelle, tossed in a tarragon cream sauce made by boiling down cream until lightly thickened with a small handful of chopped tarragon leaves and, again, some lemon zest, finished with a squeeze of lemon at the end, together with barely cooked fresh peas and strips of smoked salmon or trout.

Smoked Trout with Cucumber and Radish Salad and Tarragon Mayonnaise

Kalonji, also known as black onion seeds, sound terrifically exotic and rare, but I can buy them in my local supermarket. If you are lucky enough to have a proper Indian food store near you, they are sure to sell them, too. They have a lively, nutty taste, and the flecks of black set off the colours of the salad beautifully. However, if you can't get hold of any, substitute sesame seeds that you have dry-fried a shade darker in a heavy frying pan.

SERVES 4

150g (5 oz) **smoked trout fillet**, sliced thinly if you can

½ **cucumber**, peeled, cut in half lengthways

12 **radishes**, sliced

½ teaspoon **salt**

2 tablespoons **rice vinegar** or **white wine vinegar**

½ teaspoon **kalonji** (black onion seeds) (optional)

FOR THE MAYONNAISE:

leaves of 1 large sprig of **tarragon**

1 **egg yolk**

½ teaspoon **French Dijon mustard**

1 tablespoon **lemon juice**

60ml (2 fl oz) **lemon olive oil** or **extra virgin olive oil**

90ml (3 fl oz) **groundnut** or **grapeseed oil**

salt

to serve: thinly sliced **brown bread**, lightly toasted

• Leave the trout fillet aside for the moment. Start with the cucumber and radishes. Using a teaspoon, or a melon-balling knife, remove the seeds of the cucumber, then slice it into pieces about the thickness of a £1 coin. Mix with the radishes and salt. Cover and set aside for quarter of an hour. Now knead the cucumber and radishes with your hands for a minute or so, then transfer to a colander. Squeeze out excess water with your hands. Transfer the vegetables to a clean bowl, and stir in the vinegar and kalonji. Cover and leave in the fridge for at least 30 minutes until needed.

• To make the mayonnaise, begin by pounding the tarragon leaves and a little salt to a paste in a mortar. Work in the egg yolk, mustard and lemon juice. Mix the two oils in a jug. Drip them in, whisking constantly, and keeping on drip, drip, dripping, until a third of the oil has been used. Now you can increase the flow of the oil to a slow, steady trickle, always whisking all the time. Keep on going until the oil is all incorporated. Taste and adjust seasonings, adding more salt or lemon as needed.

• To serve, arrange one quarter of the trout on each plate with a little of the cucumber and radish salad, a mound of tarragon mayonnaise, and a slice of bread.

Smoked trout is immensely variable in quality, so you may have to undertake a bit of sampling before you hit on some that is worth buying again. The best smoked trout I've come across was made by a small producer in Devon – the flesh was moist and firm, with just the right trace of salt and smoke to it. Good enough to use in a starter like this one, where lacklustre fish gets no disguise. Less than wonderful smoked trout is best turned into a pâté by processing it with equal quantities of cream cheese, lots of lemon juice and a fair sprinkling of cayenne pepper. If there is no decent smoked trout to be had in your vicinity, try smoked salmon with this salad and replace the mayonnaise with a wedge of lemon.

Le Cake aux Herbes

SERVES 8

220g (8 oz) **butter**, well
  softened, plus a little extra
  for greasing

4 **eggs**

200g (7 oz) **plain flour**

2 teaspoons **baking powder**

3 cloves **garlic**, crushed

3 tablespoons chopped
  parsley

1 tablespoon chopped
  tarragon

2 tablespoons chopped **chives**

salt and **pepper**

This year, this excellent herb-heavy savoury cake has been absolutely the thing to serve with drinks around the little patch of France we visit. The small drinks party is an essential element of our summers in the Touraine; we sit around a few bottles of local wine with a pot of rillettes, cheesy biscuits and whatever else is to hand. Le cake aux herbes is something a little more substantial to nibble on as the sun sets and the next bottle is opened.

It also happens to make a fine starter, served warm from the oven in thick slices, with a tomato and olive salad dressed with best olive oil and balsamic vinegar.

Don't feel that you have to stick with the herbs suggested here. Use whatever you have to hand – I've included fresh thyme leaves, dill and chopped sage, even finely chopped nasturtium leaves. The trick is to use loads, but to balance the more dominant herbs, such as those listed above, with plenty of softer ones, such as parsley and chives.

• Pre-heat the oven to 180°C/350°F/Gas 4. Grease a loaf tin – I use a longish one that measures 21.5 x 6.5cm (8½ x 2½ in), but a more standard one of roughly 19 x 9cm (7½ x 3½ in) will do just as well, as long as you allow for a slightly longer cooking time.

• Separate 2 of the eggs, and reserve the whites. Beat the egg yolks, one at a time, into the butter, and then the whole eggs, again one at a time. Sift the flour and baking powder and beat in, in three batches. Now mix in the garlic, herbs, and plenty of salt and pepper.

• Whisk the 2 reserved egg whites until they form stiff peaks and fold into the cake mixture. Scrape into the loaf tin, and bake for about 25 minutes until firm to the touch. When you take it out of the oven, you will see butter bubbles welling up. Ignore them. Check by plunging a skewer into the centre of the cake. If it comes out clean and dry, the cake is done. Cool for 5 minutes in the tin, then turn out on to a wire rack. Eat warm or cold, in thick slices, with a fine glass of red wine to wash it down.

Wild Salmon Confit

SERVES 6

6 portions **wild salmon fillet**,
  weighing about 170g (6 oz)
  each
juice of 1 **lemon**
approximately 600ml (1 pint)
  goose fat, **duck fat** or **olive
  oil**
2 **bay leaves**
1 large sprig of **thyme**
2 sprigs of **tarragon**
coarse salt and lots of freshly
  ground **pepper**

to serve: **lemon wedges**

The dish I remember most vividly from the couple of times I had the good fortune to eat at Pierre Koffman's restaurant, La Tante Claire, was a darne (a thick steak) of wild salmon that had been poached in goose fat. The flavour was exquisite, and it was not in the least greasy. When I was clearing out the kitchen cupboards recently, I came across a couple of tins of goose fat gathering dust at the back. At long last I tried making 'salmon confit' for myself. It is simplicity itself, and an excellent way of cooking salmon. Duck fat also works similar wonders, but if you don't happen to be roasting a duck or goose in the near future, you can buy goose fat in tins from smart delicatessens. Failing that, you can go for a more Mediterranean approach by using extra virgin olive oil.

Wild salmon is leaner and has a better flavour than farmed, which makes it particularly suitable for this method of cooking. The pickled samphire on page 54 partners the salmon excellently.

• Pre-heat the oven to 140°C/275°F/Gas 1. Season the salmon with salt, pepper and lemon juice, rubbing them gently all over the fish. Leave for at least half an hour before cooking. Now spoon a third of the goose or duck fat, or olive oil, into an ovenproof dish large enough to take all the salmon in a close-fitting single layer. Arrange the salmon pieces in it, skin side down. Spoon over the remaining fat, which should at least come up to the level of the fish, or even cover it. Tuck the bay leaves, thyme and tarragon down among the fish. Cover with foil or a lid and then cook for 12–18 minutes in the oven, basting once or twice with the fat if it does not quite cover the fish. Test to see if the fish is done – the insides should still be a touch translucent at the centre.

• To serve, lift out of the fat and drain briefly on kitchen paper. (You could later strain and reuse the fat, but only for cooking fish.) Arrange on a plate with the lemon wedges and get it to the table quickly, while still hot.

Scallop and Corn Chowder

SERVES 4 AS A MAIN COURSE

8–12 meaty **scallops**

4 rashers **streaky bacon**, cut into strips

1 large **onion**, chopped

2 cloves **garlic**, chopped

1 tablespoon **plain flour**

600ml (1 pint) **fish stock**

1 **bay leaf**

1 good sprig of **parsley**

2 large **potatoes**, diced small

1 large **carrot**, diced small

3 fresh **corn-on-the-cob**

300ml (½ pint) **single cream**

salt, freshly ground **black pepper** and **cayenne pepper**

to serve: a little chopped fresh **parsley**

Main-course soups are not associated with summer, but this one deserves its place towards the end of the season, at that moment when the August warmth develops a chill edge of an evening to remind you that autumn is on its way. Just about then, home-grown sweetcorn should be ripe enough to pick, but make sure that it hurtles from the stalk to the pan to enjoy it at its best. If you don't grow it yourself, buy from a local farm shop or farmers' market where they can reassure you that it was picked no more than 24 hours earlier at the very outside.

Since scallops are such choice morsels, be sure to cut the potato and carrot into tiny dice, all of about half a centimetre (¼ inch) across, to make a fittingly elegant chowder rather than a rough, chunky seaman's version.

• Separate the corals from the whites of the scallops, then slice each white into 2 or 3 discs, depending on thickness. Cover and store in the fridge until needed.

• Place a deep pan over a moderate heat. Add the bacon strips and cook, gently at first, until the fat begins to run, then raise the heat to crisp and brown the bacon. When it is ready, scoop out with a slotted spoon and reserve. Now cook the onion and garlic gently in the bacon fat (if absolutely necessary, add a spot of butter or oil to the pan), until tender. Next sprinkle over the flour and stir in well. Gradually mix in the stock and bring to the boil. Add the herbs, potatoes and carrot, and salt and pepper, and simmer until the vegetables are almost tender.

• Meanwhile, slice the corn kernels off the cobs. Add to the stock, along with the cream and a little cayenne, bring back to the boil and simmer for another 5 minutes or so. Finally, stir in the scallops with their corals and two-thirds of the reserved bacon. Draw off the heat and let it stand for 2–3 minutes, before serving scattered with the remaining bacon and parsley.

Scallops

The ideal scallop, the *nec plus ultra* of scallops, the very apex of scallopdom, is the diver-caught scallop that has been individually pulled by hand from the rock or the seabed, probably somewhere off the west coast of Scotland, and reaches you, the customer, live in its shell. There is a high premium to be paid for these pampered, lovingly harvested shellfish, but it does guarantee a perfect sweet, silky mouthful of heaven – assuming, that is, they have been well handled all along the supply line from diver to fishmonger.

Let us move on to the second best, one rung down the ladder, the ranking that most of us will have to be content with: fresh scallops, probably dredged from the seabed, which cuts the cost somewhat, usually sold off the shell and ready to cook. Frozen scallops come a poor third, lacking the essential sweet shellfish-magic. The problem with either of these (but particularly frozen) is that they might have been soaked in water, which is a shabby trick indeed. Why? Because they soak up that water and it makes them look plump and inviting, the flesh paling to a virginal white. I suspect that, like me, you will object to paying a relatively high price for something that has been bulked out with water that you can get virtually free from your kitchen tap. A fresh, unsoaked scallop will have a less pure, gently off-white colour, but if in doubt ask.

Over in America they sell scallops shorn of their lovely orange roe (the coral), which is a crying shame as it is quite as good as the white meat. I am told that the roes go into pet food but I don't suppose those stateside pooches know how very lucky they are. Do not make the same kind of mistake in your kitchen, however much you love your animals. For most recipes the orange roe is detached from the thick white cylinder, but should be cooked with it. While you are pulling the roes away, check around the sides of the white and remove any remaining black lines of intestine, as well as the tough white connecting muscle.

Scallops need only the bare minimum of cooking. Too long in the pan and they lose everything that makes them worth paying for – they become chewy and dull in flavour, dry and lifeless. Unless you are using them in a soup, like the chowder opposite, the best way to cook them is with a big bold heat. I love seared scallops, the whites halved horizontally first. Begin by wiping a heavy-based frying pan with a smear of oil, then heat it up until viciously hot. In go the scallops, one by one, hissing on the surface of the pan without overlapping, then turned over some 30–45 seconds later for a second spurt of heat, again around 30–45 seconds. And that's it – a squeeze of lemon, salt and pepper, and they are ready to eat. Mmmm. If you get them in the half shell, try steaming them with a shake of fish or soy sauce, a little finely chopped garlic, ginger and chilli, and a touch of sesame oil – they'll take around 5–6 minutes.

Summer Lasagne with Goat's Cheese

SERVES 6

the kernels of 1 **corn-on-the-cob**, or about 110g (4 oz) **frozen sweetcorn**, thawed

400g (14 oz) **courgettes**, sliced thickly

a good handful of **green beans**, topped and tailed, or **runner beans**, stringed, and sliced

a little **olive oil** for greasing

250g (9 oz) fresh sheets of **lasagne**, white or green

150g (5 oz) **goat's cheese**, derinded and roughly crumbled or chopped

around 30–45g (1–1½ oz) freshly grated **Parmesan**

FOR THE TOMATO SAUCE:

1 **onion**, chopped

2 tablespoons **extra virgin olive oil**

2 cloves **garlic,** chopped

150ml (5 fl oz) **red wine**

1 **bay leaf**

1 sprig of **thyme**

1kg (2 lb 4 oz) **fresh tomatoes**, skinned and roughly chopped, or 2 x 400g **tins chopped tomatoes**

continued overleaf

What to do when the courgettes begin to gallop and swell too fast to keep up with? Bake them and stuff them and deep-fry them, mash them and blanch them and toss in herby vinaigrette for a salad and... well, plenty of options, really, if you put your mind to it. This is just one of many, but one that fits our family well, consisting, as it does, of one mushroom- and pepper-hating vegetarian among meat-eaters.

The secret of a good lasagne lies in the two sauces, both of which need more time than they are often given, and both of which can be made in advance. In other words, this is not a dish to make in a hurry. I usually make double quantities since a layered but unbaked lasagne freezes well.

• The first thing to embark upon is the tomato sauce. Fry the onion in the olive oil until tender without browning, then add the garlic and fry gently for a few seconds more. Pour in the wine at arm's length (the fat will spit furiously at you) and throw the bay leaf and thyme into that. Boil for a couple of minutes.

• Next add the tomatoes, honey, tomato purée and parsley. Season with a little salt and plenty of pepper, and then turn the heat down as low as it will go. Leave the sauce to burble contentedly for 2 hours, stirring every quarter of an hour or so to prevent catching. If it is getting too thick, or threatens to burn, pour in a slurp or two of water. When the sauce is done, stir in the sweetcorn and simmer for another 2–3 minutes. Taste and adjust seasoning, making it nicely punchy, and fish out and discard the bay leaf and thyme sprig.

• The white sauce is made in quite the usual way. In other words, warm the olive oil over a gentle heat and stir in the flour. Stir for about 30 seconds and draw off the heat. Add the milk a slurp at a time, stirring it into the flour and oil mixture thoroughly each time, until the sauce is creamy. Now you can add the milk in generous helpings, again stirring in efficiently each time. Return to the heat and bring up to the boil, stirring, then reduce the heat and simmer very genteelly for at least 5–10 minutes, stirring frequently to

1–2 tablespoons **honey**

1 tablespoon **sun-dried tomato purée**

2 good tablespoons chopped **parsley**

salt and pepper

FOR THE WHITE SAUCE:

2 tablespoons **extra virgin olive oil**

30g (1 oz) **flour**

600ml (1 generous pint) **milk**

30g (1 oz) freshly grated **Parmesan**

salt, **pepper** and a touch of freshly grated **nutmeg**

prevent catching. The sauce should be moderately thick, but still pourable. If it has reduced down too much, stir in some extra milk. Stir in the Parmesan and season well with salt, pepper and nutmeg. If not using immediately, spear a small knob of butter on a fork, and rub over the surface to prevent a skin forming. Warm the sauce up gently before using, so that it is runny enough to spread easily.

• Pre-heat the oven to 200°C/400°F/Gas 6. Bring a pan of lightly salted water to the boil and blanch first the courgettes for about 3 minutes after they come back to the boil, and then the green beans or runner beans, for 4–5 minutes, draining each vegetable thoroughly.

• Now for the fun bit. Take a shallow ovenproof dish (about 20 x 27cm/8 x 11 in) and grease lightly with olive oil. Smear a thin layer of the tomato sauce over the base of the dish. Cover sparsely with sheets of lasagne, tearing them up so that they do not overlap. Now ladle half the remaining tomato sauce over the lasagne and spread out thinly. Dot half the courgettes, half the green beans or runner beans and then half the goat's cheese over the sauce. Next spoon over about one-third of the white sauce – it doesn't have to cover every last square millimetre of tomato and vegetable, but get it roughly evenly smoothed over.

• Repeat these layers of pasta, tomato sauce, vegetables and white sauce. Cover with another layer of pasta, then spoon the last of the white sauce over the sheets of lasagne, spreading out and scraping the last drops out of the pan so that the pasta is completely covered. Sprinkle evenly with the Parmesan, and then bake for 30–40 minutes until golden brown and bubbling. Let it settle for 5 minutes before cutting into large squares and serving.

Duck with Cherries

Duck with cherries may sound like a tired culinary cliché, but it only got to that state because duck and fresh cherries are such brilliant partners. Do not for one minute imagine that this can be reproduced with soggy tinned cherries. As a dish it quite rightly has a limited season: the few weeks of cherry time that we get each year.

I never bother stoning the cherries – it seems mean to deprive everyone of the chance to play Tinker, Tailor, Soldier, Sailor.

SERVES 8

2 **ducklings**, weighing around 2.5–2.8kg (5–6 lb) each

1 large **carrot**, diced

1 **onion**, chopped

2 sticks **celery**, diced

1 **bouquet garni**, consisting of a few stalks of parsley, 2 good sprigs of thyme, 2 bay leaves and 1 small sprig of sage, tied together with string

750ml (1¼ pints) **fruity red wine** (1 bottle)

750ml (1¼ pints) **duck** or **chicken stock**

2 tablespoons **redcurrant jelly**

450g (1 lb) **fresh cherries**

salt and **pepper**

• Pre-heat the oven to 220°C/425°F/Gas 7. Wipe the ducks dry with kitchen paper. Prick their skin all over with a skewer, or a fork if the tines are sharp, so that the fat can run out more easily as they cook. Season generously with salt and pepper. Sit the ducks on a rack over a roasting tin, and slide it into the oven. Turn the heat down to 180°C/350°F/Gas 4, and leave to cook for 2½ hours.

• During that time all you need do, whenever you've a mind to, is drain off the fat that has gathered in the roasting tin – brilliant stuff for sautéing potatoes. Once you've harvested your first crop of fat, take 1 tablespoon of it and heat it up in a frying pan. Add the carrot, onion and celery and sauté until the vegetables are tender and lightly browned. Now add the bouquet garni and wine, bring up to the boil, stirring thoroughly, then boil hard until reduced by half. Add the stock and boil again until reduced by about a third to a half, giving a syrupy sauce. Now stir in the redcurrant jelly until it has melted, then strain the vegetables out of the sauce and pour into a small pan. Add the cherries and a little salt and pepper, and simmer for about 2 minutes. Taste and adjust seasoning. Reheat when needed.

• When the ducks are cooked, turn off the oven and leave the door ajar. Let them rest like this (or in another suitably warm place, supposing you need the oven for something else) for about 15 minutes. Using a sharp knife or poultry shears, cut each duck into four pieces – cutting first from head to tail end, along the breast bone and through the back bone, to give two halves, then simply dividing each half in two. Serve while still warm, with the reheated sauce.

Smoky Chicken Kebabs, with Sautéed Fennel and Pepper

The Spanish answer to paprika is smoked pimentón, an extraordinary spice made of dried smoked peppers that have been finely ground up. It can be mild or hot, depending on the fieriness of the original peppers. I use it in all kinds of dishes – it marries beautifully with anything tomatoey, is lovely with fish, and gives chicken a marvellous lift. At last you can buy it here, from good delis and some of the larger supermarkets.

Here I've combined it with tarragon and garlic to make a pungent marinade for chicken, which is set off nicely by the sautéed fennel and peppers. I use the same marinade on tofu (or, loath though I am to admit it, Quorn), for my vegetarian daughter, so that she doesn't feel left out.

The kebabs and vegetables go together exceptionally well, but it is not obligatory to serve them as an ensemble. Either half of this equation is good enough to stand on its own.

SERVES 4

8 **chicken thighs**, skinned and boned and cut into 2.5–4cm (1–1½ in) pieces

FOR THE MARINADE:

2 cloves **garlic**, peeled

leaves of 1 large sprig of **tarragon**

1 **red chilli**, deseeded and roughly chopped

1 teaspoon **smoked pimentón**

1 teaspoon **tomato purée**

2 tablespoons **balsamic** or **sherry vinegar**

4 tablespoons **extra virgin olive oil**

coarse salt and freshly ground **black pepper**

• To make the marinade, pound the garlic, tarragon leaves and chilli, with a couple of big pinches of salt, to a rough paste in a mortar. Now work in the pimentón, tomato purée, vinegar, olive oil, a little extra salt, and pepper. Pour over the chicken pieces and turn to coat each piece. Leave for at least half an hour, preferably an awful lot longer – let's say up to 24 hours, covered, in the fridge.

• It makes life easier if you cook the fennel and peppers in advance, then reheat just before serving. Trim the fennel and reserve any green feathery fronds. Halve the bulb and slice thinly.

• Heat the olive oil in a wide frying pan over a high heat and add the peppers. Sauté for about 4–5 minutes, then add the fennel and sauté for another 4 minutes until the peppers are tender and the fennel is softening but retaining a mite of crispness. Now add the garlic and olives and stir them around a couple of times. Take off the heat and add two or three big squeezes of lemon juice,

FOR THE FENNEL AND PEPPERS:

1 large head of **fennel**

2 tablespoons **extra virgin olive oil**

2 **red peppers**, deseeded and cut into strips

2 cloves **garlic**, finely chopped

90g (3 oz) **black olives**

½ **lemon**

salt and **pepper**

to serve: **lemon** or **lime wedges**

and season with salt and pepper. Reheat and sprinkle with the reserved fennel fronds, roughly chopped, just before serving.

• Pre-heat the grill or barbecue thoroughly. Thread the chicken pieces on to 8 skewers, then grill or barbecue for about 9–10 minutes, turning once, until browned and cooked through. Serve on a bed of the sautéed fennel and pepper with lemon or lime wedges.

Coronation Chicken

SERVES 8–10

2 fine **organic chickens**,
  poached (see page 77)

FOR THE SAUCE:

60g (2 oz) chopped **onion**

1 tablespoon **sunflower oil**

2 teaspoons **mild** or **medium
  curry powder**

1 heaped teaspoon **tomato
  purée**

100ml (3½ fl oz) **red wine**

60ml (2 fl oz) **water**

1 **bay leaf**

1 slice **lemon**

a dash of **lemon juice**

6 **dried apricots**

450ml (¾ pint) **mayonnaise**

3 tablespoons lightly whipped
  cream

salt, **pepper** and **sugar**

to garnish: a little **cayenne** or
  paprika and a little chopped
  parsley or sprigs of **curly
  parsley**

A cliché? What? Coronation chicken and summer buffets? Well, I really don't care. When it is made properly, with decent free-range chicken, proper mayonnaise, and dried apricots not apricot jam, it is a concoction of considerable merit. Oh, and a great dish for a summer buffet.

It was created in 1953 for the coronation lunch of Queen Elizabeth. I imagine that the ingredients list must have seemed as odd then as it does now. Quite how anybody came up with the strange reduction of wine, curry powder and tomato purée is beyond me. Still, it works, and for that I am glad. Fifty years on it still tastes very good.

• To make the sauce, begin by softening the onion in the oil without browning. Now add the curry powder, tomato purée, wine, water, bay leaf, slice of lemon and dash of lemon juice. Simmer, uncovered, for 5–10 minutes or until reduced by about half to two-thirds, then strain. Leave to cool.

• Put the apricots in a pan with barely enough water to cover. Simmer until very tender, then liquidise, adding a little extra water if needed. Leave to cool. Take the mayonnaise and add the strained curry and tomato purée and the apricot purée, and salt, pepper and sugar (if needed) to taste. Fold in the whipped cream.

• Strip the meat from the chickens and tear into bite-sized pieces. Toss in enough of the flavoured mayonnaise to coat nicely. Arrange on a plate, garnish with a sprinkling of cayenne or paprika and parsley, and *voilà* – all you need now is a cathedral and an archbishop and you're laughing, your majesty!

Chickens

Think Sunday lunch. Think family sitting round the table. Think resplendent golden roast chicken arriving on the table, plump and glistening, thighs akimbo, skin saltily crisp, its rich savoury scent wafting round the room, perhaps a notion of stuffing poking out provocatively. Sounds good? Well, so it should, but the question is: what will it taste like?

It ought to taste as good as it looks, with flesh that has substance and juiciness, and a distinct flavour of pure meaty chicken, deepening as the colour darkens at the thighs. This is what you get with a proper, out-there-pecking-about sort of a bird. A true free-range fowl that has got its feet dirty, pecked at worms and felt the wind and the rain on its feathers. A bird that has lived a relatively long and happy life, doing the kind of thing that chickens like best.

A dismaying number of people have no idea what a happy chicken tastes like. Instead, they believe that a mouthful of wet cotton-wool pap, the hallmark of a broiler chicken, is the real thing. Here we are, a nation of animal-lovers, who throw communal hands up in horror at the thought of nasty foreigners force-feeding geese for foie gras, but who think it quite reasonable to raise chickens for their own tables in horribly confined cages (average amount of space per bird is about the size of two postcards) where all their natural instincts are smothered.

Perhaps it is a grim mercy that their lives are so short.

When you do have your (free-range) chicken, make sure to squeeze every last penny's worth out of it. In practice, this may mean filling it with a terrific stuffing so that everyone loves you and the meat stretches that bit further; making a small pot of chicken liver pâté (fry the liver in butter, then process with a little extra butter, a wee slug of sherry or brandy, a few herbs, salt and pepper, and serve lightly chilled to spread on toast) if the innards are included; the rest of the giblets can go into the stockpot with the carcass, but before you sling that in, pick off all the remnants of flesh to add to a main-course soup, made with the stock and enriched with diced vegetables and pasta shapes.

For summer salads, and any dishes that require cold chicken (such as Coronation Chicken opposite), poaching is by far the best way of pre-cooking the bird, keeping the meat beautifully moist. Put the whole bird into a large pan and add a carrot, roughly sliced, an onion, quartered, and perhaps a roughly chopped leek and/or stick of celery. Tuck a generous bouquet garni in too. Pour in enough water just to cover the chicken, then bring up to the boil. Simmer very gently for around 60 minutes, depending on size, until cooked right through. Take off the heat and leave to cool in its poaching liquid. Use the chicken as required but don't forget to strain the poaching liquid which is now the very best of chicken stocks.

Fricassee of Pork, Potatoes, Peas and Parsley

A light, summery fricassee laced with lemon for its freshness and verve. Two fundamentals to bear in mind: first, you must use real stock, not a stock cube, as the flavour permeates the whole dish, and second, only free-range pork will deliver the kind of taste that a simple dish like this demands. Serve it in soup plates, and make sure everyone has a spoon to scoop up the sauce.

SERVES 4

500g (1 lb 2 oz) **new potatoes**, thickly sliced

1 small **onion**, sliced

45g (1½ oz) **butter**

200g (7 oz) shelled **fresh peas**

300ml (½ pint) **chicken** or **vegetable stock**

5 tablespoons chopped **parsley**

finely grated **zest** and **juice** of 1 large **lemon**

1 **pork fillet**

2 **egg yolks**

salt and **pepper**

• Fry the new potatoes and onion in 30g (1 oz) of the butter in a deep frying pan, until the onion is tender, without letting it brown. Add the peas, stock, parsley, lemon zest, salt and pepper. Bring up to the boil, then reduce the heat and simmer gently until the potatoes are tender.

• Meanwhile, cut the pork on the diagonal to produce 1cm (scant ½ in) thick slices. With the heel of your hand, press each one out to a thickness of about 5mm (¼ in). Heat the remaining butter in a frying pan until foaming, and fry the pork for about 1½ minutes on each side until just cooked through. Keep warm.

• Whisk the lemon juice into the egg yolks, then whisk in a few tablespoons of the hot stock from the potatoes and peas to warm the mixture through. Turn the heat right down to a mere thread under the potato pan, add the pork, and then stir in the lemon-egg mixture. Cook for a minute or two longer, without boiling, until the sauce has thickened very slightly. Taste and adjust seasoning, and serve while still hot.

Peas

We used to grow our own peas, but now that we rely on the more green-fingered staff at the market garden down the road to produce our peas, there's one thing I really miss. That's strolling around the garden with a pea pod in one hand, pulling out the tiny fresh peas and popping them straight into my mouth, one by one. The taste of a newly picked pea, savoured for a few brief seconds out in the fresh air, is a miniature tonic, a sign that all is right with the world (whatever state it is actually in), a moment of sensory perfection.

Quite why anyone bothers cooking really fresh new season peas is a bit of a mystery. They are nicer raw, or perhaps just heated through for a few minutes in a touch of butter, long enough to raise their temperature, but not so long that they lose their sweet vitality. Even youthful fresh peas that have hung around in the pod for a day or so are still good enough to shell and throw raw and crisp into a salad, or to stir through pasta with warmed olive oil, crisp shreds of pancetta, garlic and freshly grated Parmesan.

Do not assume, however, that all peas in their pods are worthy of this treatment. In bigger shops – not all of them, I dare say, but in too many in my experience – what lands up on the shelves are the rejects from the processing plant. Yup, the ones that were too big and old, or too damaged, to make it into the freezing plant. So look at the pods and consider. Are they dry and papery? Are they particularly fat and peculiarly hard?

Are they heavily blemished? If the answer to one or more of these questions is yes, then you can guarantee that the peas are well past their prime. They might be worth it for soup, especially if you have access to a ham knuckle or the end bone of a Parma ham (ask in delis what they do with them, and reserve one if you can) to add depth and bring out the best in the peas, but otherwise don't bother.

The odd blemish on stiff, bright green pods is not a sign for concern, on the other hand. That just suggests that they weren't sprayed to within an inch of their lives while they grew. If the pods are fundamentally in a healthy state, the likelihood is that the peas inside are in fine fettle too.

Once the peas have grown beyond the tiniest new state, then blanching them makes sense, but don't overdo it. A few minutes in salted simmering water is all that's required, just enough to soften them. Or, better still, cook them vaguely *à la française*. In other words, pile them into a pan with a large knob of butter and a small shredded lettuce, together with a few herbs (parsley, chervil, savory, lemon thyme), a couple of thinly sliced spring onions, if you have them, salt and pepper, perhaps a scraping of nutmeg, and a splash of water to prevent catching. Cover them tightly and cook over a low-medium heat, shaking the pan once or twice (or giving it a stir), for some 20 minutes. The peas themselves and the lettuce will contribute quite enough juice to prevent scorching. The lettuce, which almost melts away, also adds its own sweetness, making up for any coarseness on the part of the peas.

Spiced Fillet of Beef with Green Sauce

This is one of the best ways of cooking a handsome chunk of fillet of beef – a real treat, as tender as butter, and one that takes well to being pepped up with plenty of pepper. If you don't like too much spicy heat, reduce the quantity of peppercorns and increase the coriander.

The sauce is based on Italian salsa verde, but with the sorrel and anchovy essence has a more northerly feel. If you are to eat the beef cold (I think this suits it best), make the sauce after cooking the beef so it retains its bright green colour, but if the beef is to be consumed hot, make the sauce first.

When buying the fillet of beef, ask for a central piece of a fairly uniform thickness so that it cooks evenly.

SERVES 4–6

650g (1 lb 7 oz) piece of **fillet of beef**

1 tablespoon **black peppercorns**

1 tablespoon **coriander seeds**

FOR THE SAUCE:

about 45g (1½ oz) **parsley leaves**

about 45g (1½ oz) **sorrel leaves**

leaves from 3 good sprigs of **mint**

1 slice **white bread**, crusts removed

2 squeezes of **lemon juice**

2 teaspoons **anchovy essence** or **anchovy sauce**

1 level teaspoon **caster sugar**

150ml (5 fl oz) **extra virgin olive oil**

salt

• Pre-heat the oven to 220°C/425°F/Gas 7. Crush the peppercorns and the coriander seeds coarsely together. Tip into a shallow plate. Tear off a large square of foil and lay next to the plate. Roll the fillet of beef in the crushed spices, making sure that it is pretty evenly coated (but leave the ends bare). Lift the beef on to the foil and wrap up tightly.

• Heat a heavy frying pan over a high heat until outrageously hot. Place the foil parcel of beef in it and leave to cook for 2 minutes. Give the roll of beef a quarter turn and cook for another 2 minutes. Repeat twice more, so that you have given the beef a total of 8 minutes in the pan. Transfer immediately to the oven and roast for a further 8–10 minutes. Take out, turn over and leave to stand for 5 minutes, if serving hot, or until cool, if serving cold. Slice thinly.

• For the sauce, place all the herbs in a processor, tear the bread roughly and add to the processor. Squeeze in the lemon juice and add the anchovy essence or sauce, sugar and a touch of salt. Process until finely chopped, then gradually trickle in the olive oil, keeping the motor running all the time. Taste and adjust seasoning. Serve with the thinly sliced beef.

Green on Green Summer Salad

In many parts of the Middle East they use the softer-leaved herbs almost as salad leaves, mixing them together whole in generous handfuls. Nothing more than the most elemental dressing is needed to bring them together. I've borrowed that idea here, marrying the herbs with some of the best of summer saladings, and crisp green vegetables.

SERVES 6–8

150g (5 oz) **green beans**, topped and tailed

4 cos **lettuce leaves**, shredded

100g (3½ oz) raw, **fresh, shelled peas**

1 small **fennel bulb,** trimmed, quartered and very thinly sliced

a handful of **rocket**

a handful of **fresh spinach leaves**

a handful of **basil leaves**

a handful of **mint leaves**

3 tablespoons roughly chopped **chives**

2 tablespoons roughly chopped **parsley**

2 tablespoons chopped **dill** or the leaves of 2 sprigs of **tarragon**

FOR THE DRESSING:

juice of ½ **lemon**

5 tablespoons **extra virgin olive oil**

salt and **pepper**

• Blanch the green beans in lightly salted boiling water for about 4–5 minutes until barely tender. Drain and run under the cold tap, then drain again. Cut in half. When cool, mix with all the salad ingredients.

• Whisk the lemon juice with salt and pepper, then whisk in the oil. Taste and adjust seasoning – the dressing should be just a touch sharp on the tongue, and with a fair measure of salt to it. Just before serving, toss the salad with enough of the dressing to coat.

Mint

Is mint the new basil? Well, perhaps not quite, but damn near. Mint is a vastly underrated herb. It is just made for the summer months, with its capacity to bring an instant waft of freshness to all manner of foods. If you've ever tried a tomato and mint salad, dressed with a touch of balsamic or red wine vinegar, good extra virgin olive oil, salt and pepper, you will know what an extraordinarily felicitous combination it is, and one that can certainly stand its ground against the onslaught of tomato and basil salads.

What else is it good for? Obviously, it is excellent with lamb, but when you next make mint sauce, use the best wine vinegar and huge amounts of fresh mint to turn one of our national oddities into the success story that it deserves to be. Peas and mint and new potatoes and mint we all know, but to be honest, how much impact does a well-boiled sprig of mint make? Far better to make up a mint butter (process softened butter with roughly chopped mint, pepper and a squeeze of lemon juice) and to dot that over the cooked peas or new potatoes to give them a breeze of menthol.

It works deliciously in green salads, too – just throw the leaves in, roughly torn up if they are on the big side, or if you want a smoother, more unctuous dressing, liquidise the mint (loads of it) with the vinaigrette to form a viridian blend. Mint blesses fish, particularly white fish, brought into play in a salsa possibly, or stirred through a buttery hollandaise (which makes it more or less a sauce paloise), or pounded to a paste with salt, then worked into mayonnaise to serve with cold poached salmon or kebabs of monkfish. And if the fish has come off the barbie, then a knob of that mint butter (add a little finely grated lemon zest, too) will again do wonders.

Mint and sweet things is trickier. I've never much cared for mint and chocolate together and I swear that After Eights have shrunk in recent years. Where I do use it, bruised first with the end of the rolling pin, is in summer fruit salads – especially with melon, another cool summer customer, peaches and raspberries. I have added mint, finely chopped, to cheesecakes, and it is an unexpectedly good addition.

When you are buying mint to grow, look first of all for a spearmint, and if you can find Moroccan spearmint, so much the better for it has the truest minty scent. Peppermint is much, much stronger and needs to be used with discretion if you don't want every meal to taste like toothpaste. Despite its name, applemint does not taste of apples, but just brings a very pure mintiness to food. Its drawback for some are the downy leaves, though once they are chopped up no one will be any the wiser. Remember that it is sensible to grow mint in a container, as long as you water it well in hotter times. Planted straight in the ground, it has a tendency to run riot.

Roast Tomato, Rocket and Feta Salad

Roasting tomatoes in a hot oven brings out all that is best in them, intensifying their inherent flavour, caramelising their natural sugars and infusing them with a subtle waft of garlic and herbs. I love them hot and I love them eaten at room temperature. Matched with rocket and feta, they make a perfect summer salad. You could serve it as a first course, or even as a light lunch with lots of first-rate bread and some cheese and fruit to follow. It also makes a good partner for a helping of grilled fish or chicken.

SERVES 4

5–6 tablespoons **extra virgin olive oil**

6 **plum tomatoes**, halved lengthways

4 cloves **garlic** (not peeled)

1 big sprig of **thyme**

1 tablespoon **white wine vinegar**

3 handfuls of **rocket**

110g (4 oz) **feta cheese**, diced or crumbled

a few **basil leaves**, roughly torn up

salt, **pepper** and a pinch or two of **sugar**

• Pre-heat the oven to 220°C/425°F/Gas 7. Use a little of the oil to grease a roasting tin generously. Arrange the plum tomato halves in it, cut sides up, and tuck the garlic and thyme among them. Drizzle over a tablespoon of oil, then season with salt, pepper and a pinch or so of sugar. Roast for about 35–45 minutes, until very tender and patched here and there with brown. Cool and reserve until needed.

• Make a quick dressing by whisking the remaining oil with the vinegar, salt and pepper. Taste and adjust the balance of flavours, adding a little more oil if it is on the sharp side. Just before serving, toss the rocket in enough dressing to coat, and then top with the feta and roast tomatoes (and cloves of garlic, if you wish). Drizzle over some of the juice from the roasting tin, and finish with a flurry of basil.

Green or Wax Beans with Tomato and Cumin

Where once it was the glut of runner beans that characterised mid and late summer, increasingly it is the courgette and the fine French and other long green beans that vie for supremacy. I'm on the invaders' side, personally, and although I sigh sometimes when a gardening friend bowls up swinging a bag of beans or another courgette (we grow both), they are versatile enough to avoid total overkill.

This recipe marries east and west, with butter and tomatoes and cumin and coriander all taking a heap of green beans, or those lovely long yellow wax beans, into a higher realm. It takes minutes to do, and you don't even have to skin the tomato, unless you really can't stand tiny bits of tomato skin in your food.

SERVES 3–4

250g (9 oz) **fine green beans**
(French beans) or **yellow wax beans**
30g (1 oz) **butter**
1 **tomato**, chopped
1 small clove **garlic**, crushed
½–1 teaspoon **ground cumin**
chopped fresh **coriander**
salt and **pepper**

• Cook the beans in salted water until almost done, but still slightly *al dente*. Drain thoroughly. Shortly before serving, melt the butter in a saucepan and add the beans and all the remaining ingredients. Stir over a medium heat until the tomato has softened and collapsed. Taste and adjust seasonings and serve.

Courgette Fritters with Parmesan

SERVES 4–6

450g (1 lb) small **courgettes**

4 tablespoons **flour**

1 teaspoon **ground cinnamon**

¼–½ teaspoon **cayenne pepper**

2 **eggs**, beaten

90g (3 oz) fine **breadcrumbs**

45g (1½ oz) finely grated **Parmesan**

salt

olive oil and/or **sunflower oil** for frying

to serve: **lemon wedges**

We all love courgette fritters, whether they are made with new-season petite courgettes or the larger late-season whoppers. So much so, that the clans tend to gather in the kitchen ready to scoff them as soon as they come out of the pan. Ideally, I like to serve them as a side dish, but often it seems simpler to go with the flow and let everyone pick at them as they down pre-dinner drinks. If you choose this option, put a bowl of mayonnaise flavoured with chilli and basil or coriander on the table for dipping into.

• Quarter the courgettes lengthways. If they are very small and fresh from the garden, use them just as they are. If they are larger, cut the quarters into lengths of about 7.5cm (3 in), give or take. Spread out in a colander and sprinkle lightly with salt. Leave for half an hour to degorge, then rinse and pat dry.

• Mix the flour with the cinnamon, cayenne pepper and a little salt in a shallow dish or plate and place near the hob. Set the bowl with the beaten egg next to it. Mix the breadcrumbs and Parmesan in another shallow dish, and place next to the eggs.

• Heat a 1cm (scant ½ in) depth of oil in a frying pan over a moderate heat until a cube of bread dropped into the oil fizzes moderately and browns in 45 seconds. If it browns more quickly than that, the oil is too hot. Add a little more cold oil and turn the heat down. If the oil around the bread barely fizzes at all, then the oil is too cool, so turn the heat up.

• Taking a few of the bits of courgette at a time, coat each one thoroughly in the seasoned flour, shake off excess, then dip into the beaten egg. Finally coat thoroughly in the breadcrumb mixture, and slip gently into the oil. Fry for about 4–6 minutes until golden brown, then drain briefly on kitchen paper before serving with wedges of lemon to squeeze over them.

Courgettes

There comes a point in the summer when I meander up the garden to inspect the courgette plants. It seems to take an age for the courgettes to grow large enough to eat and woe betide any child who kicks his ball in this direction.

When those first courgettes are ready to pick, we treat them with ceremony. These little finger-sized darlings are usually too few to make more than a couple of mouthfuls per person, but their flavour is so concentrated and new that we don't mind. To stretch them out, we cook them tempura-style (see opposite for the batter and method, which incidentally is great on the flowers, too), or arrange one solo, lightly steamed, atop each person's mound of buttery tagliatelle, tossed with fresh herbs and Parmesan. They are consumed with suitable admiration and enthusiasm.

Later when courgettes are plentiful we branch out. Courgettes fried in olive oil with lots of garlic added at the end, can either be tossed copiously in with pasta, or just dressed with red wine vinegar and roughly chopped mint, then left to cool for the following day. Griddled courgettes are pretty wonderful too – cut them into long slices around 5mm (¼ in) thick, brush with olive oil and cook on a horribly hot griddle pan until tender and striped with black-brown lines. Eat them just as they are, hot and seasoned with salt, or dress with lemon juice and olive oil and plenty of chopped herbs to enjoy at room temperature.

Larger courgettes can be grated, then salted to force out all the water that has diluted their flavour. Once rinsed and squeezed dry, stir-fry them in butter for a few minutes, and finish with a touch of cream and lemon for a rich accompaniment to chicken or pork. Or mix the shreds (again salted and squeezed) with a little flour and beaten egg, and fry tablespoonfuls to make small courgette pancakes with tender centres and crisp, whiskery edges.

Courgettes that have reached commercial size (in other words, have an ample girth of around 4cm or 1½ in) are big enough to stuff, or at least to bake, halved lengthways underneath a blanket of breadcrumbs and finely grated Parmesan, dotted with butter. To stuff them proper, first halve and scoop out some of the inside with a teaspoon or melon baller to make a rudimentary canoe. Arrange in a buttered or oiled dish, tucked up close to each other for mutual support. Next make up an inspiringly and passionately seasoned stuffing – based on breadcrumbs, or sausagemeat and crumbs, perhaps, with added nuts or raisins, fried onions and garlic, chilli, spices and herbs, and so on and so forth – and stuff the courgette boats with this, mounding it up nicely in each half. Drizzle a little stock or a glass of white wine over the courgettes, scatter with more breadcrumbs and with cheese if you like, dot with butter or finish with a drizzle of olive oil then bake in a moderate oven until the courgettes are tender but have not yet collapsed. There you are – a fine supper and no doubt about it.

Spiced Courgettes and Broad Beans with Tamarind

SERVES 4

400g (14 oz) **courgettes**, thickly sliced

1kg (2 lb 4 oz) **broad beans** in their pods, or 350g (12 oz) shelled broad beans

2 tablespoons **sunflower** or **grapeseed oil**

1 heaped teaspoon **cumin seeds**

a good ¾ teaspoon **ground cinnamon**

a good ¼ teaspoon **turmeric**

1½ tablespoons **tamarind purée** (see opposite)

salt and **pepper**

to serve: 2 generous tablespoons chopped **coriander** and a little **extra virgin olive oil**

Although you could eat this warm, I prefer it at room temperature, after it has sat around long enough for the flavours to soften and blend. So make it a few hours or even a day in advance, adding the coriander and olive oil just before serving.

• Tip the courgettes into a colander. Sprinkle with salt and leave to degorge for at least half an hour. Rinse and pat dry.

• Shell the broad beans, then blanch the beans in boiling salted water for 3 minutes. Drain and rinse under the cold tap. Now, using your fingernails or a small knife, slit open the tough greyish skin and extract the delicious bright green bean imprisoned inside.

• Fry the courgettes in the oil over a moderate heat, until tender and patched with brown. Keep a plate by the cooker and take out slices as they brown, so that you don't overcook them.

• Once they are all done, return the cooked ones to the pan, together with the spices and the broad beans, and stir well. Cook for another 30 seconds or so, then pour in the tamarind, and season lightly with salt and pepper. Stir for a minute or so, then taste and adjust seasoning. Tip into a shallow dish, and leave to cool. Scatter with coriander, drizzle over a little olive oil, and serve.

Tamarind

The tamarind is a handsome evergreen tree that originated in Africa but now grows widely right across South-east Asia as well as the Caribbean. It's not something that you are going to find in every back garden here, nor will it be popping up at the local farmers' market, but its big European claim to fame is that it provides an essential ingredient for Worcestershire sauce.

The part that matters, if you like to cook and eat, is the soft, tart pulp cushioning the seeds inside the lengthy tamarind pods. Occasionally I have come across the fresh pods, but usually it is sold here in semi-dried blocks. They look like slabs of chocolate fudge, marred by the inclusion of bits of pod and any number of seeds. You will find them on rare occasions in supermarkets, but Asian food shops are a far better bet. The blocks keep well (I usually nestle mine somewhere in the back of the fridge), so it is worth buying when you see it even if you won't be using it immediately.

Most recipes call for a tamarind paste or purée, which contributes a unique, fruity acidity to food. You *can* buy the paste ready prepared in some supermarkets, but this short-cut substitute lacks the immediate, invigorating power of home-made. Besides, it is relatively expensive and doesn't keep so well once opened. Preparing your own is a quick job, anyway. All you do is pour 150ml (5 fl oz) of very hot water over 30g (1 oz) tamarind pulp in a bowl. Break up the pulp a bit, then leave to soften for around 20 minutes. Mash it with a fork, mix it roughly, and then rub as much of the liquid and pulp as you can through a sieve. Chuck out the seeds and other debris, and what you have left is the tamarind purée, paste, liquid or whatever you care to call it.

Tamarind has a hundred and one uses, probably more. Diluted and sweetened it makes a keen drink for a hot day, but on the whole I save it for tempering spicy dishes, adding a sharpness that is so different from that of lemon or lime. Not that it has to be reserved for foods laden with spice; I've thrown it into salad dressings, too, as a replacement for lemon juice or wine vinegar. It makes a marvellous companion to fish, especially the meatier, chunkier ones like tuna and swordfish. Use it in a marinade, or simply rub some over the surface along with a touch of oil, salt and pepper before barbecuing or searing.

Broad Beans

The broad bean is our one, very own, native European bean. The rest, the haricots and kidneys and string beans and green beans, are new world interlopers. Fresh broad beans demand application. They are not the material of ten-minute suppers, but that's not necessarily a bad thing. There's something to be said for setting aside ten minutes to undertake an undemanding, potentially soothing job. Shelling broad beans should be a peaceful pleasure, accompanied by a good record, an intriguing play on the radio, or congenial company. When time is on our side, I share the task with the children and anyone who cares to join in, sitting on the lawn (or the kitchen floor, if it is teeming with rain), vying for who can raise the largest mound of emptied pods in the shortest amount of time. To keep the harmony I may have to redistribute some of my heap, but I'm willing to lose the winner's title in order to preserve my team of willing helpers.

Very small early season beans can be eaten raw, as they are in Italy, served as an antipasto with Parma ham and thin slivers of Parmesan, but trouble hoves into view as they mature. For many, eating full-sized broad beans is a penance. The source of woe is that tough, grey-green outer skin. Take that away (and yes, this does mean extra preparation time, but it's time extremely well spent) and, lo and behold, you are left with the most delectable bright green beanlets, which will convert the most ardent bean-hater. If you've never tasted fresh, skinned broad beans, then now is absolutely the perfect time to try.

PREPARING BROAD BEANS

When buying broad beans in their pods, it's handy to know that the pods make up about two-thirds of the weight, i.e., for 500g (1 lb) shelled beans, you will need to purchase 1.5kg (3 lb) beans in their pods.

To shell the beans, break open the pod by squashing along the 'seams' then pulling open (fingernails are handy at this point). Run your finger down the inside to loosen the beans themselves.

To skin fresh broad beans, drop the shelled beans into a pan of boiling water and simmer for 1–2 minutes. Drain, then, using your fingernail or a small sharp knife, slit open the pale outer skin and squeeze out the inner beanlet. Finish the cooking in fresh boiling salted water – exact time depends on the size of the beans, but it should only take a further 4–5 minutes. When done, the raw leguminous taste will have disappeared, leaving a soft, mealy-textured bean with a marvellous flavour.

FROZEN BROAD BEANS

Broad beans freeze very well. I usually ignore packet instructions for cooking, instead letting them thaw out, then skinning them as above, before giving them a final blanching in boiling salted water for about 3 minutes to finish the cooking process.

Sloppy Strawberry and Raspberry Mousse

This is a gelatine-free mousse (that's why it is sloppy), a quick confection of a thing that has become very popular around our house in the summer. I like it made with a blend of strawberries and raspberries, but you could just as well use blueberries, tayberries, loganberries, and so on. Eat as soon as it is made to get it at its most moussey. If you have to leave it to stand for a while (in the fridge, up to 24 hours), then fold the separated mousse that has floated to the top back into the body of the mixture before spooning into bowls.

Since it contains raw egg white, the usual warning must be trotted out: although the risk of salmonella poisoning is infinitesimally small, it's sensible not to serve this to the very young or very old, or to invalids or pregnant women.

SERVES 4

200g (7 oz) **strawberries**, hulled

125g (4½ oz) **raspberries**

45g (1½ oz) **caster sugar**

150g (5 oz) thick **Greek yoghurt**

1 **egg white**

• Mix the strawberries, raspberries and 15g (½ oz) of the sugar. Crush roughly with a fork, or a potato masher, producing a deeply uneven mush. Mix in the yoghurt.

• Whisk the egg white until it forms soft peaks. Sprinkle over the remaining sugar, then whisk again until very thick and glossy. Fold lightly into the fruit mixture. Divide between bowls, and serve at room temperature.

Strawberries

There are, as far as I can tell, three critical elements when it comes to properly strawberry-ish strawberries, with the perfect balance of sweet and sharp. The first and I believe the most important is the variety. It is rare that I come across an Elsanta, for instance, that thrills. Big it may be, but that counts for nothing. The smaller Mara des Bois, on the other hand, is nearly always stunning, richly scented and totally bursting with the kind of flavour that reminds you of what a strawberry really is meant to taste like. This variety is enormously popular across the Channel in France and I am glad to report that it is beginning to make inroads here. All power to it, I say.

The second critical element is freshness. The sooner it is eaten, the better the strawberry tastes. Time, even in relatively small doses, takes its toll. A couple of days away from the plant and the fruits are already dulled down, the highs ironed out to a uniform mediocrity. In practice this means grow your own, or pick your own, or at least buy from a farm shop where they can assure you that those punnets were filled that very day, or at most the day before. Then it is up to you to eat them as quickly as possible.

The third element is the right degree of sunshine – not overly hot, but plenty of it – as the berries redden to plumptious ripeness. Rain in moderation is fine, but too much swells each strawberry to an ungainly, watery bulk, diluting the taste and precipitating rot.

Since there's precious little we can do about the weather, it makes sense to concentrate on variety and freshness. Recent years have, at last, seen a handful of mostly small-scale growers begin to experiment with varieties, breaking away from the all-pervasive Elsanta and its similarly high-yield, disease-resistant, heffalump-sized, dismally dull brethren. Marvellous for commerce, deeply disappointing for consumers. To be fair, if the season is good, and Elsantas are eaten within 24 hours of picking, they are not bad, but I've yet to taste one that can compete with the finest-flavoured varieties. If you want the kind of strawberry that makes you sigh with pleasure and utter phrases like, 'I'd forgotten what a strawberry really tastes like!', you will have to search beyond the common mass.

As with all of the best of our fruit, the trick is to follow the varieties as they ripen one after the other through the season. That way you can get each one at its best. If you are not growing your own, then befriend your local strawberry producer and ask which varieties they grow, in what order they peak, and ask them to print the name of the variety on the punnets if they don't already. And if they, too, have been seduced by the Elsantas of the strawberry world, suggest tactfully that they might, for a short row or two, just for a season or two, risk a little novelty in the hope of making their more discerning customers extremely happy.

Strawberry and Elderflower Creams

An easy pudding of prettiest pink that marries strawberries and cream in time-honoured fashion, sprucing them up with a shake of elderflower cordial. Home-made cordial is best (see page 56), but these days the ones you can buy are good too.

SERVES 6

500g (1 lb 2 oz) ripe **strawberries**, hulled

3 tablespoons **elderflower cordial**

85g (3 oz) **caster sugar**

4 leaves **gelatine**

300ml (½ pint) **whipping cream**

2 strips **lemon zest**

• Set aside 6 small, choice, but not overripe strawberries. Process the remaining strawberries with the cordial and sugar.

• Submerge the leaves of gelatine in a dish or roasting tin of cold water (see page 98) and leave to soak while you heat up the cream. Bring the whipping cream and the lemon zest slowly to the boil, then draw off the heat. One by one take the gelatine leaves out of the water, squeeze out excess water and stir into the cream. Cool until warm, remove the lemon zest, then mix with the strawberry purée. Spoon into stemmed glasses or ramekins and leave in the fridge to set (3 or 4 hours will do nicely). Bring back to room temperature before serving.

• Halve the reserved strawberries, and arrange 2 halves on the top of each strawberry cream, then serve.

Strawberry and Lime Cheesecake with Strawberry Sauce

A gorgeously creamy, pale pink cheesecake, splashed with small pieces of red strawberry. The lime gives a subtle freshness to the mixture, which brings out the flavour of the strawberries, but to really emphasise the strawberry flavour serve it with a simple strawberry coulis.

By the way, using leaf gelatine is incredibly easy (see page 98), so if you've battled with powdered gelatine before and given up in despair, try again. Most big supermarkets and good delicatessens now sell leaf gelatine, so you should be able to find it without any trouble. If you can only find powdered gelatine, sprinkle one sachet evenly over the hot single cream after you have taken it off the heat and whisk until it has all dissolved.

SERVES 8

FOR THE BASE:
220g (8 oz) **digestive biscuits**
110g (4 oz) **unsalted butter**, melted

FOR THE FILLING:
3 leaves **gelatine**
150ml (5 fl oz) **single cream**
300g (10½ oz) **cream cheese**
125g (4½ oz) **caster sugar**
finely grated **zest** and **juice** of 2 **limes**
300g (10½ oz) ripe **strawberries**, hulled and chopped
150ml (5 fl oz) **whipping** or **double cream**, whipped
1 **egg white**

FOR THE SAUCE:
250g (9 oz) **strawberries**
juice of 1 **lime**
sugar, to taste

• Crush the biscuits finely, then stir in the melted butter. Mix thoroughly so that all the crumbs are soaked in butter, then press evenly into the base of a 24cm (9½ in) loose-bottomed flan or tart tin. Leave in the fridge to set while you make the filling.

• Half fill a roasting tin with cold water and submerge the gelatine leaves in it. Leave to soak and soften for 5 minutes. Bring the single cream to the boil, then draw off the heat. Straight away, take the gelatine leaves out of the water, squeezing out excess, and stir them into the cream one by one. They will dissolve instantly. Leave to cool for a few minutes.

• Put the cream cheese into a bowl with the sugar, half the lime zest and the lime juice. Beat together until smooth and creamy. Mix in the single cream mixture and then the chopped strawberries. Next fold in the whipped cream. Whisk the egg white until it forms stiff peaks, then fold into the cheesecake mixture. Now pour the whole lot into the tart tin and smooth down lightly. Chill until set, then sprinkle with the remaining lime zest.

• To make the sauce, put all the ingredients in a processor or liquidiser and blitz. Taste and add more sugar if needed. Serve with the cheesecake.

Gelatine

Once upon a time, domestic cooks were offered no choice when it came to gelatine. Powdered or powdered and that was that. The powdered stuff does the job OK, but in my experience it can, on occasion, be a royal pain to get it to dissolve perfectly and avoid those lingering and rather repulsive tiny globs of tacky gelatine that spoil the odd mouthful of something otherwise quite delicious.

If you have found yourself avoiding making dishes that contain gelatine, try your hand again with leaf gelatine. It dissolves perfectly in an instant, every single time. No worry, no hassle; no wonder professional chefs have been using it for decades. They've kept mighty quiet about it, too. But the secret is out now and, for the first time in my cooking lifespan, it is easy to buy as well. Good delis have it, but that's nothing new, and not much help if you don't live anywhere near one. Finally, though, supermarkets are beginning to catch up. Most of the bigger ones stock leaf gelatine, even if it does take a bit of tracking down among the endless aisles. For some strange reason it is not always displayed alongside powdered gelatine, which would seem logical.

I always keep a couple of packets in the store cupboard, which means I can knock up a real fruit jelly in five minutes flat. It takes no longer than making up those vile artificially coloured and flavoured jelly cubes – I've timed both, so I can say this with some assurance – and what you end up with is infinitely nicer, not to mention far healthier. Real jelly is one of those simple puddings that usually delight both children and adults, but if you want to exclude the youngsters, then you can blend booze into the juice as well to make a strictly grown-ups-only kind of jelly. I've had notable successes with Campari and orange jellies, white wine and vanilla jellies, and apple brandy and apple juice jellies, among others. The permutations are endless.

The method is the same in all cases. Here's what you do. Take a pint (600ml) of liquid, let's say orange juice with raspberry purée stirred in. Pour it into a pan and set over a moderate heat. Now half fill a roasting tin with cold water and lay four gelatine leaves in it, pushing them down gently so that both sides are dampened (they'll bob back up to the surface, but that's fine). When the juice is good and hot, but not boiling, stir in sugar to taste – heating develops the natural acidity so you'll need a little sugar, even with a supersweet juice like pineapple. Draw off the heat, and then one by one take the softened gelatine leaves out of the cold water, quickly slough off excess water and drop into the hot juice. Stir once and the leaf will have dissolved like magic. Once all the leaves have melted away, pour the juice into glasses or small bowls or whatever you choose to serve it in, leave to cool and then transfer to the fridge to set. It will take a good few hours (I always allow at least four), so be patient.

For creamy mousses and other dishes involving gelatine, soak the leaves in the same way, and heat up whatever liquid there is in the recipe to dissolve them in.

Blueberry and Orange Trifle

SERVES 6

10 **ladies' fingers** (a.k.a.
 sponge finger biscuits or
 Savoiardi biscuits), each
 snapped in half

5 tablespoons freshly squeezed
 orange juice

1 tablespoon **orange-flower
 water**

300ml (½ pint) **whipping** or
 double cream

FOR THE CUSTARD:

425ml (15 fl oz) **creamy milk**

4 **egg yolks**

2 tablespoons **plain flour**

2 tablespoons **caster sugar**

1 teaspoon **vanilla extract**

FOR THE BLUEBERRIES:

250g (9 oz) **blueberries**

85g (3 oz) **caster sugar**

finely grated **zest** and **juice**
 of ½ **orange**

TO DECORATE:

toasted **flaked almonds**

angelica (optional)

ratafia biscuits (optional)

An admission. Until a year or so ago, my children had never tasted a home-made trifle. The truth is that not only had I never made them a trifle, but I had never ever made a trifle in my life. I seem to have inherited, albeit subconsciously, something of a blind spot for them. I am ashamed, and indeed chastened. To prove that I was a changed woman who had seen the light, I made a trifle. Well, when I say 'a trifle', I mean my own personal take on a trifle. I don't much like sponge cake soaked in alcohol. So, no alcohol, which makes it child-friendly, and no soggy sponge. Instead, I have soaked ladies' finger biscuits in a little orange juice. I also like a touch of freshness against the richness of the custard and cream, here in the form of lightly cooked fresh blueberries sharpened with a little orange. So here it is, my first attempt at a trifle.

• Pile the biscuits loosely into a glass bowl or dish if you have one, or an ordinary but presentable bowl if, like me, you don't. Mix the orange juice and orange-flower water and spoon over the biscuits. Leave to soak.

• Now make the custard. Bring the milk up to boiling point. Meanwhile, beat the egg yolks with the flour and sugar. Whisk in the hot milk, then pour the mixture back into the pan. Stir over a moderate heat and bring up to the boil. Simmer for about 3 minutes, then draw off the heat and stir in the vanilla extract. Pour the hot custard over the biscuits and leave to cool and set.

• To make the blueberry compote, set aside around a dozen blueberries for decoration, then put all the rest, together with the sugar and orange zest and juice, into a pan. Bring up to the boil, stirring until the sugar has dissolved. Simmer for about 4 minutes, then leave to cool until barely tepid. Spoon over the custard and leave to finish cooling. Whip the cream until it holds its shape nicely, but not too thickly, and pipe or spread over the blueberry compote. Decorate with almonds, the reserved blueberries, and angelica and ratafia biscuits if using.

Cream

Summer is not a time for creamy food, but it is a time for cream. I'm not being contrary – at this time of year most of us instinctively head for salads and grilled foods, light salsas, relishes, lots of fresh herbs and fresh fruit, and so on and so forth, and the last thing we want are the creamy sauces that belong to colder-weather dinner parties. Aah, but what do we pour over those sexy, vibrant heaps of raspberries, strawberries, loganberries *et al*? Cream, of course. Towards the end of June, when the gooseberries are ripe and plump, what is essential for conjuring up a gorgeous gooseberry fool? Yup, it's cream again. What sets off everybody's favourite summer pudding? It has to be a small slick of cream. And how could we forget that this is the high season for cream teas: on holiday, at the village fête, or just at home out on the lawn.

How often, though, do we get the chance to buy really high quality cream? I don't suppose many of us ponder the fact that if the difference between mass-produced and farmhouse cheese is so massive (and it is), then surely the same should be true of cream (and it is). Unlike ordinary single or double cream, for instance, a really good unpasteurised Jersey cream is far more than just a rich and luxurious consistency. It has a distinct taste that turns strawberries and cream into something genuinely worth shouting about (assuming the strawberries are good, that is). Even pasteurised Jersey cream, with its beautiful primrose-yellow colour, can be a noticeable treat when made with care in a small dairy.

It is not just the regular creams that bear the badges of their production on their sleeve, as it were. Clotted cream varies enormously. The difference between a commercial clotted cream and a genuine farmhouse one is astonishing. The latter has a thick golden crust that is almost chewy, masking a buttery stand-your-spoon-up-in-it drift of cream in which you can almost distinguish the clover that Daisy had been munching out in the fields.

I dare say you can find remarkable crème fraîche in this country, but I've yet to be introduced to any that match the cream I buy from the stall in the corner of the market I go to every summer in France. It is no bigger than a side-table, stacked high with crème fraîche and butter churned by the ever-elegant Breton farmer's wife, her hair swept up high as if she has just stepped out of the hairdressing salon. Her cream is to die for, so firm it is almost grainy, yellow and lemony. It is unpasteurised, which means it needs to be used up quickly, especially when the weather is hot and thundery, but that's no problem.

The moral of all this is if you have a small local dairy then patronise it as often as you can, or head straight to the neighbourhood shops that sell their products. Even if you consider their output less than superior, here is one place where you, the customer, can have direct impact. If the dairyman doesn't know that you want something a cut above the standard, educate him politely, and encourage others to do the same. Heavens above, we have so much lush green grass in this country, we really ought to be able put the world's most devastating cream on our tables.

Roast Peaches with Shortbread and Redcurrants

A quick and appetising summer pudding, this is an anglicised version of the Italian dish of baked peaches with amaretti filling. It is best made with home-baked shortbread, but high-quality bought will do. Serve it plain, or with runny or whipped cream, Greek yoghurt or scoops of ice cream.

SERVES 4

4 **ripe peaches**, white or
   yellow

45g (1½ oz) softened **unsalted butter**

85g (3 oz) **shortbread**,
   crumbled

175g (6 oz) **redcurrants**,
   stringed, or **blueberries**

30g (1 oz) **light muscovado sugar**

4 tablespoons **water**

• Pre-heat the oven to 220°C/425°F/Gas 7. Halve the peaches, remove stones and pull off the skins. Use a little of the butter to grease an ovenproof dish and arrange the peach halves in it, cut sides up. Mash the shortbread with the remaining butter to form a thick paste. Divide into 8 small portions, roll each into a ball and press down lightly into the stone cavity of each peach half. Scatter redcurrants or blueberries and the sugar over and around the peaches, then spoon the water into the dish. Roast for about 20 minutes, basting once with their own juices. Serve hot or warm.

Redcurrants

This year we will at last have redcurrants in the garden, and for that I am mighty thankful. There is no summer fruit more beautiful than a skein of translucent redcurrants, glinting seductively in the sunshine. They may not provide the immediate hit that a raspberry or strawberry bestows in the mouth, but their worth is undeniable. Encapsulated in each ruby sphere is a burst of intense, tart, sweet juice that fairly vibrates with radiant health.

Somehow, and I won't bore you with the ins and outs of the story, we have never before had the chance to harvest our own crop, and only now are we approaching the first proper season for our new, handsome, standard redcurrant bush. I am already counting the little pots of redcurrant jelly, relishing the fact that now it will be economically viable to make plenty of the recipe I like best – equal weights of currants and sugar boiled up together for exactly 7 minutes before being tipped into a jelly bag to drip through.

Incidentally, if you try this at home, have the jars sterilised and ready to go before you put the fruit on to cook as the juice sets with indecent haste, waiting for no tardy drying of pots. The yield is small, but the sheer intensity of the jelly makes up for that, especially later on in the autumn and around Christmas when it comes out of the cupboard to go with a rack or leg of lamb or to dissolve into Cumberland sauce for the ham.

The rest of the redcurrants will be used in summer pudding, in sauces for pork or perhaps a quickly cooked duck's breast, in my mother's delectable *Ribiselkuchen* (see page 106), and any number of other puddings where their blessed acidity brings out the best in other fruit. It does occur to me that I might be overestimating the yield from one lonely bush, but in that case we shall just have to plant a second and maybe even a third. After all, redcurrants freeze beautifully (as do blackcurrants, incidentally), so if we are overrun with a surfeit, we shall stash them swiftly away in the cold and return to them in the middle of winter.

Summer Fruit Compote with Red Wine and Rosemary

A lightly cooked mix of summer berries is a great standby. It's the kind of thing that can be served hot, warm or cold as the whim takes you. The obvious way to employ it is spooned over scoops of vanilla ice cream, or perhaps even white chocolate ice cream. I love it ladled on top of thick Greek yoghurt. For a more dinner-partyish dessert, use it as a sort of coulis, spooning it around a warm cake (something like the Gooseberry Sauce Cake on page 108) and finishing with a scoop of beaten mascarpone or crème fraîche.

A compote like this one also freezes well, and there's something very reassuring about finding a tubful of summer fruit tucked away at the back of the freezer in colder months.

SERVES 4–6

700g (1 lb 9 oz) mixed summer berries: **blackcurrants, raspberries, tayberries, loganberries, redcurrants, white currants, blueberries, blackberries**

1 glass **red wine** (around 150ml or 5 fl oz)

250g (9 oz) **caster sugar**

1 sprig of **rosemary**

1 **vanilla pod**, slit open

• Put all the ingredients into a saucepan. Bring up to the boil, stirring frequently until the sugar has dissolved. Lower the heat and simmer for 3 minutes. Draw off the heat and eat hot, warm or cold, removing the vanilla pod and rosemary twig just before serving.

Summer Pudding Sorbet

This sorbet carries the deep, deep concentrated flavour of midsummer in every mouthful. The yield may seem, at first glance, rather small, but such is the power and delight of the blend of fruit that you will find that a small serving proves enormously satisfying.

The addition of a whisked egg white is unnecessary if you are using an ice-cream maker but will lighten the texture of a hand-whisked ice. Try it, but remember all the usual strictures about serving raw egg, i.e., it's not for the very elderly, the infirm, the very young or pregnant women.

SERVES 4

600g (1 lb 5 oz) mixed summer berries – such as **blackcurrants, redcurrants, raspberries, tayberries, blueberries, boysenberries, gooseberries, early blackberries** (but not strawberries)

220g (8 oz) **caster sugar**

1 **vanilla pod**

2 tablespoons **crème de cassis** or **crème de mûres** or **ruby port**

1 **egg white** (optional)

• Put the fruit into a pan with the sugar and vanilla pod and set over a low heat until the juices begin to run. Raise the heat and stir until the sugar has dissolved. Bring up to the boil, then simmer for 4 minutes. Draw off the heat and strain, pressing down on the mass of fruit to extract every last drop of juice. Extract the vanilla pod, rinse and return to the sugar jar. Stir the crème de cassis, crème de mûres or ruby port into the juice. Taste and add a little more sugar if you think it needs it, remembering that the chill of the freezer will soften the sweetness a little. Chill the juice.

• Freeze in an ice-cream machine if you have one. If not, pre-set your freezer to its coldest setting. Pour the juice into a shallow freezer container and freeze until the sides begin to set. Break up the edges and push into the centre of the container, then return to the freezer. Repeat once more. When the sorbet has just about solidified but is not yet rock hard, take it out of the freezer again, scrape into the processor and process until smooth and slushy. Whisk the egg white quickly, if using, to form stiff peaks, and fold into the sorbet mixture. Return to the freezer to finish freezing.

• Move the sorbet from the freezer to the fridge about 40 minutes before serving to soften.

Redcurrant Meringue Tart

This Austrian tart takes me straight back to my childhood. My mother made it once or twice every year in the brief currant season and this is her recipe, though it was originally given to her by an old friend. *Ribiselkuchen*, to give it its proper name, is a pudding of deliciously contrasting textures and flavours. There's the thick biscuity almond base, slightly softened by the juice of the tart redcurrants that form the central layer, topped by a soft cloud of fluffy meringue, its edges caramelised in the heat of the oven. Bliss... and if you want to gild the lily, serve it with a puddle of single cream.

SERVES 8

FOR THE ALMOND PASTRY:
150g (5 oz) **lightly salted** or **unsalted butter**
110g (4 oz) **caster sugar**
4 **egg yolks**
85g (3 oz) **ground almonds**
270g (9½ oz) **plain flour**

FOR THE REDCURRANT LAYER:
450g (1 lb) **redcurrants**
110g (4 oz) **caster sugar**

FOR THE MERINGUE:
4 **egg whites**
110g (4 oz) **caster sugar**

• Process the butter with the sugar until evenly mixed. Add the egg yolks, then the ground almonds and flour. Process to form a stiff dough. Press the dough evenly into the base of a 23cm (9 in) tart tin. Chill for half an hour.

• Pre-heat the oven to 190°C/375°F/Gas 5. Bake the base for about 30 minutes until firm and biscuity. Strip the redcurrants from their stalks, then mix with their sugar. Whisk the egg whites until they form stiff peaks, then add 55g (2 oz) of the sugar and whisk until glossy and smooth. Fold in the remaining sugar.

• Raise the heat in the oven to 220°C/425°F/Gas 7. Spread the redcurrant mixture over the base, trying as best you can to leave a narrow border bare all around the edge. Then pile on the meringue, taking it right over the bare border, completely enveloping the redcurrants. Use a fork to tease up the meringue into peaks, then pop into the oven for a final 10–15 minutes until the meringue is touched with brown and just firm. Serve warm or cold, with or without cream, as the spirit moves you.

Cherry Pie with Thyme

Cherry pie is one of America's great contributions to homely gastronomy. This particular version is taken mostly from *The Joy of Cooking* by Irma S. Rombauer, Marion Rombauer Becker and Ethan Becker, a real classic of American home-cooking. The thyme, however, is entirely my contribution, adding a subtle, hard-to-define scent that works an extra spot of magic. Lemon thyme is especially good, but plain thyme is almost as successful, and if you happen to be lucky enough to own a bush of orange thyme, then that's definitely the one to go for.

The cream-cheese pastry, by the way, is a joy to handle, and tastes pretty damn fine, too.

SERVES 6–8

FOR THE PASTRY:
300g (10½ oz) **plain flour**
2 tablespoons **icing sugar**
large pinch of **salt**
170g (6 oz) chilled **unsalted butter**
170g (6 oz) **cream cheese**
60–80ml (2–3 fl oz) **single** or **double cream**

FOR THE FILLING:
1kg (2 lb 4 oz) **cherries** – sour or sweet, stoned
240g (8½ oz) **caster sugar** if using sour cherries, or 140g (5 oz) if using sweet
2 teaspoons fresh **thyme leaves**
juice of ½ small **lemon**
3 rounded tablespoons **cornflour**

• To make the pastry, sift the flour with the icing sugar and salt. Using a pair of knives or a pastry blender, cut in the butter and cream cheese until the mixture resembles a pile of coarse breadcrumbs with the odd larger knobble here and there. Now add enough cream to mix to a soft dough. Gather up to form a ball, knead very briefly to smooth out, divide in two, then chill for at least 1 hour.

• Pre-heat the oven to 220°C/425°F/Gas 7. Roll out half the dough to line a 23cm (9 in) pie plate or shallow tart tin. Line and chill in the fridge until needed. Roll out the second half to form a circle to cover the tin, lay on greaseproof paper and chill until needed.

• Mix the cherries with all the remaining ingredients. Let the mixture stand for 20 minutes, then stir once more. Pile into the lined pie plate in a gently swelling mound. Brush the edges of the pastry crust with water, then lay the pastry lid on top. Trim the edges, then crimp together firmly. Cut a hole in the centre of the pie to allow steam to escape. Bake for 20 minutes then reduce the heat to 180°C/350°F/Gas 4 and bake for a further 30–40 minutes until the thickened cherry juices bubble up through the central steam hole. If the pastry is darkening too rapidly, cover loosely with foil. Serve the pie warm or cold, with cream.

Gooseberry Sauce Cake

SERVES 8–10

280g (10 oz) **self-raising flour**

1 teaspoon **baking powder**

½ teaspoon **salt**

110g (4 oz) **caster sugar**

110g (4 oz) **demerara sugar,**
 plus a little extra for sprinkling

110g (4 oz) **butter**, melted

2 **eggs**

300ml (½ pint) unsweetened
 stewed **gooseberries**

1 teaspoon **vanilla extract**

Oh my, but we love this cake. It is so buttery and tender and moist with the flavour of gooseberries permeating it gently but clearly. Best eaten slightly warm from the oven, with a cup of coffee or tea, or even as a pudding, perhaps jazzed up with a raspberry or strawberry coulis, or more stewed gooseberries folded into whipped cream. Having said that, it also keeps beautifully, staying moist and firming up over a matter of a day or two.

It is based on American apple-sauce cakes, so in the autumn try it again, replacing the gooseberries with home-made apple sauce. It also works brilliantly with Rhubarb and Honey Compote (page 42) or even puréed stewed plums. If you use sweetened stewed fruit, decrease the quantity of caster sugar to 60g (2 oz).

• Pre-heat the oven to 180°C/350°F/Gas 4. Line the base of a 23cm (9 in) cake tin with non-stick baking parchment and butter the sides.

• Mix the flour with the baking powder, salt and the two sugars. Make a well in the centre and add the butter, eggs, stewed gooseberries and vanilla extract. Beat the whole lot together well, then pour into the tin. Smooth down lightly, then sprinkle another 1½–2 tablespoons demerara sugar evenly over the surface. Bake for about 45 minutes, until firm to the touch. Test by piercing the centre with a skewer. If it comes out clean the cake is done. Let the cake cool for at least 15 minutes in the tin before turning out.

Gooseberries

The burden of the gooseberry is that it is loved and loathed in equal measure. As much as it has given pleasure to the multitude, so it has provided penance to the unlucky. It shares this perplexing status with rhubarb, another source of pain and joy depending on your point of taste. Both fruit share an innate sourness, which presumably is why so many take against them.

Temper the sourness of either – though here I am more concerned with gooseberries than rhubarb – with ample sweetness in the form of sugar and perhaps a touch of honey, soften it further, if you wish, with cream or suitable stodge, and the taste proper can emerge unhindered.

My parent's gooseberry bush was more of a thicket than anything else, stuck at the end of a long garden, well out of sight of the house.I don't think it was ever nurtured, but as far as I remember it produced fruit enough for many years until eventually it succumbed to geriatric lack of fertility and had to be grubbed up. I mourned its passing, probably because it had rarely been junior Sophiewho had to pick the wretched drupes.

Now that I, adult Sophie, am the beneficiary of several gooseberry bushes, all, I am glad to say, in fine fettle, I understand why my mother and father failed to replace the lost thicket. Picking gooseberries is painful work.

I brace myself to do it, and though I don't regret the scratches and piercings that ensue (gardening gloves may reduce the damage but mine don't seem to do away with it),I can't say that I relish them either. I do, on the other hand, relish the gooseberries themselves, and that is why I am prepared to suffer.

Do I think that the difference in flavour between bought and home-grown gooseberries is exceptional? Sorry, no. I just like the idea of having them there at my disposal for those few special summer weeks. I still thrill to the first of the gooseberry fools, and I love gooseberry crumble and gooseberry cake, and gooseberry jam and gooseberry chutney. I want to have mackerel or salmon and gooseberry sauce just once or twice, and perhaps stray into the territory of gooseberry stuffing or gooseberry curd.

You can tell from this that I am not enormously adventurous when it comes to gooseberries. I don't create deeply unusual gooseberry dishes. I don't try to jazz them up with chilli and lemongrass, or coriander and balsamic vinegar, or whatever the current favourites are. I can't see the point. With such a short season there is barely enough time to work through the classic gooseberry repertory, which is what I look forward to from the moment I spot the first tiny nascent berries on those thorny branches. Why mess around, when I know that the recipes I return to every year are so very satisfying? Sometimes familiarity is the hottest option around.

Buttermilk Scones

MAKES ABOUT 14 x 5CM (2 IN) SCONES

220g (8 oz) **plain flour**

1 level teaspoon **bicarbonate of soda**

¼ teaspoon **salt**

45g (1½ oz) **unsalted butter**

1 tablespoon **golden syrup** or **golden caster sugar**

roughly 185ml (6–7fl oz) **buttermilk** or **soured cream**

Isn't it amazing that something as simple and innocent as a scone can cause so much angst? Will they rise? Should there be eggs in the recipe? Self-raising flour or plain? And so on and so forth. No wonder so many people (and coffee shops) end up buying ready-made scones, if they eat them at all. A pity, as a good scone, though frivolous and utterly unnecessary to everyday life, is still an item of great joy when freshly baked. And there's the rub. They never taste quite as perfect when reheated, and I've yet to taste a commercial scone that hits the mark. Never fear, for a good scone is within everyone's reach.

After years of trying different recipes, I think that this is the best so far. Very light and buttery, wonderful with clotted cream and Rhubarb and Strawberry Jam (see page 113).

• Pre-heat the oven to 200°C/400°F/Gas 6.

• Sift the flour with the bicarbonate of soda and the salt. Rub in the butter. Make a well in the centre and add the syrup or sugar and enough buttermilk or soured cream to make a soft but not sticky dough. Pat or roll out, on a floured surface, to a thickness of 1.5cm (generous ½ in). Use a 5cm (2½ in) biscuit cutter to stamp out rounds, lay them on a floured baking sheet and brush the tops with a little milk. Bake for about 10 minutes until well risen and lightly browned. Serve warm with clotted cream (or butter) and jam.

Buttermilk

Once upon a time, buttermilk was the liquid left behind after churning cream until a golden knob of butter had formed. Left standing around in the dairy, it would sour in the most delightful way, developing mild acids that thickened the liquid just a little. The result was a deliciously refreshing drink when chilled, and worked wonders in cooking, particularly in baking.

These days, real buttermilk is almost extinct, certainly as far as you and I are concerned. Presumably it still exists, as there's no shortage of butter, but it must be siphoned off for use in something else. Certainly I don't recall ever seeing it for sale. We must console ourselves instead with cultured buttermilk. Quite how close it is to the original I can't tell you, but as a cooking ingredient it works just fine, even though as a drink it doesn't do it for me. Cultured buttermilk is made by introducing a bacterial culture to skimmed milk. As the positively beneficial bacteria do their thing they produce a mild acid that makes the milk thick and lightly creamy, with a pleasing buttery lemony sharpness. The process is much the same as that of making yoghurt or crème fraîche, though the culture itself is a little different.

In the summer I blend buttermilk with strawberries or raspberries and sugar to make an all but instant fruit sauce, excellent spooned over warm pies or crumbles or cold ice creams and sorbets. Primarily, however, buttermilk is used in baking, often in combination with bicarbonate of soda. The acidity of the buttermilk sets the bicarb fizzing, and deletes the dirty yellowing that bicarb solo can produce. They come together, perhaps most famously, in Irish soda bread, but across the Atlantic they are married in cakes and pancakes with great aplomb. Indeed, in the States, buttermilk is a staple of down-home country cookin', besides being an essential in the baking repertoire. It is also used as a dip for moistening chicken or fish before coating in crumbs or flour and frying. Now that seems like the kind of idea that's well worth hijacking if you have a little buttermilk left at the bottom of the tub.

Rhubarb and Strawberry Jam

Everyone loves home-made strawberry jam, but I'm not sure that this classic combination of rhubarb and strawberry isn't even nicer with the particular sharp edge that rhubarb brings. Use the thinner stems of rhubarb and strawberries that are just a tad underripe. Discard any fruit that has even the tiniest hint of softness or overripeness, otherwise your jam will not keep.

As the rhubarb and strawberries steep in the sugar overnight, their juices begin to ooze out, ready to form the basis of the jam.

MAKES ABOUT 2.5KG (5 LB)

1.4kg (3 lb) garden **rhubarb**, weighed without leaves

500g (1 lb 2 oz) **strawberries**, hulled

1.6kg (3½ lb) **granulated** or **preserving sugar**

3 **lemons**

a square of **butter muslin** (from a fabric shop)

• Trim the ends off the rhubarb stems, then cut into 2cm (¾ in) pieces, pulling away any tough strings as you work. Cut the strawberries in half. Take a large, non-metallic bowl and layer rhubarb, strawberries and sugar in it, finishing with a layer of sugar. Halve the lemons, squeeze their juice, then put the shells and all the pips and pulpy bits from the squeezer into a bowl. Cover and stash in the fridge. Pour the lemon juice over the fruit and sugar. Cover that, too, and leave overnight at room temperature, unless the weather is particularly hot and stormy, in which case you had better find room for it in the fridge.

• Next day, cut the shells of the lemons into quarters, and then pile up with the pips and pulp in the centre of the square of muslin. Tie the edges together firmly around them, using a long piece of string, to form a little bag. Scrape the fruit and sugar mixture into a preserving pan, tie one end of the string to the pan handle and bury the bag in among the fruit.

• Slowly bring the contents of the pan up to the boil, stirring gently until the sugar has completely dissolved. Once it is boiling, leave to bubble away merrily for around 15 minutes, then start to test for a set (see page 114). Once it is ready, draw off the heat and discard the bag of lemon debris. Skim off any scum, ladle the jam into hot sterilised jars, seal and label. Once cooled, pack the jars away in a cool, dark cupboard.

Jam Essentials

The making of jam is absolutely a science, overlaid with the deceptive patina of quaint country pursuit, not to mention thatched cottages, roses round doors and grannies in mob caps. Forget all that claptrap and remember only this: that a) home-made jam is one of those small pleasures that make the daily grind of getting up in the morning bearable, and b) even if you don't want to take a degree in the science of jam-making, it is worth knowing the basics and following the rules to get it right.

So, here come the basics. The purpose of all that boiling up of fruit and sugar is not primarily gustatory pleasure (that's just a positive attribute), but preservation of seasonal excess. Sugar is the preservative in question, and you need it in sufficient quantity to keep the finished jam from developing unwelcome growths and moulds. So don't start reducing sugar quantities in an attempt to make a low-sugar jam unless you can store the jam in the fridge and devour it all within a few weeks. And be prepared to settle for a soft-set jam...

By some genius stroke of scientific coincidence, the percentage of sugar needed for successful preservation is much the same as that required for the perfect set. To get a nice set, you need to hit the golden ratio of sugar, acid and pectin, a substance present in many fruit, particularly when they are just a mite underripe. Very sharp fruit, like cooking apples and redcurrants, are usually blessed with high volumes of pectin. In very ripe or overripe fruit, the pectin levels drop dramatically. That's why it is better to include some underripe fruit among the piles that go into the preserving pan, and why you should always chuck out overripe fruit (which may also introduce moulds to the jam).

The tests for setting are pretty straightforward. A sugar thermometer is a useful guide – the jam needs to reach a temperature of 105°C (220°F), which is the boiling point for the correct saturation of sugar for setting. Unfortunately, this is not absolutely to be relied on – thundery weather, for instance, upsets the barometric pressure, and sends the thermometer out of kilter.

The less obviously scientific saucer-method is actually surer. Here it is: you chill a stack of 3 or 4 saucers (or plates or whatever) in the fridge before you start boiling up the jam. Once said jam has been boiling for a few minutes (or if you are using a sugar thermometer, once it rises close to 105°C/220°F), drip a couple of drops of the juices on to an icy-cold saucer. Pull the jam off the heat while the drips cool for a minute or so, just in case you've already hit the perfect spot. Now nudge the edge of one of the drips with your fingernail, pushing it in gently towards its centre. If the jam surface wrinkles then, bingo, it is done. If not, haul the jam back on the heat and carry on boiling, then test again a few minutes later.

To sterilise your jam jars (another important measure, assuming you want your jam to last through the winter), first wash them with soapy water, then rinse thoroughly and let them drip dry, upside down, without touching the insides. In fact, from now on, make sure that you don't touch the insides at all, neither with your hands nor a tea towel nor anything else that might introduce invisible mould spores or bacteria.

Next arrange the jars upside down on a rack in an oven pre-heated to 140°C/275°F/Gas 1, and leave them there for at least half an hour, until the jam is ready to pot. In most instances, the jars should be very hot as the jam is ladled into them, so don't get them out of the oven until you need them.

Filling and sealing the jars is another exercise in making sure that your jam stays in prime condition. A jam funnel, which you can buy from a good cookware shop, is a brilliant help with getting the very hot jam into the jars without dribbling it down the outsides. The heat of the jam itself will help to knock off unwelcome infiltrators. As soon as the jam is in, cover the surface with a disc of waxed paper. These discs come in the packs of jam-pot covers you can buy in cookware shops and supermarkets, but you will undoubtedly have to cut them to size so they sit flat on the surface of the jam, covering the exposed surface area. The idea here is to make a smooth seal between jam and waxed paper so no nasties can lodge underneath.

Finally, finally, get that lid screwed on tight as quick as you can, while everything is still enormously hot. As the air between jam and lid cools, it will shrink to create a partial vacuum, which is a deeply hostile environment as far as any jam-spoilers are concerned.

What? No lids? OK, this is where the jam-pot covers come in. Take one and swiftly dampen it in cold water, pat dry, then stretch over the top of the jar and secure with an elastic band. As it dries fully, it will smooth out to form a brilliantly taut, airtight cover.

Finally, let me assure you that there is loads more to say about the science of jam-making, but if you want to delve in further and deeper you will have to invest in a book dedicated solely to preserving food. It is a fascinating subject considering how very simple the basic ingredients are. Well, I think so anyway.

Fennel Water Biscuits

MAKES AROUND 25–30

½–¾ teaspoon **fennel seeds**, **aniseed**, **caraway seeds**, **crushed green peppercorns** or **cumin seeds**

110g (4 oz) **plain flour**

¼ teaspoon **salt**

45g (1½ oz) **butter**

2 tablespoons **milk**

3 tablespoons **water**

I've always found most commercial cheese biscuits (i.e. biscuits made to accompany cheese, not those with cheese in them) and crackers pretty tedious. Their only enjoyable quality is the impossible 'three crackers in a minute' challenge. I've not tried downing three home-made water biscuits in a minute so I can't tell you how they compare on that front, but in every other respect they are definitely to be preferred. They are also supremely easy to make, and you can play with the basic recipe by adding different spicings as mood dictates. I happen to be particularly partial to a hint of aniseed, so good with most British cheeses, and you could also substitute other spices, such as caraway seeds, crushed green peppercorns (freeze-dried, not in brine) or cumin.

• Pre-heat the oven to 190°C/375°F/Gas 5. Dry-fry the fennel seeds briefly, then cool and crush roughly in a mortar. Sift the flour with the salt and stir in the fennel seeds. Bring the butter, milk and water to the boil together in a small pan, then pour into the flour, stirring with a knife to form a soft but not sticky dough (you may not need all the liquid).

• Knead for a few minutes to smooth out. Roll out as thinly as you can on a lightly floured board. Stamp out 5cm (2 in) circles or cut out diamonds, and lay on a greased baking sheet. If you fancy flat biscuits, prick all over with a fork. For blistered ones, leave well alone. Gather up the trimmings, knead to form a smooth ball, then roll out and stamp out more biscuits.

• Bake the biscuits for 8–10 minutes until a pale mottled tan, turning the trays round once so that they cook evenly (you may need to hoick some out early if they are browning too swiftly). Cool on a wire rack and store in an airtight tin.

Malted Bread

This is not the traditional malt loaf, darkly sticky and chewy, but an altogether lighter affair. I've jettisoned the raisins and reduced the malt extract to make a proper bread rather than something that is verging on cake. In other words, it makes great sandwiches, goes very nicely with a slice or two of cheese or a bowl of soup, or can be eaten just as it is with a smear of butter or cream cheese, toasted or not as the fancy takes you.

The malt extract (which you can buy from shops that sell home-brewing gear) provides enough sweetness and adds its own nutty flavour, but to give it a touch more substance I use a mixture of white and brown bread flours.

MAKES 1 LOAF

450g (1 lb) **strong white bread flour**

150g (5 oz) **strong wholemeal bread flour**

1 teaspoon **salt**

30g (1 oz) **butter**

1 sachet (7g) **easy-blend yeast**

100g (3½ oz) **malt extract**

a little **oil**

a little **milk**

• Mix the flours with the salt and rub in the butter. Stir in the yeast, then add the malt extract and enough water to form a soft but not sticky dough. Knead energetically for 5–10 minutes until smooth and silky, and good and elastic. Rinse out the mixing bowl and oil lightly. Turn the dough in the bowl to coat it in oil, cover with a damp tea towel and leave for at least an hour until doubled in bulk.

• Punch back, then knead again briefly. Shape into a ball and place on an oiled baking sheet. Cover again with a damp tea towel and leave to rise again until doubled in size.

• Pre-heat the oven to 220°C/425°F/Gas 7. Brush the surface of the bread with milk (go lightly, so that you don't deflate the risen bread), then bake for about 25 minutes until the loaf sounds hollow when tapped on the base. Brush again with milk about 3 minutes before it is done. Cool on a wire rack before slicing.

Cornish Saffron Buns

MAKES 12

2 large pinches of **saffron threads**

60ml (2 fl oz) **hot water**

500g (1 lb 2 oz) **strong white flour**

½ teaspoon **salt**

200g (7oz) **unsalted** or **slightly salted butter**

85g (3 oz) **caster sugar**

1 sachet (7g) **easy-blend yeast**

220g (8 oz) **mixed raisins, currants** and **sultanas**

45g (1½ oz) **candied orange** and **lemon peel**, chopped

170ml (6 fl oz) **milk**

TO FINISH:

a little **extra milk**

demerara sugar

OK, this is not the kind of bun you're going to be knocking up blithely at the drop of a hat, but they are so utterly divine that it's worth trying your hand at them one slow weekend. Just imagine how impressed all and sundry will be when you pop these on the table for Sunday breakfast or tea.

The yeast dough is gilded with saffron and enriched with so much butter that it is positively obscene. Add to that a gentle studding of dried fruits and a small amount of best candied peel and you have one of the most delicious creations in the history of British baking. Honest. Especially when they are eaten still warm from the oven.

All that butter in the dough means that it needs plenty of warmth to rise (too cold and the butter congeals, holding the dough solid and quite incapable of movement) and plenty of time too. That's why I prefer to make them in the summer, though if the weather is a bit chilly you may still need to put the bowl of dough in the airing cupboard or even in front of a fan heater to keep it snug.

• Dry-fry the saffron threads in a heavy-based frying pan over a moderate heat for a few seconds. Tip into a bowl and, when they have cooled slightly, crumble them roughly. Add the hot water and leave to steep for at least an hour, or better still overnight.

• Mix the flour with the salt. Rub in the butter, then add the sugar, yeast, dried fruit and candied peel. Pour in the saffron and enough of the milk to form a soft but not sticky dough. Knead the dough in the bowl for a good 10 minutes until smooth and elastic. Cover with a damp tea towel, then leave in a warm place until doubled in bulk. As the dough is so rich, this will take much longer than you might expect even in a warm spot – say 3–4 hours.

• Punch the dough down, knead again briefly and then divide into 12 pieces. Flour your hands lightly and roll each one into a ball. Place on greased baking trays, leaving plenty of room for each one to expand. Cover again with a damp tea towel and leave to rise once more until doubled in bulk. This time allow around 2 hours, again in a warm place. If you want to cook the buns first thing in the morning, time proceedings so that you can leave them to rise at room temperature overnight. If they still seem a bit small in the morning, sit them on top of a warmed hot-water bottle to give them a bit of encouragement!

• Pre-heat the oven to 180°C/350°F/Gas 4. Bake for 20–25 minutes, until the buns are golden brown. Take out and quickly brush the tops with milk, sprinkle with demerara sugar and return to the oven for a final 3–4 minutes. Cool on a wire rack.

Lemon Barley Water

MAKES ABOUT 750ML (1¼ PINTS)

300g (10½ oz) **pearl** or
   pot barley
1 **lemon**
75g (2½ oz) **caster sugar**
icing sugar (optional)

Discovering how to make real lemon barley water was a bit of a revelation for me, though it shouldn't have been as the name says it all. You mix the water from cooking barley with lemon and a little sugar and that's all it is. What you end up with is one of the most refreshing drinks you can down when you're hot and thirsty (or just fancy a cool drink). It's the kind of drink that is made for sunny days at the cricket pitch or tennis court, whether you're taking part or watching from the sidelines. Far superior to the stuff that comes in bottles, and besides, brewing up your own means it can be as sweet or as tart as you like.

• Bring the barley and 2.5 litres (4¼ pints) water to the boil, skim off any scum that rises to the surface and simmer for 20 minutes. Draw off the heat.

• Pare the zest from the lemon in long strips using a potato peeler. Stir into the hot barley water with the caster sugar, then leave to cool. Strain and discard the barley and lemon zest. Squeeze the lemon and stir the juice into the liquid, taste and, if necessary, sweeten a little more with icing sugar, or add more lemon juice if it could do with an extra shot of acidity. You may even want to add a little more water to soften the flavour. Whatever adjustments you make, the critical thing is to serve your lemon barley water thoroughly chilled… even if it's raining and the cricket/tennis has been called off.

autumn

Pumpkin, Smoked Haddock and Lime Soup

My son Sidney and I tackled the Hallowe'en pumpkin with suitable glee and enthusiasm, all ready to carve out the gap-toothed smile of our jack-o'-lantern. It was Sid who insisted on pumpkin soup for supper – quite rightly, under the circumstances. We roasted the pumpkin seeds to nibble at later on, and dined royally on this soup together.

Pumpkin is the most 'delicate' of the winter squash fraternity. In other words, it is bland and needs boosting if it is to be anything more than soothing. This combination with smoked haddock and energising lime makes a delicious soup, with plenty of life to it. The haddock gives it a pleasantly grainy texture.

SERVES 4–6

500g (1 lb 2 oz) peeled and deseeded **pumpkin**, roughly chopped

1 **onion**, chopped

1 **bouquet garni** (sprig of thyme, rosemary and parsley and a bay leaf tied together with string)

2 tablespoons **extra virgin olive oil**

300g (10½ oz) undyed **smoked haddock** fillet

250ml (8 fl oz) **milk**

juice of 1½ **limes**

finely grated **zest** of 1 **lime**

salt and **pepper**

• Mix the pumpkin, onion, bouquet garni and oil in a large pan. Sweat over a low heat, covered, for 10 minutes, stirring once or twice. Meanwhile, place the haddock in a shallow dish and cover with boiling water. Leave for 5 minutes, then pour the water off into a measuring jug. If necessary, add more water to bring the level up to 450ml (¾ pint). Flake the haddock, discarding skin and bones.

• Add the flaked haddock to the pan, together with the soaking water, salt and pepper. Bring up to the boil, then reduce heat and simmer for a further 5–8 minutes. Draw off the heat. Liquidise in two batches, then return to the pan with the milk. Reheat without boiling, then stir in the lime juice. Taste and adjust seasoning, and serve, sprinkled with grated lime zest.

A FUNKIER VERSION WITH SOUTH-EAST ASIAN OVERTONES
Sweat one or two deseeded, chopped red chillies and a 1cm (½ in) length of fresh ginger, peeled and chopped, with the onion and pumpkin. Replace the milk with coconut milk. Top each bowlful of the finished soup with a little chopped spring onion and coriander leaf, as well as the lime zest.

ROASTED PUMPKIN SEEDS

When you are cleaning out the inside of your pumpkin, scrape, tug and cut out all the seeds and their slimy threads. Pile into a bowl. Cover with warm water and work the seeds from the threads, gently massaging and swishing around. The majority will soon rise to the surface. Scoop them out and dry roughly on kitchen paper. Tip on to a baking tray, and add a generous slug of extra virgin olive oil, then a merry slurp or two of soy sauce, and finally a shake or two of Worcestershire sauce. Mix it all together with your hands, then roast for about 10 minutes at 180°C/350°F/Gas 4, stirring once or twice, until the seeds are a rich toasty brown. Cool and then munch – they should be crisp enough to enjoy whole, but if not, return to the oven for a few more minutes to finish cooking through.

Squashes Galore

I've long harboured a passion for winter squashes. It's a family of vegetables that takes in large and small, warty and smooth, brightly coloured and dully muted with consummate ease. The commonest is still the pumpkin, so prevalent in the run-up to Hallowe'en. Being more watery than all the others it is the least inspiring in flavour, but it is still worth cooking in soups and pies as long as you back it up with plentiful seasoning. My real favourites include the onion squash and the red kuri, as well as smaller one-portion squashes such as the charming Little Dumpling squash and the elfinly pointed Acorn squash. One star quality of all these squashes is their longevity. Whole, they keep in a dry place, not too warm but sheltered from frost, for weeks if not months, never losing out on flavour. You need to check them frequently just in case they develop any soft squishy patches, in which case you should cut out the rot and use the remaining squash immediately.

Naturally, their colour and sweet chestnutty taste are their greatest appeal. When I'm short on preparation time, I bring this to the fore simply by cutting them into thin crescent wedges, removing seeds and loose fibres, tossing in olive oil and salt, and roasting, skin and all, in the oven until tender. With five minutes extra to play with, I remove skin as well, cut the pumpkin into 5cm (2 in) cubes and it's ready to roast around a pheasant or a guinea fowl. With good seasoning and the addition of warm spices such as nutmeg, cinnamon and allspice, steamed or baked squash is perfect for mashing, with or without potato depending on how sweet you like your final purée, but definitely with a large knob of butter.

I love sautéed squash, too, this time cut into small cubes of around 1cm (½ in) in size. Sauté them just like potatoes, seasoning towards the end of cooking time, and finishing with a sprinkle of parsley and shavings of Parmesan.

With the smaller, one-per-person squashes, the easiest way to deal with them is to lop off a 'lid', scoop out the seeds, and drop into the central cavity a knob of butter or a little cream, along with a small sprig of thyme or rosemary, or a grating of nutmeg, then replace the lid and bake gently, surrounded by a few tablespoonfuls of water, until tender. This way, they make a neat little first course that will amuse both children and adults.

Maple-roasted Carrot and Ginger Soup

This soup is one I came across in New England, when I headed off there to see maple syrup being tapped in its snowy woods. Now it is something I make whenever carrots are cheap and plentiful and there's a nip in the air. In other words, I make it frequently! It works just fine in smaller quantities as a first course soup for a dinner party, though we might well down it in larger quantities as the mainstay of a simpler family meal.

The original, by the way, was created for a maple syrup producer's chow-down in one of the restaurants of the New England Culinary Institute in Vermont.

SERVES 8

1kg (2 lb 4 oz) **carrots**

2 **onions**, cut into eighths

4cm (1½ in) length of **root ginger**, cut into matchsticks

4 cloves **garlic**, peeled

3 tablespoons **sunflower oil**

4 tablespoons **maple syrup**, preferably Grade B, dark

1.5 litres (2½ pints) **chicken** or **vegetable stock**

salt and **pepper**

to serve: a little chopped **lovage**, or chopped **chives**

• Pre-heat the oven to 220°C/425°F/Gas 7. Cut the carrots into pieces very roughly the thickness and length of your little finger. Place them in a roasting tin with all the rest of the ingredients except the stock and lovage or chives. Mix thoroughly with your hands, then smooth down lightly. Roast for some 45–60 minutes, turning occasionally, until the vegetables are very tender and patched here and there with brown.

• Cool slightly, then scrape into a liquidiser, including as much as you can scrape off of the brown sticky residues at the bottom of the tin. Add half the stock and liquidise until smooth, adding more stock if your liquidiser cup can take it, and the soup needs it.

• Pour into a saucepan, stir in the last of the stock, and then taste and correct the seasoning. I find that it usually needs a fair amount of salt to balance out the sweetness. Heat up well just before serving, and sprinkle each bowlful with chopped lovage or chives.

Warm Pear, Stilton and Watercress Salad

SERVES 4

2–3 ripe or nearly ripe **pears**

juice of ½ **lemon**

4 tablespoons unrefined
  sunflower oil

110g (4 oz) **watercress**

1½ tablespoons **balsamic**
  vinegar or **verjuice**

85g (3 oz) **Stilton**, or **Oxford**
  Blue, derinded and crumbled

1 heaped tablespoon
  sunflower seeds

salt and **pepper**

Putting pears with Stilton and watercress is nothing original, but it is something very good, and well worth repeating. I like this version, where they come together in a warm salad. Many fruits become more acidic when heated, but not pears. Actually, their sweetness is enhanced, which makes this a fine way of using slightly unripe pears to their best advantage. You can prepare everything but the pear in advance, if that makes life easier.

Unlike everyday sunflower oil, which has been chemically stripped of flavour to produce a neutral base, unrefined sunflower oil retains the sweetly nutty flavour of sunflower seeds. It is sold in good delis and some health-food shops. Pumpkin seed oil is similar, but if you can't get either then a mixture of bland sunflower oil and hazelnut oil, or a light extra-virgin olive oil, is very nearly as good.

• Not too long before serving, peel, quarter and core the pears, and slice lengthways. Toss quickly in the lemon juice to prevent discoloration.

• Put the oil on to heat in a wide frying pan. When hot, drain excess lemon juice from the pears and add the slices to the pan. Fry over a fairly brisk heat, turning frequently, until tender and spotted with brown here and there. While the pears cook, either place the watercress in a heatproof serving bowl or divide between 4 plates. Drizzle over the balsamic vinegar or verjuice, and season lightly with salt, generously with pepper. Scatter over the Stilton or Oxford Blue.

• When the pears are nearly done, add the sunflower seeds to the pan and cook for a few minutes more until they begin to brown. Now spoon the hot pears, sunflower seeds and oil over the watercress. Take the salad straight to the table, and toss quickly if in a single big bowl.

How to Cook a Giant Puffball

Lucky you! You've found a swollen, creamy white puffball, a dead ringer for some enormous alien egg, laid bizarrely in the green grass of a field. Take it home, invite all and sundry around and fry it up in giant slices, in best butter with lots of garlic and a splash of white wine. The soft porous flesh of the puffball is mild and tender, and takes on these flavours with delectable charm.

First wipe your puffball clean with a damp cloth. Don't deluge it with water as it will soak it all up like a sponge. Cut into slices about 1cm (½ in) thick. Chop about as many cloves of garlic as slices, assuming the cloves are small and the slices big. Large

cloves? One to every two or three slices, then. Chop plenty of parsley pretty finely. Open a bottle of white wine, pour yourself a glass, pour others a glass, but leave a good glassful or more in the bottle for cooking.

Melt a large knob of butter with a splash of sunflower or grapeseed oil in a wide frying pan. If you have many slices to cook, use two frying pans simultaneously. When the butter is foaming, lay slices of puffball in the pan, without overlapping. Fry over a moderate heat until brown underneath, then turn. Fry for a few minutes more, until the underneath is lightly tanned, then sprinkle over the garlic. Fry for a little longer until it has softened. Now tip out as much of the browned butter as you can, return the pan to the heat and add a fresh knob of butter, sprinkle with parsley, salt and pepper, and then, when the butter has melted and started foaming, slug a good splash of white wine in around the slices of puffball. Turn them in the buttery winey juices for a minute or two, then serve up, either just as they are, or on toast, which will absorb the juice.

Pheasant Pâté

SERVES 6–8

1 plump **pheasant**, including
   livers if available
2 tablespoons **brandy**
300g (10½ oz) **belly of pork**,
   minced
175g (6 oz) **veal**, minced
6 **juniper berries**, crushed
finely grated **zest** of 1 **lemon**
2 **shallots**, very finely chopped
2 cloves **garlic**, very finely
   chopped
2 teaspoons fresh **thyme**
   leaves
2 tablespoons chopped
   fresh **parsley**
1 **egg**
6 tablespoons **dry white wine**
around 220g (8 oz) x 3mm
   (⅛ inch) thick sheet **pork**
   back fat, or thinly sliced
   streaky bacon
2 or 3 **bay leaves**
salt and **pepper**

We don't make pâtés often enough. They are simple to construct, all the better for being cooked several days in advance, and make for an excellent first course or a fine light lunch or picnic (just supposing the weather is clement enough) with bread and salad.

Since you will probably have to ask your butcher to mince the belly of pork and veal together for you, this recipe is not compatible with supermarket shopping. Good. A decent butcher needs support, and in return you will get meat that has true succulence and flavour. Make the most of him or her.

If you don't fancy cutting up the pheasant, you can still make a good pâté by substituting a chicken breast for the pheasant.

• First skin the pheasant, then cut off the breasts. Cut into slices about 1cm (½ in) thick. Mix with the brandy and leave to marinate for 2 hours.

• Strip as much of the remaining flesh as you can from the pheasant carcass, discarding tough tendons and sinews. Chop it finely, and chop the livers finely too, if you have them. Now mix with all the remaining ingredients, excluding the sheet of pork back fat or streaky bacon and the bay leaves. When the breast pieces have notched up their allotted time in the brandy, drain off the juices and mix them in too.

• Fry a small knob of the mixture and taste to check the seasoning. Adjust accordingly.

• Preheat the oven to 170°C/325°F/Gas 3, and put the kettle on to boil. Line a 1-litre (2-pint) capacity terrine with the pork back fat or streaky bacon. Cut a few strips from the remainder to decorate the top. Spread one-third of the minced meat mixture over the base of the lined terrine, then arrange the marinated breast over that. Repeat these layers, then dollop on the rest of the minced meat mixture. Press into place, mounding it up gently. Arrange the strips of pork fat or streaky bacon and bay leaves prettily on top. Cover the dish with a rectangle of greased foil. Stand in a roasting tin, and pour enough very hot water around it to come about 2.5cm (1 in) up the sides. Bake for 1½–2 hours until just firm to the touch and shrinking well away from the sides of the dish. Remove the foil for the last 20 minutes or so of the cooking time, so that the top can brown a little.

• Lift the dish out of the roasting tin, cover with a new sheet of foil and weight down with a couple of tins of baked beans or consommé or whatever you have stashed away in your larder. Once the pâté is cool, transfer to the fridge until needed.

• Serve thickly sliced, with cornichons, pickled walnuts and/or a vibrant fruit chutney, and great bread.

Savoy Polenta with a Smoky Chickpea Sauce

With one vegetarian in the family, we end up eating a good deal of meat-free or almost meat-free dishes. For Florence I make this without the bacon, while the rest of us appreciate the extra depth it gives to the sauce. Either way, it comes as a very welcome autumnal dish, rib-sticking and satisfying.

Spanish smoked paprika (sometimes sold as pimentón) is a gem of a spice, giving an almost addictive smoky note to all kinds of dishes. It brings a taste of the barbecue to foods that have never seen the heat of glowing charcoal – very handy on a rainy day when everyone is longing for a touch of sun.

SERVES 6

FOR THE SAUCE:

1 **onion**, chopped

2 cloves **garlic**

125g (4½ oz) **bacon**, diced, or cubed **pancetta** (optional)

2 tablespoons **extra virgin olive oil**

2 teaspoons **smoked paprika** (pimentón)

1 small sprig of **rosemary**

2 tablespoons chopped fresh **parsley**

2 x 400g (14 oz) tins chopped **tomatoes**

1 teaspoon **caster sugar**

1 x 400g (14 oz) tin **chickpeas**, drained, or 240g (8½ oz) cooked chickpeas

salt and **pepper**

FOR THE POLENTA:

350g (12 oz) shredded **savoy cabbage**

350g (12 oz) quick-cooking **polenta**

30g (1 oz) **butter**

to serve: freshly grated **pecorino** or **Parmesan**

• To make the sauce, fry the onion, garlic and bacon or pancetta slowly in the oil until tender and lightly touched with brown here and there. Sprinkle over the smoked paprika, add the rosemary and half the parsley and stir around for a few seconds. Now tip in the tomatoes, season with the sugar, salt and pepper, and simmer gently for 30–60 minutes (the longer the better), adding a splash of water if it threatens to get too thick and burn. Now mix in the chickpeas, and simmer for a further 15 minutes. Try a taste and add more salt or pepper if needed. Reheat when ready to serve.

• Bring 1.5 litres (2¾ pints) water to the boil in a large pan. Add the cabbage and salt and bring back to the boil. Now pour in the polenta in a slow, steady stream, stirring as you do so. Cook for as long as required (check the packet – it should be between 1 and 5 minutes), then stir in the butter. Taste and adjust seasoning. As soon as it is done, scrape out into a warm serving bowl. Ladle the sauce over it, and scatter with the last of the parsley. Serve immediately, passing the grated cheese around for everyone to help themselves.

Bacon

I've become increasingly fussy about bacon. Well, it varies so very much, and it's only relatively recently that it has become easier to buy really good quality dry cured bacon. A few years ago it seemed like real bacon was on the verge of extinction. Oh sure, here and there, if you knew where to look, you could track down a rare specimen of a slowly matured, lovingly handled rasher, but most of us were landed with nothing more than damp, floppy, brine-injected, over-salted and over-lean and over-pink mass-produced meat. Dismal. Thank heavens, then, for those bacon stalwarts who refused to give in, and carried right on making proper bacon, determined that the perfect British breakfast was not to be demeaned. Now anyone who wants to really enjoy bacon and eggs in the morning, or to inject that superb savoury flavour that only cubes of bacon can bring to sauces and stews and other composite dishes, should be able to satisfy their craving. I'm lucky. Near me I have at least three purveyors of lovely bacon, made from pigs that have led happy free-range lives, dry cured, with the right balance of salt to innocently sweet flesh. The first two I found at the farmers' market and the third was recommended to me by a fellow food-writer. There are others, but these three make bacon that suits my taste just perfectly.

Roast Monkfish with Bacon, Prawns and Tomatoes

This is a dish for the end of the crop of tomatoes, those ones that linger on into early autumn, grabbing the last of the warm sunshine to turn from green to red.

The monkfish 'joint' can be prepared a few hours in advance, ready to be whipped into the oven whenever suits you. The salt of bacon and the sweetness of the prawns and roasted vine tomatoes are nigh on miraculous against the firm juicy flesh of the monkfish. If you can't get cherry tomatoes on the vine, which look particularly pretty, use halved small tomatoes instead, arranging them cut-side up around the fish, and seasoning well. A pinch or two of sugar will help to bring out their full flavour.

SERVES 4–6

1–1.5kg (2–3 lb) **monkfish** tail

2 tablespoons chopped fresh **parsley**

1 clove **garlic**, chopped

finely grated **zest** of 1 **lemon**

100g (3½ oz) cooked, shelled **prawns**

250–280g (9–10 oz) best unsmoked **streaky bacon**

2 tablespoons **extra virgin olive oil**

400g (14 oz) **cherry tomatoes** on the vine

salt and **pepper**

to serve: **lemon wedges**

• Ask the fishmonger to trim away the skin of the monkfish tail, and the thin grey skin that lingers underneath, then to fillet the monkfish carefully for you. Don't leave the bone behind – it is excellent for fish stock.

• Back at home, pre-heat the oven to 200°C/400°F/Gas 6. Pile the parsley, garlic, lemon zest and prawns together on a chopping board and chop together until very finely minced. Season the fillets lightly with salt and generously with pepper. Now, sandwich the fillets together with the prawn mixture.

• Now, this is where it gets a touch fiddly, but by no means impossible. Have faith. Lay the monkfish sandwich before you on the board, and wrap the bacon fairly evenly around it, tucking the ends underneath to hold them in place. Take a long length of string and tie it around the thicker end of your bacon-wrapped bundle, then wind it round the length of the bundle as best you can, to keep the bacon in place – I usually go once down and once up, but you may be able to get away with less if you are nimble fingered. Tie securely at the end. Well done!

• Oil a large ovenproof serving dish with a little of the olive oil. Lay the monkfish in it. Arrange the tomatoes, still on their vines, all around and drizzle the remaining olive oil over them. Season with salt and pepper. Roast for 25 minutes.

• To serve, snip off the string with a pair of scissors (also useful for snipping up the tomato vines), then cut the monkfish into thick slices with a sharp knife. Serve with tomatoes, pan juices and lemon wedges.

Escalopes de Poulet Vallée d'Auge

SERVES 4

4 skinned **chicken breasts**

45g (1½ oz) **butter**

500g (1 lb 2 oz) (or even a little more) **eating apples**, cored and cut into eighths

3 tablespoons **apple brandy** (sometimes sold as cider brandy) or Calvados

250ml (8 fl oz) **whipping** or **double cream**

a dash of **lemon juice**

salt, **pepper** and freshly grated **nutmeg**

Poulet Vallée d'Auge comes from just across the Channel, in Normandy, where their apples are almost as good as ours. Like them, we are now distilling marvellous apple brandy – something well worth looking out for in specialist shops – and our cream, when it is good primrose-yellow Jersey cream, can be outstanding. Add happy free-range chicken and, lo and behold, you have an outstanding dish that suits Britain just as well as it does the north of France.

Although traditionally the chicken is pot-roasted in butter and flamed Calvados, I find this version, made with thin chicken escalopes, every bit as good and a little quicker to conjure up. The surprising thing about this extremely quick method of cooking chicken is that it turns out more juicy and moist than chicken cooked in practically any other way.

To make your life easier, cook the apple slices in advance as they will be reheated nicely in the cream sauce.

• Using a sharp knife, slice horizontally through the centre of each chicken breast, without quite cutting it in half, so that you can open it out like a magazine. Lay between two sheets of greaseproof paper, or clingfilm, and bash with a rolling pin until flattened to a thickness of around 5mm (¼ in).

• Melt half the butter in a wide frying pan over a moderate heat. When foaming add the apple slices and brown on both sides. Once they are on the go, melt the remaining butter in a second large frying pan and heat until foaming. Lay as many of the chicken escalopes as will fit comfortably in a single layer in the pan and fry until lightly browned on the underneath (around 1½ – 2 minutes). Turn over and fry on the other side for a couple of minutes until cooked through. Keep warm while you cook the remaining escalopes, then return to the pan, overlapping the escalopes so that they fit in comfortably.

• Now add the apple brandy, warm through briefly, then ignite by tilting the pan towards the flame, if you cook on gas, or at arm's length with a match if you use an electric hob. Shake the pan gently as the flames flare, until they die down. Finally, tip in the apples, with their juices, season with salt, pepper and nutmeg, then pour in the cream. Let the cream bubble up around the chicken and apples until lightly thickened, then stir in a squeeze of lemon juice. Taste and adjust seasonings and serve with boiled new potatoes, and maybe some spinach, or green beans.

Quick Duck Confit, with Damson and Juniper Relish

Nothing in cookery is original. Or at least very, very little. This recipe is based on a dish I ate in Brown's Restaurant in Oxford. Duck and plums is a well-respected combination, but what pleased me about their rendition was the addition of juniper berries to the cooked plum relish. Since there were plenty about, I chose to use little damsons, rather than the larger plums favoured in the restaurant.

Both duck and relish can be cooked well in advance – several days, if that makes life easier – and reheated when called for.

SERVES 4

4 **duck thighs**
½ tablespoon coarse **salt**
1 teaspoon **black peppercorns**
1 teaspoon **coriander seeds**
5 **juniper berries**
110g (4 oz) **duck** or **goose fat**, or **lard**

FOR THE RELISH:

450g (1 lb) **damsons**
45g (1½ oz) **demerara sugar**
10 **juniper berries**, crushed
a good sprig of **thyme**

• Dry the duck thighs on kitchen paper. Pound the salt with the peppercorns, coriander seeds and juniper berries until all are roughly crushed. Rub the mixture into the skin of the duck thighs and leave for 1–3 hours. Pre-heat the oven to 130°C/250°F/Gas 1. Now melt the duck or goose fat or lard over a gentle heat. Rinse the duck thighs and pat dry. Place in a close-fitting, ovenproof dish. Pour over the melted fat. Cover with foil and then cook in the oven, turning the pieces every half hour or so, for about 1½ hours or until thoroughly cooked through and tender. Leave to cool in the fat. If not using immediately, cover with a clean piece of foil and store in the fridge.

• To make the relish, put the damsons, sugar, juniper and thyme into a heavy-based saucepan and add a dash of water. Place over a moderate heat and cook gently until the juices begin to run. Raise the heat a little and cook, stirring occasionally, until the damsons are tender, having split their skins. Draw off the heat, and leave to cool. Store in a covered bowl until needed.

• To finish the dish, pre-heat the oven to 220°C/425°F/Gas 7. Take the pieces of duck out of their cooking fat and lay on a baking tray. Roast for 20–30 minutes, until crisp, browned and heated right through to the core. Warm the relish gently, and then serve with the duck.

Pheasant and Partridge

I'm not so much of a country girl that I go stomping off in wellies and Barbour on the trail of the local shoot. I come from a cat household, no dogs at all and certainly no guns. *But* I do take very kindly to the occasional offering from friends who derive considerable enjoyment from the mud and damp of autumnal treks across the sodden stubble and the leaf-mouldy woodlands. Each to their own, I say, from the warmth of the kitchen, armed with nothing more than a steaming cup of coffee and a sharp knife.

When the game is coming in direct you do have to be prepared to do a little work, and over the years I've slowly learned that it is easier to skin than to pluck, and I've realised as I pull the innards out that perhaps I might have managed that biology O-level after all. Skinning and eviscerating are both fascinating as long as you are not too squeamish, but if you want detail, you'll have to invest in a copy of my book *Feasts for a Fiver*, published some years ago.

If these processes are not your cup of tea, then the nearest game dealer is the place to go for pheasant and partridge in the autumn months when they are young and tender. Supermarkets increasingly offer feathered game for sale, but the prices are usually higher, and there's never anyone who can give you advice on cooking or the relative merits of male versus female. Nor, indeed, will you ever know where your birds were raised and whether they have any connection with the landscape you see around you.

There's no great mystery to cooking pheasant and partridge once they are fully prepared. If you can roast a chicken then you can roast pheasant or partridge with only minor adjustments to method. The biggest difference is that these wild birds are leaner and so have a tendency to dryness. The best way to combat this is to ask your butcher for a sheet of pork back fat, then to cut a square per bird and tie it over the breast with string. The rest of the fat can go into the freezer ready for next time. Streaky bacon is a good second option, though it can be a little too domineering in flavour for the flesh of the bird. Sliding a few wedges of apple or onion into the central cavity along with a good knob of butter or even a spoonful of Greek yoghurt will also help both flavour and moistness. I roast pheasant at 190°C/375°F/ Gas 5 for about 45 minutes, while partridges do better at the slightly higher temperature of 220°C/425°F/ Gas 7, and take only about half an hour. Both will need to be basted frequently as they cook.

Older birds caught post-Christmas are probably better stewed, braised or pot-roasted. You can adapt any casseroled chicken or guinea fowl recipe, allowing enough cooking time to soften the well-exercised muscles of winter birds.

Roast Partridge with Grapes and Walnuts

Neat and tender, partridges are blessed by a touch of sweetness in the form of halved grapes, and the slight milkiness of new season autumnal walnuts. If I can find Muscat grapes, I grab them straight away for this dish as they have a particularly scented sweetness that lifts them way above the rest, but as their season is short, I usually have to resort to whatever variety of grapes is to hand. This year, I was lucky enough to be given some surprisingly plump and well-flavoured red grapes grown in my village, which were very good in this recipe.

SERVES 4

4 **partridge**

250g (9 oz) sweet **grapes**, halved and deseeded if necessary

45g (1½ oz) **butter**

4 squares of **pork back fat**, or 4–6 rashers **streaky bacon**

150ml (5 fl oz) **Madeira**, or a medium-sweet white wine

100ml (3½ fl oz) **game** or **chicken stock**

85g (3 oz) **walnut halves**

salt and **pepper**

• Pre-heat the oven to 220°C/425°F/Gas 7. Season the partridge with salt and pepper. Push 2 grapes (i.e. 4 halves) and a small knob of the butter inside each bird. Tie squares of pork fat, or strips of bacon cut in half, over the breast of each one. Place in a roasting tin and pour over the Madeira or white wine and the stock. Roast for 25 minutes or so, until cooked through, basting *frequently* with the liquids. Remove the pork fat and return to the oven (having basted the birds again) for 5–10 minutes until beginning to colour. Now add the grapes and walnuts to the tin and return to the oven for a final 5 minutes or so to finish browning the birds. Transfer them to a warm serving dish, scoop the grapes and walnuts out too with a slotted spoon, and spoon around the birds. Let them rest in a warm place for 5 minutes while you finish the sauce and get vegetables sorted.

• Taste the pan juices – if they are a touch on the weak side, boil down for a few minutes to concentrate. Now add the remaining butter in small pieces and shake over the heat until it has dissolved into the sauce, thickening it lightly. Spoon over the birds, grapes and walnuts, and serve.

The coal-black seeds of black onion, also known as kalonji or nigella, have a delicious nutty flavour. They can sometimes be found in the spice racks of big supermarkets, or in Asian food stores, where you will also be able to buy the best value tamarind in dark brown, sticky blocks. Sesame seeds can be substituted for the black onion seeds if you really can't find any.

And if all that sounds rather foreign and exotic, then the lamb itself and the pedestrian nature of the vegetables will bring it back down to our own corner of the earth. By the autumn, lamb is a little firmer in texture and the taste is fuller, both qualities that make it well suited to being cooked at length, unlike spring lamb which requires speed and a light touch.

Spiced Roast Lamb Chops with Roots and Alliums

This is a mildly spiced, all-in-one dish of lamb with loads of vegetables, and although the list of ingredients looks rather lengthy, there's actually nothing much to the cooking part except mixing everything together in the roasting tin.

SERVES 4

30g (1 oz) **tamarind** (see recipe introduction, and page 91)

200ml (7 fl oz) very hot **water**

6 **carrots**

12 small **new potatoes**

3 large **parsnips**

3 **red onions**, quartered

1 head of **garlic**, divided into cloves but not peeled

4 tablespoons **sunflower oil**

½ teaspoon **ground turmeric**

2 teaspoons **cumin seeds**

1 teaspoon **black onion seeds** (also known as kalonji or nigella seeds)

4 meaty **lamb chops**

coarse **sea salt** and lots of freshly ground **black pepper**

• Pre-heat the oven to 220°C/425°F/Gas 7. Put the tamarind into a bowl and pour over the hot water. Leave to soak for about 20 minutes, mashing the tamarind pulp down with a fork every now and then. Give it one final squish and mash and mix, then rub the liquid through a sieve, pressing through as much of the soft tamarind pulp as will be parted from the seeds and fibres. Stir the tamarind liquid.

• Cut the carrots in half lengthways. If the new potatoes are a touch on the large side, halve them. Quarter the parsnips lengthways, then cut out the tough inner core. Put all the ingredients, except the chops, into a roasting tin. Turn so that the vegetables are coated in the oil and tamarind mixture. Cover with foil and cook in the oven for 30 minutes. Remove the foil, give the vegetables a good stir and nestle the lamb chops down among them, making sure that they are coated in the juices. Return to the oven and roast, uncovered, for a further 40–50 minutes, stirring once or twice, until the chops are cooked and the vegetables are all very tender and patched with brown. Check once in a while and if the dish is beginning to look a little dry, add a touch more water. When they are done, serve immediately.

Double Lamb Chops with Red Onion *and* Balsamic Vinegar

We're lucky enough to have a fantastic butcher in the village, and his double lamb chops are spectacular. I cook them with respect – not too much fiddling around, but enough to bring out their fine qualities to the full. The sweetness of the slowly cooked vegetables and the acidity of the vinegar are enormously complementary to the meat. This recipe will work well with any good, chunky lamb chops.

SERVES 4

1 **red onion**, chopped

1 large **carrot**, finely diced

1 stick **celery**, finely diced

1 clove **garlic**, chopped

2 tablespoons **extra virgin olive oil**

2 teaspoons chopped **savory**, or 1 teaspoon chopped **tarragon** or finely chopped **rosemary**

1 tablespoon chopped fresh **parsley**

2 tablespoons **balsamic vinegar**

4 **double lamb chops**, or any other large, chunky lamb chop

salt and **pepper**

• Pre-heat the oven to 220°C/425°F/Gas 7. Mix the onion, carrot, celery, garlic and 1 tablespoon of the oil in a heavy frying pan that can go into the oven handle and all (or has a detachable handle). Cook over a fairly gentle heat, stirring frequently, until the vegetables are touched here and there with brown, and sweet and soft. Don't rush this stage – it should take a good 15 minutes or more. Draw off the heat and stir in the savory, tarragon or rosemary and the parsley, balsamic vinegar, and salt and pepper.

• Meanwhile, heat the remaining oil in a second frying pan and swiftly brown the chops on both sides. Lay them on the cooked vegetables, season with salt and pepper, and transfer to the oven for 5–10 minutes depending on how well cooked you like your meat. Serve while still hot, making sure each chop is accompanied by some of the vegetables and their sticky juices.

Spiced Venison and Chestnut Stew

SERVES 6

2 tablespoons **sunflower** or
   extra virgin olive oil
1 **onion**, halved and sliced
1 clove **garlic**, chopped
2.5cm (1 in) length of **root
   ginger**, finely chopped
2 tablespoons **flour**
1½ teaspoons **ground
   cinnamon**
1 teaspoon **ground cumin**
¼ teaspoon **ground mace**
1kg (2 lb 4 oz) trimmed diced
   venison braising steak
100ml (3½ fl oz) **red wine**
1 tablespoon **tomato purée**
220g (8 oz) **carrots**, sliced
200g (7 oz) cooked, peeled
   chestnuts
1–2 tablespoons **redcurrant**
   or **quince jelly**
salt and **pepper**

You know that feeling, when you really need comfort food, something that steams and caresses the tastebuds, makes you feel loved and warm? This could be the answer; it certainly worked a small spell of magic the chilly day our central heating died on us.

If you are a conscientious cook, you will peel and cook the chestnuts yourself – allow about 350–425g (12–15 oz) raw ones to get the right amount – and the flavour will be infinitely superior (see page 204). But, let's face it, it is a nasty, painful job I am prepared to suffer only once or twice a year so for this stew, I'd use vacuum-packed, ready-cooked chestnuts almost every time.

• Pre-heat the oven to 150°C/300°F/Gas 2. Heat about ½ tablespoon oil in a wide frying pan and fry the onion, garlic and ginger gently until very tender and beginning to brown here and there. Scrape into an ovenproof casserole dish.

• While the onion is cooking, mix the flour with the cinnamon, cumin, mace, salt and pepper and turn the diced venison in this mixture. Add another tablespoon of oil to the frying pan and raise the heat to medium. Brown about a third of the floured venison, add to the casserole and then repeat twice with the remaining venison, adding the last of the oil when needed. Sprinkle any leftover flour over the meat in the casserole. Pour the red wine into the frying pan and bring up to the boil, scraping in all the sticky brown stuff on the bottom of the pan. Stir in the tomato purée, and pour over the meat. Add the carrots and enough hot water to almost cover the meat. Clamp a lid on and stash in the warm oven. Leave to bubble gently (if it is doing more than that, then turn the heat down a few degrees) for 1½–2 hours.

• Now stir in the chestnuts and return to the oven for 5 minutes to heat through. Last but not least, stir in the redcurrant or quince jelly to taste, and adjust seasoning. Serve straight away over buttered noodles, spring onion mash or even polenta, or reheat thoroughly (adding a little more water if necessary), when hunger hits.

Buttered Cabbage with Poppyseeds and Lemon

white or green cabbage,
  lightly blanched
butter
zest of lemon, finely grated
poppy seeds
juice of lemon
salt

This is so good that I'd be happy to eat it by itself, but you are probably more restrained than me, so try serving it with roast or grilled chicken, or even with roast feathered game.

• All you do is heat the butter until sizzling and toss in the cabbage, lemon zest and a sprinkling of poppy seeds. When it is good and hot, add a generous squeeze or two of lemon juice, and some salt if it needs it. Now it's ready to eat.

Roast Cabbage

cabbage
extra virgin olive oil
cloves of garlic
coarse salt
balsamic vinegar (optional)

This is so easy, but if you've never tried it before, such a revelation, that you'll wonder why the world and his aunt have not been cooking cabbage this way for ever. It works with all sorts of cabbage, but the best I find are the conical pointed cabbages, which have a particularly attractive sweetness, and leaves that are not quite as densely packed as, say, a standard white cabbage.

• Pre-heat the oven to around 200°C/400°F/Gas 6 – a little warmer or a touch cooler is fine if you are cooking something else in there at the same time. Trim your cabbage, removing tougher outer leaves, then cut into four lengthways if it is fairly small, and eight if it is large and healthy. Place in an ovenproof dish and drizzle generously with the oil. Add the whole cloves of garlic (unpeeled), and season with the salt. Turn the pieces of cabbage so that they are completely coated in oil. Roast for around 30–40 minutes until tender at the heart, and browned fairly generously at the edges, basting occasionally as they cook. Finish, if you wish, with a small slurp of balsamic vinegar, and serve. Excellent with steak.

Asian Slaw

So simple you can barely call it a recipe – but it certainly makes for a vibrant take on a standard coleslaw.

SERVES 3–4

¼ **white cabbage**, finely
  shredded

1 **carrot**, grated

1 teaspoon toasted **sesame
  seeds**

1 tablespoon **sesame oil**

juice of ½ **lime**

½ medium hot **chilli**, very finely
  diced

1 teaspoon very finely diced
  root ginger

1 heaped teaspoon **light
  muscovado sugar**

salt or a few shakes of **fish
  sauce**

• Not too difficult, this one – just mix all the ingredients and it's done!

Cabbages

I've had a sort of epiphany with regard to cabbage over the past couple of years. Sure, I quite liked the stuff in a disinterested kind of a way, but of late this has changed quite, quite radically. I've finally seen the light – cabbages in their many forms have enormous potential, a fact that is largely ignored. Not surprising, when you encounter that ghastly smell of stale elderly and overcooked cabbage that lingers so grimly in cheap dining rooms, sad boarding houses and even school canteens where they should be encouraging children to eat their greens, not putting them right off.

Cabbages have a complex flavour that needs a touch of cosseting. At the very least the dutiful cook should ensure that her shredded cabbage is never over-boiled. Three or four minutes in vigorously boiling salted water is generally quite enough. Add a touch of butter (or something more fancy like a drizzle of lemon olive oil), and you have an admirable side dish, every bit as good as more expensive veg.

There is an exception to the quick cooking rule (isn't there always an exception?) which takes you to the opposite extreme; in other words, cabbage can be very good when braised for an awfully long time (say, an hour or more over a low heat in a tightly lidded pan) with, perhaps, a knob of butter, a few spoonfuls of water or, better still, stock, salt and pepper.

This is not where the cabbage story ends. Roast cabbage is fantastic and so is fried (try it fried in olive oil until tender but patched with brown, adding lots of chopped garlic and a crumbled dried chilli towards the end of the cooking time). A truly fresh cabbage makes for a fantastic salad, which is why coleslaw caught on initially, though now commercially made slaws have ruined the reputation of this handsome salad. I love cabbage in more complex dishes, for instance in a quiche (see page 21), or a soup with beans and chunks of potato.

A Savoy cabbage is by far the most handsome, with its crinkly dark green leaves that beg only the lightest of cooking and the addition of butter, lemon and perhaps some whole caraway seeds. But these days I find myself favouring the humbler white cabbage, with its cannon-ball density, or the less compact but sweetly, succulent pointed cabbages. I'm less smitten with miniature cabbages that have followed in the wake of other small vegetables as I can't fathom a good reason for cooking cabbage whole, even at that small size.

The point, though, is that we should not consider this common, cheap vegetable of lesser importance or value than fancier vegetables that garner more attention. Celebrate the common cabbage!

Leeks with Red Wine and Bacon

SERVES 4–6

2 tablespoons **olive oil**

675g (1½ lb) **leeks**, trimmed, and halved, first lengthways, then across

2 rashers of **back** or **streaky bacon**, cut into strips

150ml (5 fl oz) **red wine**

150ml (5 fl oz) **chicken** or **vegetable stock**

salt and **pepper**

One of my favourite leek recipes, which takes them from a humble standby to star status. This way of cooking them works well for older or younger leeks, but avoid the hugest, fattest, most stringy logs of leeks, which have to be sliced thinly if they are not to be impossible to eat. I like this dish both hot and at room temperature, as a starter with a good chunk of bread to suck up the juices, or as a side dish. Once cooked, the leeks keep well, covered, in the fridge, for up to five days.

The recipe comes originally, I think, from Elizabeth David, but I learnt it from that wonderful chef Joyce Molyneux. The bacon is my addition, but only worth including if it is of good quality, lightly smoked or green, not too salty, and with a sweet flavour.

• Heat the oil in a wide frying pan. Add the leeks and bacon, and fry for about 5 minutes until the leeks are patched with brown and the bacon is cooked and crisp. Now pour in the wine, stock, salt and pepper. Bring up to the boil, then cover and simmer for 5 minutes. Uncover and simmer for a further 5–10 minutes until the leeks are tender. Lift them out on to a serving dish, and if necessary, boil down the juices in the pan until you have just a thin film covering the bottom. Taste and adjust seasoning, then pour over the leeks. Serve hot or cold.

Apple and Bacon Mash

SERVES 4

700g (1 lb 9 oz) floury
potatoes, peeled and cut
into large chunks

310g (11 oz) **cooking apples,**
peeled, cored and cut into
chunks

30g (1 oz) **butter**

4 rashers **streaky** or **back
bacon,** cut into strips

2 tablespoons chopped
fresh **chives**

salt

There's a magic moment in the early autumn when the first of the garden's maincrop potatoes and the first of the apples coincide. The children disappear outside to gather produce and earthworms, and soon a basket of potatoes, topped with a few sour cooking apples, appears on the kitchen table. Occasionally the worms are included, but it is not something I encourage.

Their coincidence makes the German dish of *Himmel und Erde* (heaven, for the apples, and earth, for the potatoes) inevitable. It is a surprising and welcome mixture, the apples imparting a mild, fruity sourness to a rich buttery mash. We like it even better with plenty of crumbled, crisp old-fashioned bacon stirred in. Great with sausages, chops, fish (particularly cod or salmon), and other elemental, plainly cooked main courses.

• Put the potatoes into a pan with water to cover and salt. Bring up to the boil, and simmer until the potatoes are almost done. Now drain off about two-thirds of the water, and add the apples to the pan. Mix in, then cover and cook gently until the apple is soft enough to mash into the potato. Add the butter and beat in well to make a smoothish purée.

• While the potatoes are cooking, fry the bacon in its own fat, slowly at first until the fat runs, then raising the heat to crisp it up. Stir about three-quarters of the bacon, with its fat, into the mash, together with most of the chives. Spoon into a big warm bowl and sprinkle with the remaining bacon and chives.

Autumn Potatoes

The potato is taken for granted. We love them, and it's hard to credit that when they were first brought over from the new world we regarded them with intense suspicion and mistrust. Now that we understand that they don't cause grievous bodily harm, we give them hardly a minute's thought as we stuff them into our shopping baskets. Cheap and plentiful and filling.

So, it may come as a bit of a shock to encounter a relatively pricey pile of earth-laden potatoes at a farmers' market. Just the other day, I heard a customer at my local farmers' market complaining that she didn't see why she should pay for the muck that was still clinging to the healthy-looking spuds piled up high in the chilly autumn air. Here's why: they will taste fantastic, and she would surely notice the difference if she was prepared to shell out those very few extra pence. My mum, who knew a thing or two, always chose 'dirty' potatoes over pre-cleaned ones. That veil of soil helps to seal in moisture and flavour, preserving more of the taste of freshly dug potatoes. It will also go some way to cloak them from the light, so they have less chance of developing those unpalatable green patches that have to be cut out. I still follow my mum's

example, even though I do find myself groaning occasionally as I scrub the potatoes at the sink. It really doesn't take an awful lot longer, and the end result is far more satisfying.

The other bonus of buying at a farmers' market, or direct from a farm shop, is that you may get a chance to try varieties that don't often make it to the supermarket. Believe me, there are literally hundreds of fabulously named potatoes, in a stunning array of hues from ivory through dusky pink to deep purple-black, that are total strangers to the mega-buyers of the retail world. Given that potatoes are such a staple in our diet, it makes sense to explore the possibilities of flavour to the full. How pleasing to be able to experience such variety, while all the time staying on familiar territory.

Cauliflower with Sun-dried Tomatoes, Garlic and Capers

A good and dramatic way to dish up a cauli in its full glory. The piquancy of the dressing does wonders for the flavour. If time is short, you may prefer to break the whole head down into florets for swifter cooking and, though you lose in dramatic impact, the flavour will be unimpaired.

SERVES 6

1 whole **cauliflower**, especially the green Romanesco, or the purple-headed cauliflower

4 tablespoons **extra virgin olive oil**

2 cloves **garlic**, chopped

3 pieces **sun-dried tomato**, chopped

1 tablespoon small **capers**

1 **red chilli**, deseeded and chopped (optional)

salt and **pepper**

• Trim the leaves off the cauliflower and cut a deep cross in its base so that it cooks evenly. Either steam it whole, microwave (about 7 minutes on full power, but check frequently), or boil as follows: pour 5cm (2 in) water into a large pan, season with salt and bring up to the boil while you make two long straps from lengths of foil folded in half then in half again. Lay one strap across the other to form a cross, sit the cauliflower in the centre and pull the straps up around it to form a cradle, so that you can lift the cauliflower in and out of the pan with ease. Now, lower the cauliflower into the simmering water, cover and leave to half boil, half steam until just tender, then lift out.

• When the cauliflower is just about cooked, heat the oil in a small pan, and add the garlic, tomatoes, capers and chilli (if using). Fry over a generous heat until the garlic is beginning to brown, then draw off the heat. Drain the cauliflower if necessary, and transfer to a serving dish. Spoon the hot oil and flavourings over the cauli, and serve immediately.

Cauliflower

Cauliflowers have certainly come on with aplomb over the past decade or so. These days we are not only blessed with the plain, white-curded specimen but can feast our eyes and mouths on stunningly beautiful green Romanesco caulis with their pointed swirls, and, perhaps more predictably, purple-headed caulis that tend to lose much of their colour to the cooking water (the best way to preserve the colour is either to steam the cauli or to cook the florets in the microwave). Add to this cute little miniature cauliflowers, which may help to make the vegetable more appealing to children, and you have an extraordinary range to choose from.

The fact is, though, that they all taste pretty similar. Perhaps the Romanesco is a trifle more delicate, a little less heavy on the negative taints of the cabbage family, but to be quite honest what counts most is the cooking, and freshness. Cauliflower, of whatever hue or size, needs to be accorded considerable respect in the kitchen. Original sin is not part of the cauliflower's make-up. It starts off well, but what drags it down is being left lying around in a vegetable rack for days on end, then being overcooked in a negligent way.

Exact timing is impossible to dictate as it depends on the size of your florets, but precision is nonetheless crucial. I reckon you should be allowing something between 5 and 9 minutes of boiling, but don't trust me implicitly on this one. Keep testing, and whip the pan off the heat the very second that those ivory white chunks are barely tender, yet retain a slight resistance at the centre. Drain swiftly and serve straight away. When this is not practical, the best thing to do is to run them under the cold tap for a few seconds to arrest cooking, then reheat them later in butter or olive oil, transform them into a salad (lovely with mayonnaise, yoghurt and toasted almonds) or, perhaps best of all, turn them into the classic cauliflower cheese (see page 218) under a blanket of superlative cheese sauce.

Fresh Pear Relish

SERVES 4–6

½ teaspoon **coriander seeds**

¼ teaspoon **black peppercorns**

¼ teaspoon **fennel seeds**

2 ripe **pears**

juice of ½–1 **lemon**

½ **red onion**, finely chopped

sugar, to taste

2 tablespoons chopped fresh **coriander**

salt

Sweet autumnal pears are a delight and now that I'm blessed with my own fecund tree, I find myself branching out (excuse the pun) in the ways that I use them.

This relish is one I serve with burgers. Real burgers, that is, made from good quality meat, and grilled or griddled until just done, not as tough as leather. I will admit to not always making them myself, as I have ample access to excellent burgers from my village butcher, several of the meat-producers on the farmers' market and at least three farm shops. I've even served it with bison burgers (good flavour, low on fat), sandwiched in a toasted bun, along with slices of tomato, shredded lettuce and a few dabs of mayonnaise mashed with blue cheese. A combination I can highly recommend.

• Dry-fry the three spices, then crush roughly with a pestle in a mortar.

• Peel, quarter and core the pears, then dice or finely slice them and toss immediately in lemon juice to prevent browning. Mix with all the remaining ingredients, adding spices to taste (I reckon 1½–2 teaspoons is about right). Taste and adjust seasoning. Cover until needed.

Blackberry and Plum Streusel Tart

Plums are dropping from the trees just as blackberries start to ripen – another great, though often overlooked, combination from Mother Nature. Try them in a crumble, or better still in this Germanic crumble tart.

SERVES 8

375g (13 oz) **sweet shortcrust pastry**

250g (9 oz) **blackberries**

280g (10 oz) **plums**, halved (or quartered if large) and stoned

85g (3 oz) **caster sugar**

1 tablespoon fine **semolina** or **dry breadcrumbs**

FOR THE STREUSEL TOPPING:

200g (7 oz) **plain flour**

1 teaspoon **ground cinnamon**

85g (3 oz) **caster sugar**

75g (2½ oz) **butter**

• Roll the pastry out on a lightly floured board to form a circle large enough to line a 23cm (9 in) metal tart tin. Prick the base with a fork, then chill for half an hour. Pre-heat the oven to 190°C/375°F/Gas 5.

• Line the pastry case with greaseproof paper or foil, and weight down with baking beans. Bake for 10–12 minutes, then remove beans and paper or foil. Return the case to the oven to dry out, for about 5 minutes.

• Toss the blackberries with the plums and sugar. Sprinkle the semolina or breadcrumbs over the bottom of the pastry case. Pile in the fruit, and smooth down as best you can. To make the topping, sieve the flour with the cinnamon and mix with the sugar. Melt the butter and pour over the flour and cinnamon mixture while still hot. Using a knife, cut the mixture repeatedly until you have a mass of crumbs. Scatter thickly and evenly over the blackberries and plums, so that they are completely covered. Bake, still at the same temperature, for 25–30 minutes until golden brown. Serve hot, warm or at room temperature, with custard or cream.

Blackberries

I'm apprehensive about the ripening of blackberries. From mid-August I watch those red berries deepen in colour, changing so slowly but surely through darker burgundy into the inky-black purple that signifies ripeness and the onset of autumn. Summer is my favourite season, and I mourn the signs of its imminent departure, waiting for the day when the warmth changes and the burn has quite disappeared. Once I've passed the threshold of September, I begin to relax into the issue of autumn, and it is again the blackberries that mark this new phase of the year. The first blackberrying trip to the long hedge that unfurls down into the floor of the valley usually leaves me feeling more upbeat, ready to enjoy the colours and smells of the

This last year the harvest was phenomenal, stretching on and on far beyond the usual cut-off point of 10 October, when legend has it that the Devil spits on brambles, withering the remaining fruit away to a damp and tasteless pulp. We worked those hedges up and down, time and again, picking basketfuls of blackberries as they ripened in non-stop succession. The recipe of the season was definitely the Blackberry and Plum Streusel Tart (see page 157), bringing together one waning and one waxing fruit, while ice cream and jam were stashed away to be eaten at a later date. I have copious tubs of stewed blackberry and apple, flavoured sometimes with orange and vanilla, others with star anise for a mild burst of aniseed. I will bring it out in the middle of winter, when the taste of blackberries will again seem as exotic as it did with the first haul way back in early

Crushed Blackberry Syllabub

The boozy froth of a syllabub carries the flavour of crushed blackberries perfectly. The syllabubs will sit happily in the fridge for up to 36 hours – a thoroughly well-behaved dinner-party pud.

SERVES 6

300g (10½ oz) ripe
  blackberries
85g (3 oz) **caster sugar**
finely grated **zest** and **juice**
  of ½ **lemon**
300ml (½ pint) **double cream**
2 tablespoons **brandy**

• Crush the blackberries with the sugar and lemon zest until you have a knobbly runny mush. Stir in the lemon juice and the cream. Whip, adding the brandy when it is beginning to thicken. Carry on whipping until thick and light, but still floppy. Spoon into individual glasses. Either serve immediately, or chill until ready to eat.

Blackberry *and* Clotted Cream Ice Cream

Blackberries make a fabulous ice cream, delicious on its own, but a total winner served with a slice of hot apple pie, or a steaming baked apple. I like to leave the blackberries whole, to give some texture to the ice cream, but if you don't like the idea of all those seeds, sieve the cooked blackberries and their juices, rubbing through as much of the flesh as you can.

SERVES 6–8

450g (1 lb) **blackberries**
150g (5 oz) **caster sugar**
2 tablespoons **crème de mûres** or **crème de cassis** (optional, but good!)
220g (8 oz) **clotted cream**

FOR THE CUSTARD:
4 **egg yolks**
2 tablespoons **caster sugar**
1 tablespoon **plain flour**
300 ml (½ pint) **milk**

• Pre-heat the oven to 150°C/300°F/Gas 2. Put the blackberries into a shallow, ovenproof dish and sprinkle with the sugar. Leave to soften gently in the oven, stirring once or twice, for 40 minutes, until the juices flow copiously and the tantalising scent curls around the kitchen. Leave to cool, then stir in the crème de mûres or crème de cassis.

• To make the custard, beat the egg yolks with the sugar and flour. Bring the milk up to the boil, and pour on to the egg yolk mixture, whisking constantly. Rinse out the pan, then pour the custard mixture back in and stir over a low heat until it has thickened and the taste of raw flour has disappeared. Leave to cool.

• Beat the clotted cream until softened, then whisk in the custard and the blackberry mixture. If you have an ice-cream maker, freeze according to manufacturer's instructions. If you don't, pre-set the freezer to its coldest setting. Spoon the ice cream mixture into a shallow freezer container and leave in the freezer for about an hour, until the sides have frozen but the centre is still soft. Break up the sides and push them into the centre. Return to the freezer for another ½–1 hour until just set solid but not yet frozen hard. Scrape into the processor and process to a smooth slush, or tip into a bowl and beat hard to break up jagged ice crystals. Either way, return the mixture to the container and then slide it back into the freezer to finish freezing.

• Transfer from the freezer to the fridge about 45 minutes before serving, so that it softens enough to scoop.

Autumn-fruiting Raspberries

When we moved house at the end of August, I bemoaned the loss of our autumn-fruiting raspberries, just on the verge of yielding up bucketfuls of fruit. But, lo and behold, there in the garden of the new house were two lines of beautiful raspberry canes, already drooping under the weight of ripening berries. Yippee!

I appreciate raspberries even more in the crossover month of September and on into October than I do in late June and July. Autumn-fruiting raspberries and sleek, dark wild blackberries are the last and perhaps the best of all the soft fruit, generously easing us into autumn before the frosts set in. Both make the most superb jams (see page 165), carrying such a full burst of fresh scent in each spoonful. Better, I think, on scones than strawberry jam, and just fabulous in Poor Knights of Windsor. That was one of my favourite childhood homely puddings – raspberry jam sandwiches, fried in butter until golden brown, then straight out of the frying pan on to our plates. It was all we could do to wait long enough to let the Poor Knights cool down enough to devour.

Raspberry jam is essential for a good Linzertorte (see page 164), that most glamorous of jam tarts from Austria with its biscuity pastry, but highest praise is to be reserved for our own Queen of Puddings (see page 223), with its layer of bread custard topped with jam (raspberry or blackberry jelly, please) and finished with a light swirl of a cloud of meringue. Heavens above but we are good at puddings in this country.

Raspberry and Earl Grey Jellies

SERVES 6

450g (1 lb) ripe **raspberries**
150g (5 oz) **caster sugar**
4 leaves **gelatine**
2 **Earl Grey teabags**
juice of ½ **lemon**

to serve: thick but runny
   double cream (optional)

A pudding for a warm day in an Indian summer, or perhaps even on a chillier evening, after a sturdy meal. Jelly becomes a sophisticated, grown-up pudding when made from fresh fruit and served in stemmed glasses. Add cream for a touch of indulgence, or eat plain and naked for the pure, bright flavour.

The scent of Earl Grey tea and its slight tannic edge works well with the flavour of raspberries, but you could try, say, jasmine tea instead, to good effect. Make the jellies at least 5–6 hours before serving, so that they have time to set.

• Wield your potato masher and work the raspberries and sugar to a juicy pulp. Set aside for half an hour, stirring occasionally, so the sugar has a chance to dissolve completely. Rub through a sieve.

• Put the kettle on. Half fill a roasting tin with cold water, and lay the gelatine in it to soften. Drop the teabags into a glass or metal measuring jug, and pour in enough boiling water to come up to the 300ml (½ pint) mark. Leave for a few minutes to brew, but while it is still very hot, remove the teabags. Swiftly scoop the softened gelatine out of its bath, squeeze out excess water and then stir into the steaming tea. Now add the lemon juice and pour in the raspberry liquid. One stir and it's ready. Pour into 6 stemmed champagne flutes or small wine glasses. Leave to cool, then transfer to the fridge to set.

• Just before serving, top with a spoonful of cream if you crave a touch of richness to counterbalance the purity of the jelly.

Linzertorte

SERVES 8

150g (5 oz) **plain flour**
½ teaspoon **ground cinnamon**
pinch of **salt**
150g (5 oz) **caster sugar**
150g (5 oz) **ground almonds**
finely grated **zest** of 1 **lemon**
150g (5 oz) softened **unsalted
  butter**
2 **egg yolks**
200g (7 oz) home-made
  raspberry jam
icing sugar

I suppose you could say that Linzertorte is a glorified jam tart from Austria. The base is made of a beautifully short almond pastry, pressed out as thick as a chunky biscuit, and the filling is nothing more than a generous spread of raspberry jam, finished with a lattice of more almond pastry. With home-made jam and fresh sweet butter, however, the whole caboodle becomes a jam tart of rare and joyous distinction.

• To make the pastry, mix the flour with the cinnamon, salt, caster sugar, ground almonds and lemon zest. Make a well in the centre and then plug it with the butter and egg yolks. Using first a knife and then the very tips of your fingers, work the whole lot to a dough. Knead for a minute or so to smooth it out and then slice off around a quarter of the dough. Form the smaller and larger chunks of pastry into balls, wrap each in clingfilm, and chill for 30–60 minutes.

• Bring the larger piece back to room temperature, and press evenly into a 24cm (9½ in) tart tin. Prick all over with a fork, then spread evenly with the jam, leaving just a narrow band of bare pastry around the edge. Roll out the remaining pastry on a lightly floured surface, and cut into strips of around 1cm (½ in) wide. Lay one long strip across the centre of the tart tin, and then a second at right angles to it. Next take two more strips and lay them on either side of the first strip, leaving a gap of about 1cm (½ in) between strips. Then take two more, and lay on either side of the second strip in the same fashion. Repeat until you have formed a pretty latticework top over the jam. Trim off the trailing ends of the pastry, and press the trimmed ends neatly on to the bare borders of the pastry base. Chill for 30 minutes in the fridge.

• Slide a baking tray into the oven, and turn the dial to 200°C/400°F/Gas 6. Once the oven is thoroughly heated, place the linzertorte directly on the hot baking tray, which will give a direct blast of heat to the underneath of the pastry. Bake for 25–30 minutes, until golden brown. Cool and dust prettily with icing sugar. Serve in wedges or squares.

Raspberry Jam

**MAKES AROUND
2.8KG (5½ LB)**
30g (1 oz) **butter**
1.5kg (3 lb) **raspberries**
1.5kg (3 lb) **granulated**
or **caster sugar**

Aah, the joy of having too many raspberries – something that only comes with your very own raspberry canes. Well, it's some small consolation for growing older. Over the past seven or eight years of blessed ownership of our own fertile canes, we have experimented with various different methods of making raspberry jam, and this is the one we like best. It takes time, and doesn't ever reach a convincing set, but the flavour and colour are so very superior, catching the soul of the fresh fruit, that we don't care. The recipe comes originally from Mary Norwak's *Complete Book of Home Preserving* published by the WI and Ward Lock back in 1978.

If your harvest of raspberries is meagre, or if you only want a few pots of jam, then it is easy to reduce quantities – the basic formula is equal quantities of raspberries and sugar and a small knob of butter.

This jam method also works well for blackberries, a little on the pippy side perhaps, but the flavour is fantastic.

• Warm a preserving pan, then rub the butter over the base. Pile in the raspberries and place over a very low heat, using a diffuser mat if you have one. Leave until the juice starts to run, stirring it just once in a while. This may take some 20–30 minutes. Meanwhile, warm the sugar in a low oven.

• Once the raspberries are oozing juice, stir in the warm sugar, which should dissolve fairly easily. Leave the pan over the same low heat, stirring once in a while, for another 30 minutes or so, without ever letting it boil. Now ladle into hot sterilised jars and seal as usual (see page 114). Label and stash away snugly in your preserves cupboard.

Damson, Honey and Apple Crumble

SERVES 4

300g (10½ oz) **damsons**
250g (9 oz) prepared-weight, peeled, cored and roughly chopped eating **apples**
3 tablespoons **honey**
1–2 tablespoons **caster sugar**

FOR THE TOPPING:

200g (7 oz) **plain flour**
100g (3½ oz) **ground hazelnuts**
100g (3½ oz) **demerara sugar**, plus a little extra for sprinkling
200g (7 oz) **unsalted butter**

Everyone loves a crumble, don't they? It may be obvious, but it is still one of the great vehicles for seasonal fruits, be they gooseberries, rhubarb, apples, plums or whatever else comes to hand. The tart flavour of damsons mixed with early windfall apples (that's why I give prepared weight – roughly what I get from 3 apples with the occasional bit of bruising) is one of the best combinations with the sweet, buttery crumble on top. Ground hazelnuts make it particularly good – for the absolute best, buy them whole, and grind them yourself, a little unevenly. You can, of course, substitute ground almonds for the hazelnuts, or just use all flour. Sometimes I scatter flaked almonds, or little pine kernels, over the top before the crumble goes into the oven.

• Pre-heat the oven to 190°C/375°F/Gas 5. Stone the damsons if you have the time and the will, but remember that children (and adults) love playing Tinker, Tailor, Soldier, Sailor. Mix with the apples in a pie dish or gratin dish. Drizzle over the honey, and then sprinkle with caster sugar.

• To make the topping, mix the flour, ground nuts and sugar, then rub in the butter until the mixture resembles fine but uneven breadcrumbs. Sprinkle thickly over the fruit. Scatter over a little extra demerara sugar. Do not press down. Bake for some 25–30 minutes until lightly browned, with hot bubbles of juice burbling up round the sides. Serve at once with custard or cream. Lots of it.

Damsons and Sloes

These two come last in the cavalcade of plums that starts in the height of summer. They are not such obvious winners, too astringent and tart to be eaten fresh, but it is their harder-to-distinguish characteristics that make them special. Add sugar to soften their blow, heat or alcohol to develop their strengths, and they come into their own. Pretty little damsons with their frosted blooms are often to be had for free from hedgerows but sloes can rarely be bought. You will definitely need to track down a local bush to supply you with enough to conjure up a bottle or two of sloe gin (see below) to warm chilled insides when winter proper sets in.

I'm lucky enough to have a damson tree nestling at the very top of the garden, casting its shade over the compost heap. Every September it rains plump damsons on to the lawn below, shaming me into picking the last few bowlfuls before they too go to waste. Damson crumble is absolutely top of my list, though I save a few handfuls to cook up a relish to go with duck or pork (see page 140). I should make more use of them, I know, but they come at a time when I am barely through with the sweeter plums and already on the verge of heading off for the blackberry hedges. Then there's the return to school,

and the gearing up of work after the sloth of summer, and somehow, somehow I find myself yet again promising that next year I will definitely not let them go to waste.

TO MAKE SLOE GIN

This blissfully simple and handy recipe was given to me by a lady who was working on the tills at my local Habitat store. Obviously a consummate cook, she swapped recipes with me as she cashed up my purchases. I've not seen her there since, but if she ever reads this I would like to thank her for passing this little gem on to me. It's particularly handy if you come home from picking your sloes and don't have time to do anything with them for a day or two (or longer). Even if you are not time-short, it is still worth freezing the sloes for a day or so, as this does away with the need to prick each and every one with a needle. Spread the sloes out on a baking tray and freeze. Once frozen tip into a plastic bag and leave in the freezer. Whenever you next have a few moments to spare, take them out and tip into a kilner jar or other wide-necked preserving jar. Once they have thawed, measure them and add the same volume of gin (or vodka) and the same volume of sugar. Seal tightly and shake to mix. Leave in a cool place, shaking every now and then, for at least three months. Strain, bottle and label. Drink in small glasses, on a chilly night. Or use to enrich gravies, particularly for game, or in puddings. It is also good in the cranberry sauce at Christmas.

Quinces

There are quinces and then there are English quinces, and don't let anyone tell you otherwise. Although you can buy big, often rather green quinces from Turkey or Cyprus in the autumn, the ones to look out for are our own, smaller, golden fruit, which have an infinitely superior scent and flavour. Not so easy to find, unless you grow your own. Still, keep your eyes peeled in the autumn months, and you may find them piled at a farmers' market, or an apple day fair, or even, as I did, tucked away in a box at a local village shop. Buy them instantly, even if you can't use them straight away. They will keep for a week or two (or even longer), and will perfume your kitchen patiently until you are ready to use them.

You cannot eat quinces raw: they'd break your teeth, they're so hard. Heat is what it takes to soften them to delicious palatability. Theoretically, the flesh should be ivory under the peel, but I've found that even if it has browned, it is still good to cook, as long as it is firm. If you are not removing the skin (no need, for instance, when baking them), you will need to rub off the soft down before cooking. I love them baked – just cut in half horizontally across the middle, arrange cut sides up in a buttered ovenproof dish, dredge with sugar (they are quite astringent), spoon a few tablespoonfuls of water around them and bake for an hour or so in a moderate oven until tender – or poached (see opposite), and they also make the most superior jelly. My aunt Mary used to make a wonderful quince compote, with a touch of vinegar as well as sugar, to go with roast goose. I wish I had her recipe for it, but I fear it died with her.

When we first moved out of London, we landed up with a generous neighbour who unloaded all her quinces on us that first autumn. We baked them and poached them and made pots of jelly. We made only one mistake: as a thank you we took a jar of jelly over to her house. Sheer delight on her part as she'd never tasted it before but the following year we saw very few of her magnificent quinces – they all went into her preserving pan instead of ours! To make quince jelly, wash the down from the quinces, then chop them up roughly, skin, core, pips and all. Tip them all into a preserving pan and add 600ml (1 pint) of water for every 500g (1 lb) quinces. Bring up to the boil and simmer gently for about 1 hour until the fruit is very soft. Tip liquid and pulp into a jelly bag, and leave to drip into a clean saucepan or bowl for a good 8 hours. If you want your jelly to be clear and glinting, refrain from pressing down on the pulp, which will make it cloudy. Now measure the juice and weigh out 500g (1 lb) sugar for every 600ml (1 pint) of liquid. Stir juice and sugar together over a moderate heat until the sugar has completely dissolved, then bring up to the boil. Keep the heat high and boil swiftly until setting point is reached. Skim off all the scum, then ladle the hot jelly into sterilised jars, seal tightly and label. Quince jelly is excellent on toast in the morning, on scones with clotted cream, or even in Queen of Puddings (see page 223) instead of raspberry jam. It is also good with lamb and game, or just spooned over cream cheese and beaten with a little cream for a simple pudding.

Vanilla-poached Quinces

One of autumn's most beautiful treats: when slices of quince are poached slowly and gently for a considerable length of time, they turn a remarkable deep burgundy red. Don't mess around with them; don't try to be clever. Just keep this simple, and enjoy the colour and the equally beautiful flavour, not to mention the heavenly scent that wafts around the house as it cooks.

Once poached, the quinces will keep for a week or more, covered, in the fridge.

SERVES 8

1kg (2 lb 4 oz) **quinces**, preferably English
1 **vanilla pod** (or 4 wide strips **lemon** or **orange zest**)
450g (1 lb) **caster sugar**
around 600ml (1 pint) **water**

• Peel the quinces and cut into eighths, then remove the core. Place in a pan with the remaining ingredients. Set on the stove, give it a gentle stir, then while it heats up cut out your 'cartouche'. That's the chef's name for a circle of greaseproof paper, slightly smaller than the pan, that sits snugly on the surface of the syrup and quinces to prevent the syrup boiling away to a burnt mess. Settle it in place, gently pushing out as much of the trapped air as you can.

• Bring the syrup up to the merest whisper of a simmer, with just a few lazy bubbles rising to the surface. Now adjust the heat so that it stays at this temperature, and leave the quinces to cook gently for around 1½ hours, or sometimes even as much as two, stirring occasionally, until both the syrup and the fruit take on their characteristic dark, garnet-red colour. If it is the first time you've poached quinces, have faith – they will get there in the end. Add a little more water only if you absolutely need it.

• Once they are done, tip out into a serving bowl and leave to cool. Serve with clotted cream, golden Jersey cream, or really good vanilla ice cream.

Pears
Poached in Cinnamon Port

SERVES 4–6

4 large or 6 smaller **pears**
juice of ½ **lemon**
280g (10 oz) **caster** or
   granulated sugar
1 long **cinnamon stick**
600ml (1 pint) **ruby port**

A classic, but then many of the best recipes are. Poached pears (and quinces) were one of the regular autumnal treats when I was a child. My mother always served them in the same Chinese bowl of pale, pale jade porcelain, a cinnamon stick or vanilla pod lying among the translucent slices of fruit. Elegant enough for dinner parties, simple enough for ordinary meals too.

One of my husband William's few culinary failings is an intense dislike of pears – more the texture I eventually discovered than the taste. However, we realised that all was not lost when he was moved to taste a poached pear early in our relationship. Grudgingly, for someone who seemed to be eating with some relish, he admitted that he 'quite liked' it, and that maybe, just maybe, poached pears were all right. Luckily he has not passed on his aversion to our children, who express considerable delight at the sight of a bowl of poached pears.

The principle itself is what you really need to master here, since once that is firmly secured you can vary the flavourings and poaching liquid to your heart's content, or at least to what is to hand. You can use a plain water and sugar syrup, especially good for quinces, as long as you don't forget the vanilla pod (see page 169). For more drama, and a more intense flavour, a red liquid (not Ribena...) such as port or red wine is a fine embellishment. Although you don't get the impact of the colour, a good sweet wine – Sauternes for the extravagant, a Moscatel de Valencia or similar for the rest of us) – does a good job too. Although vanilla and cinnamon are the most obvious of spices, you can ring the changes by adding a few cardamom pods for perfume, or a star anise or two for its seductive aniseed scent. Cloves, mace, strips of orange or lemon zest, rosewater, even sprigs of fresh thyme or rosemary... they all contribute their own particular, pleasing flavour. In other words, from one simple classic you can extrapolate any number of variations.

N.B. If it seems extravagant to use such a large amount of port (it does, and indeed it is initially), be reassured that not all of it will be used up. You can reuse leftover syrup, thinned down with water, for a second batch of pears, or dried fruit – stash it in the freezer if necessary. If you forget it is there until next summer, then it is a fabulous poaching liquid for peaches, nectarines, apricots, cherries and even plums.

• Peel the pears, and halve and core if you are feeding 4 people or fewer. For up to 6, slice the peeled and cored pears moderately thickly. Squeeze over the lemon juice and turn gently with your hands.

• Put the sugar, cinnamon and port into a wide saucepan, and stir over a moderate heat until the sugar has dissolved. Bring up to a gentle boil. Slip in the pears and their juice, handling them very carefully if they are ripe. If the pears jut hopelessly out of the ruby syrup, add a little hot water, or even a slug or two more port, to bring the liquid level with the pears. Bring up to a very, very gentle simmer. Cover the lazily bubbling surface of the port and pears with a 'cartouche' (see method on page 169) of greaseproof paper, pushing it down lightly so that the surface is efficiently covered. This reduces the evaporation of the syrup. Poach the pears like this for about 30–40 minutes, turning them once or twice, until they are very tender, and slightly translucent, having taken on the colour of the port.

• Lift the pears out carefully and transfer to a serving bowl. Boil the syrup down hard (having discarded the greaseproof paper), until it is reduced by about one-third to a half. Taste a bit – it should feel syrupy in the mouth with a rich, deep sweetness. Pour some hot syrup over the pears and leave to cool. Serve with a little single cream, or with finest vanilla ice cream.

Apple Pie

SERVES 6

FOR THE FLAKY PASTRY:

220g (8 oz) **plain flour**, plus extra for rolling

pinch of **salt**

110g (4 oz) **unsalted butter**

a squeeze of **lemon juice**

60g (2 oz) **lard** or **vegetable shortening**, or more **butter**

FOR THE FILLING:

juice of ½ **lemon**

700g (1 lb 9 oz) **cooking apples**, or mixed cookers and eaters (about 6 medium apples)

1 teaspoon **cinnamon** (or alternative flavouring – see intro)

vanilla sugar or plain **caster sugar**, or **light muscovado sugar**

15g (½ oz) **butter**

1 **egg**, lightly beaten with 1 tablespoon water

Apple pie is as old as the hills, but sadly neglected these days in the welter of mascarpone and cheesecake and filo-pastry creations. I like it best made with a single layer of flaky pastry, buttery and crisp and the perfect foil to the softened apple. Though there is no reason why you shouldn't make apple pie with eating apples that stay in whole chunks, the real McCoy is made with sour cookers that dissolve to a rough purée, or perhaps a mixture of the two. Flavour it with cinnamon, or a grating of lemon or orange zest, or a couple of cloves lodged somewhere in the apple mass. Constance Spry recommended a few leaves of lemon verbena, to give an unusual lemony scent. When it is up and away in the garden, some chopped sweet cicely imparts a mildly aniseed flavour and diminishes the acidity of the apples, thus reducing the quantity of sugar needed.

Gooseberry and rhubarb pies are made in exactly the same ways (remembering to top and tail the gooseberries and pull away the worst strings on the rhubarb before chopping). Ginger in the form of diced preserved stem ginger makes an excellent addition to either, as does orange zest, or a slurp or two of elderflower cordial. Sweet cicely is, again, another time-honoured addition.

• Allow plenty of time for the making of the pastry. Start by sifting the flour with the salt and rubbing in 45g (1½ oz) of the butter. Then add the lemon juice and enough cold water to mix to a soft, but not sticky dough. Knead briefly on a lightly floured board until smooth, then roll out into a rectangle that measures roughly 10 x 30cm (4 x 12 in). Dice the lard, vegetable shortening or extra butter into small lumps and dot all over two-thirds of the pastry, leaving the lower third, nearest you, stark naked. Fold this piece over to cover one-third of the lard-dotted pastry, then flip the upper third, with its cargo of lard, over to cover the whole lot, just as if you were folding a business letter. With the rolling pin, press down on the edges to seal them together neatly. Now turn the pastry

round through 90 degrees, anti-clockwise, so that one of the sealed edges is nearest to you.

• Roll the pastry out again to a 10 x 30cm (4 x 12 in) rectangle, and repeat the folding process, using half the remaining butter. And then off you go again, rolling out, dotting with butter and folding up again, then sealing the sides. And no, you haven't finished yet, because you're going to do the same thing one last time, but this time without any fat, because you've used it all up. Altogether, you will have worked your way through this process four times, which amazingly produces a total of 81 layers! If at any time the pastry becomes sticky and over-soft with butter streaking through to the surface, wrap the pastry and rush it into the fridge for half an hour to chill, before carrying on. Once you've made your 81 layers, you will need to chill the pastry for a good half an hour before using it.

• For the filling, squeeze the lemon juice into a bowl and add some cold water (to make an acidulated bath that will keep the apples from browning). Peel, core and chop the apples roughly, piling them into the lemon water bowl as you work. Drain thoroughly, and pile into a 24–25cm (9½–10 in) circular pie plate, or other dish, mounding them up gently in the centre. Sprinkle with cinnamon and sugar to taste. Dot with slivers of butter.

• Roll the pastry out nicely on a floured board. Cut a 1.5cm (¾ in) wide strip from two sides. Brush the edge of the pie plate with a little of the egg mixture. Lay the pastry strips on it, curving them round, and gently pressing the edges together. Brush with egg wash. Now lift the remaining pastry on the rolling pin, and lay over the pie dish. Trim off the excess that hangs down. Crimp the edges together, pressing firmly but evenly so that they adhere one to another and to the dish. Use some of the trimmings to cut out leaves or other decorative shapes, and glue to the pastry with a dab of egg wash. Make a hole in the centre for steam to escape. Chill the pie for 15–30 minutes to minimise shrinkage.

• Pre-heat the oven to 180°C/350°F/Gas 4. Brush the pastry with egg wash, then sprinkle with extra sugar. Bake for about 20–30 minutes, until golden brown and crisp. Eat hot, with cream.

Apples and Pears

One of the pleasing things about living in Britain is that we have an honourable history of growing superlative tree fruit. That we fail to announce this loudly and proudly to the world at large is one of the less pleasing things about living here. Don't you think that the fact that we and we alone produced an apple of such outstanding perfection as the Cox's Orange Pippin (at least when it is freshly picked) is something to boast about? Well, I do. And not just the Cox's Orange Pippin, either. We have grown literally hundreds of different varieties here, many specific to particular regions and counties. Some will have disappeared as trees became too old to survive and, worse still, as orchards have been grubbed up to make way for easier, more profitable crops, but there are still dozens of varieties available to us all, if only we care to search a little further afield than our nearest supermarket.

Not far from where I live now, the area around the village of Harwell in Oxfordshire was renowned for its fruit trees until the late fifties and early sixties. Gradually acre after acre of orchards disappeared, dragging history with them, until now all that remain are a few relatively small patches of fecund trees and memories of a time when almost everyone in the surrounding villages worked the orchards. It's a familiar story right across much of England. The heroes are those people who are nurturing ancient orchards, replacing worn-out elderly trees with new ones, thrilling to the flavours of newly picked apples in the autumn in all their extraordinary complexity.

Some small reversal of the process of decimation has taken place over the past decade or so, and if it is to continue then it is the customer, in other words you and me, who needs to push it onwards. Come autumn, make a point of refusing imported apples (loudly), and try to make sense of the succession of apples and pears, from early Discoveries, on through Lord Lambournes and James Grieves in September to Cox's and Egremont Russets in October to Kidd's Orange Red and Suntan from November on. Search out local growers and let them know that you would rather have their produce when it is fresh and right, than the same handful of dull, over-stored and over-travelled apples offered by supermarkets. Take pleasure in one of the things that Britain does best.

Seed Cake

SERVES 6–8

2 large **eggs**

unsalted butter

sugar

self-raising flour

ground almonds

1 teaspoon **baking powder**

2 heaped teaspoons **caraway seeds**

1–2 tablespoons **milk** (optional)

An old-fashioned sort of a cake, a plain one too, but made special by the sweet anise scent of caraway seeds. The basic mixture is essentially that of a pound cake, or *quatre quarts* (four quarters) as it is called in France. In other words, equal quantities of four ingredients – eggs, flour, sugar and butter. To lift the flavour without destroying it, I replace part of the flour with almonds, which also makes it a little more moist.

Seed cake should always be baked in a loaf tin, not a round tin, and cut into thick even slices. Why? I haven't the foggiest idea, and in fact it may be just something that I've inherited from my mother and grandmother. The idea of a round one just seems downright wrong to me.

• Line the base and sides of a 22 x 10cm (8½ x 4 in) loaf tin with non-stick baking parchment or grease and flour. Weigh the eggs and then weigh out equal quantities of butter and sugar. Then weigh out two-thirds of the eggs' weight of flour, and one-third ground almonds. Melt the butter and let it cool until tepid.

• Mix the flour, baking powder, ground almonds, sugar and caraway seeds in a large bowl. Make a well in the centre and break in the eggs. Pour in the butter and mix to a soft dough, adding a little milk if necessary to give a dropping consistency. Pour into the prepared tin and bake for about 50–60 minutes, until firm to the touch. Test to see if it is done by plunging a skewer into the centre. If it comes out clean, then the cake is ready. Cool for 5–10 minutes in the tin, then turn out and cool completely.

• Serve plain – but if you want some sort of extra indulgence, spread the slices with lightly salted butter.

Burnt Butter Biscuits

Butter cooked until a nutty brown (not actually blackened) together with the seeds of a real vanilla pod is what gives these crumbly biscuits their special flavour.

MAKES 25–30

150g (5 oz) **unsalted butter**
250g (9 oz) **plain flour**
110g (4 oz) **caster sugar**
pinch of **salt**
1 **vanilla pod**
icing sugar

• Pre-heat the oven to 190°C/375°F/Gas 5. Grease two baking trays. Melt the butter in a saucepan with a pale-coloured interior (it's hard to judge the colour of the butter against black) over a moderate heat. Cook, keeping an attentive eye on it, until it colours to a rich hazelnut brown. Quickly draw off the heat.

• As the butter cooks, mix the flour, sugar and salt. Slit the vanilla pod in half, from one end to the other, and scrape the seeds out into the flour mixture (a rather sticky business at first, but persevere and let no seeds go to waste). Now add the melted butter, and mix to a mass of fat crumbs. With your hands, grasp enough crumbs to roll firmly into a walnut-sized ball. Place each one on the prepared baking trays.

• Bake for 8–10 minutes, until they turn a shade or two darker. Not easy to tell, I admit, so you will just have to trust me on timing – if the balls start to crack, you've overcooked them, and they will be a little firmer than is ideal, but still very good. Let the biscuits cool for about 2–3 minutes on the trays. Meanwhile, spread icing sugar out in a shallow plate. Handling the hot biscuits very carefully, roll each one in the icing sugar, then transfer to a cake rack to cool. Store in an airtight container, shaking more icing sugar over the base and between layers.

Walnut, Apricot and Rosemary Bread

This is a bread that goes particularly well with our hard cheeses – perfect, for instance, with a slice of nutty, mature farmhouse Cheddar, or the paler buttery Yarg, or crumbly Lancashire. It toasts well, too, in which case I like to slather it in butter and honey.

MAKES 1 LOAF

200g (7 oz) **light rye flour**

200g (7 oz) **strong wholemeal flour**

200g (7 oz) **strong white flour**

2½ teaspoons **salt**

30g (1 oz) **butter**

1 sachet (7g) **easy-blend yeast**, or 15g (½ oz) **fresh yeast** – see page 241 for notes on use

100g (3½ oz) **walnut pieces**

100g (3½ oz) ready-to-eat **dried apricots**

1 level teaspoon very finely chopped fresh **rosemary** leaves

• Mix the flours with the salt and rub in the butter. Now mix in the yeast. Add enough water to give a moderately soft, but not sticky dough. Knead the dough energetically for 5–10 minutes, until smooth and elastic. If the dough seems rather stiff and hard to handle, then knead in a little more water, just a tablespoonful at a time until the mixture eases. If it is sticky, then gradually knead in a little more strong white flour until it is easier to handle. Rinse the bowl out with warm water, and dry. Return the dough to the bowl, cover with a damp cloth and leave in a warm place to rise. It needs to double in volume; with the rye and wholemeal flour, I find that this takes a little longer than usual, say 1½ to 2 hours.

• While it is proving, spread the walnuts out on a baking sheet and whip them into a moderately hot oven – somewhere around 200°C/400°F/Gas 6 – for 5–10 minutes, checking frequently, until lightly toasted. Tip into a metal sieve and shake over a sheet of newspaper to dislodge flaky bits of skin.

• Punch the dough down, then knead briefly. Flatten it out as well as you can and sprinkle over the apricots and the rosemary. Roll it up and knead again for 30 seconds or so. Now flatten it out one more time and scatter the walnuts over the surface. Roll it up again, and knead for a few more minutes until all the bits are pretty evenly distributed and the dough has come back together nicely. Form into a rugby ball shape, sit it on a lightly oiled baking sheet and spread a little extra flour over the top. Cover with a damp tea towel and once more leave in a warm place until doubled in size.

• Pre-heat the oven to 220°C/425°F/Gas 7. Bake the loaf for 25 minutes, turning once, if necessary, so that it browns evenly. Tap the bread on its base and if it sounds distinctly hollow, then it is done. Cool on a wire rack.

Walnut, raisin and rosemary bread has become something of a modern classic, but I like to replace the raisins with apricots for their hint of tartness. I've also tried dried sour cherries, and cranberries, in their place, both of which work nicely. And of course, if you like a touch of experimenting, you could partner any one of them with toasted hazelnuts or pecans instead of the walnuts. If you can't find any light rye flour, replace it with more wholemeal flour.

winter

Celeriac and Hazelnut Soup

Celeriac and hazelnut soup is pale and creamy and extremely good. Hold back the stock cube and make the effort to brew up your own chicken stock (good butchers usually let you have chicken carcasses for a pittance), as the flavour of the celeriac and hazelnuts is not domineering enough to disguise any shortcomings.

A scattering of small croutons goes well with this soup if you want to dress it up for a special outing.

SERVES 6

100g (3½ oz) **shelled hazelnuts**

1 medium/large **celeriac**

45g (1½ oz) **butter**

1 **onion**, chopped

2 tablespoons **long grain** or **pudding rice**

1 litre (1¾ pints) **chicken stock**

juice of ½ **lemon**

85ml (3 fl oz) **double cream**

salt and **pepper**

• Pre-heat the oven to 190°C/375°F/Gas 5. Spread the hazelnuts out on a baking tray and roast until they turn a shade darker and the skin flakes off easily. This will only take some 5–10 minutes, so check regularly to prevent burning. Rub the skins off. Peel the celeriac, and cut off and discard the worst of the gnarled tangled roots at the bottom. Cut into rough dice.

• Melt the butter in a large pan over a low heat. Add the onion, rice, hazelnuts and celeriac. Stir to coat in butter, then slam on the lid and leave to sweat gently for around 10–15 minutes, stirring once or twice. Pour in half the stock, season well with salt and pepper, and bring up to the boil. Simmer gently for about 15 minutes until the celeriac and rice are good and tender.

• Let the soup cool for a few minutes, then liquidise, adding the remaining stock to thin the soup down. Return to the pan, stir in the lemon juice and then the cream, and reheat when needed, being sure to taste and balance the seasoning. Serve totally hot and steaming.

The Joy of Soup

I take it for granted that you like soup. I do. I like good soups a great deal, especially in autumn and winter. We settled down, yesterday lunchtime, to big, hot bowls of Mrs R's Borscht (see page 185). Outside the sky was grey, the rain drizzled on and on, the light even at one o'clock was half-hearted. A few spoonfuls in and the dismal weather receded from our minds, and warmth settled in.

What makes a good soup? Like all good food, the quality of the ingredients is paramount. Although, having said that, it is remarkable what you can conjure up out of the sad odds and ends of vegetables, a little past their prime, that sometimes collect in the vegetable drawer of the fridge. Essentially, however, the fresher the ingredients, the finer their flavour and the better the soup.

Mixed vegetable soups can be fantastic, but by and large restraint is the key to a truly classy soup. Two to three main ingredients – Maple-roasted Carrot and Ginger and Celeriac and Hazelnut (see page 128 and opposite) – which bring out the best in each other, give the surest results. Single-flavour soups, such as the Sorrel Soup on page 4, usually rely on a second back-up ingredient, such as potato, to carry the predominant flavour. And somewhere in the background of almost every soup an onion lurks in the shadows, essential, but unseen.

At the heart of the vast majority of good soups, however, is the stock. Now, although water is sometimes acceptable when other flavours are strong enough to need no boost, in most instances you definitely require an animated stock to carry the tastes that will give the soup its character. The stock is the backbone, and without it, a soup will fall flat and lifeless. Stock cubes can be used in emergencies, but they don't do nearly such a good job as real stock. In more delicately flavoured soups – say a plain potato soup or a Vichyssoise, or the Celeriac and Hazelnut Soup on the page opposite – a stock cube would be a disaster, as it is impossible to disguise.

You don't have to get fancy and cheffy when making stock, but getting into the habit of chucking chicken bones, whenever you have them, and a few vegetables and seasonings into a large pan of water and cooking them gently together for a couple of hours will stand you in good stead. Stock freezes well, and you will be glad that you made the effort.

Equipment requirements are minimal – sharp knife and chopping board, a capacious saucepan, a liquidiser for smooth soups (so much more effective than a processor), a wooden spoon, a ladle and a big bowl – and the effort-time-results ratio so well loaded in the soup's favour, that soup-making should be taught to every novice cook as soon as they are strong enough to lift a full saucepan without danger of slippage. Put soup making on the school curriculum, and we'd soon have a happier, healthier nation.

Brussels Sprout and Caramelised Onion Soup

An unexpectedly good soup, with all the fresh, nutty flavour of Brussels sprouts, tempered by the sweetness of the onion. Even those who profess to loathe sprouts will not be dismayed by this transformation.

SERVES 6

450g (1 lb) **onions**, sliced

30g (1 oz) **butter**

1 tablespoon **caster sugar**

450g (1 lb) **Brussels sprouts**, trimmed and halved

1 generous sprig of **thyme**

1.15 litres (2 pints) **light chicken** or **vegetable stock**

salt and **pepper**

to serve: **soured cream**, **crème fraîche** or **Greek yoghurt**, and **paprika** or **cayenne pepper**

• Put the onions into a pan with the butter, cover and sweat over a gentle heat for about 30–40 minutes until the onions are incredibly tender and soft. Sprinkle over the sugar and cook, uncovered, for another 10–15 minutes or so until the onions are lightly coloured, and jammy looking. Add the sprouts and thyme and stir around. Pour in the stock and season with salt and pepper. Bring up to the boil and simmer for around 10 minutes until the sprouts are just tender. Cool slightly, remove the thyme sprig, and then liquidise in two batches. Reheat gently if needed then taste and adjust seasoning. Serve piping hot, with a spoonful of crème fraîche or yoghurt in each bowlful, and a light dusting of paprika or cayenne.

Mrs R's Borscht

SERVES 4–6

450g (1 lb) **uncooked beetroot**, peeled and grated
1 large **carrot**, finely diced
1 **onion**, chopped
110g (4 oz) **white cabbage**, shredded
2 teaspoons **caster sugar**
1 **bay leaf**
2 tablespoons **lemon juice**
1.5 litres (2½ pints) hot **chicken** or **beef stock**
salt and **pepper**

to serve: **crème fraîche** or **soured cream** and chopped fresh **parsley**

My next-door neighbour, Juliet Rickard, is one of those seemingly insouciant cooks – 'Oh, I just put in a little of this and a little of that' – who always turns out superb meals. She doesn't bat an eyelid at the prospect of dealing with half a dozen pheasant, feathers, guts and all, or a glut of beetroot and beans. She makes one of the best beetroot soups I've ever tasted and this is her recipe... more or less. I should point out that she begins with a really good home-made stock and ultra-fresh home-grown beetroot, and therein lies a large chunk of her success. Oh, and she is dedicated to her slow-cooker, which is what she uses for this, leaving the ingredients to cook overnight.

• Pre-heat the oven to 140°C/275°F/Gas 1. Pile all the ingredients into a casserole dish, stir, cover and then leave in the oven for 4 hours, until all the vegetables are very tender.

• Allow to cool a little, remove the bay leaf and then liquidise until smooth. To serve hot, spoon into bowls and finish with a spoonful of cream and a scattering of parsley. A few croutons or crumbled, grilled bacon are both excellent additions.

• To serve cold, chill in the fridge. Serve thick and lightly jellified, again with cream and parsley or chives. No croutons or bacon please.

Double-cheese Flatbreads

We eat these cheese breads cut into oozing wedges as a hunger-quencher before the main course, or with soup, or indeed as the main matter of a salady lunch. The original recipe is from East Europe, or, to be more precise, Georgia, though I came across it in a riveting American book called *Flatbreads and Flavours* by Naomi Duguid and Jeffrey Alford, published in 1995.

My version contains whatever cheese we have in abundance in the larder, but the best combination so far has been this one of Stilton and Yarg, one sprightly and big, the other mild and sharp. Pure Stilton, would, I think, be too overwhelming, even though the cheese filling is spread very thin between the two layers of yoghurt dough.

MAKES 4

FOR THE FILLING:

60g (2 oz) derinded **Yarg**, or **Lancashire cheese**, crumbled

30g (1 oz) derinded **Stilton** or other blue cheese, crumbled

1 tablespoon **Greek yoghurt**

1 small egg, or ½ large **egg**

1 tablespoon finely chopped fresh **parsley**

FOR THE DOUGH:

270g (9½ oz) **Greek yoghurt**

approximately 350g (12 oz) **plain flour**, plus extra for rolling out

½ teaspoon **salt**

1 rounded teaspoon **baking powder**

a little **oil** for greasing baking sheets

• Pre-heat the oven to 230°C/450°F/Gas 8. Grease one large baking sheet. To make the filling just mash the two cheeses with a large fork, then work in the other ingredients.

• For the dough, begin by measuring the yoghurt into a bowl, then add about three-quarters of the flour, the salt and baking powder. Stir into the yoghurt, gradually adding more of the flour until you have a workable dough that is no longer horribly soft and sticky. Tip out on to a floured work surface and knead for around 3–4 minutes, sprinkling with flour as required, until smooth and silky. Divide into four pieces.

• Roll each ball out to form a circle of around 20cm (8 in) in diameter. Place a generous tablespoon of the filling in the centre. Now gather up the edges over the filling, pinching them together firmly to cover it completely. Flour your hand and gently press down on the gathered dough, flattening it out again, and easing the filling out towards the edges. Turn over and press down a little more on the other side, again edging the filling out evenly, and thinning the pastry to a thickness of around 0.5–1cm (¼–½ in). Lay on the oiled sheet, while you make the other pastries. Don't worry if the odd worm of filling bursts its way out of the edges – no doubt it wouldn't if you were an expert Georgian cook, but you aren't, so don't worry, as the pastries will still turn out fine.

• Bake the breads for 6–10 minutes until puffed and golden brown. Eat while still warm.

Baked Eggs with Leeks and Smoked Salmon

I used to cook baked eggs for my supper when I was a student – an economical and soothing dish for a cold night. I still enjoy them, though by and large I've transferred them to a position at the beginning of a relatively light meal, dressing them up with a little smoked salmon (a good way of using up odds and ends) for good measure.

For a more substantial main course, I'd cook two per person, and bake the whole lot together in one shallow gratin dish, still set in a bain-marie of hot water. Otherwise the method and cooking times remain much the same, as long as the eggs are not vastly overcrowded and you are not cooking huge numbers. Do double-check, however, that the egg whites are perfectly set before whisking the dish irrevocably out of the oven – undercooked translucent albumen is not appetising.

SERVES 4

60g (2 oz) finely chopped white
of **leek**, or **spring onions**

25g (scant 1 oz) **butter**

3 tablespoons **single cream**

45g (1½ oz) **smoked salmon**,
roughly chopped

4 **eggs**

salt and freshly ground **black
pepper**

• Pre-heat the oven to 180°C/350°F/Gas 4. Sweat the leek or spring onions in the butter in a covered pan over a low heat until soft – around 5 minutes.

• Put the kettle on to boil. Arrange four ramekins in an ovenproof dish and divide the cooked leek evenly between them. Spoon 1 teaspoon cream over the leeks in each ramekin, and season with pepper. Pour enough boiling water around the ramekins to come a good centimetre (½ in) up their sides. Swiftly and smoothly transfer them to the oven for 5 minutes to heat through.

• Now, working speedily so that you don't lose too much heat from the ramekins, take them out of the oven, divide the smoked salmon between them, then break an egg into each one. Trickle one more teaspoon of cream over each egg, and season with pepper and a touch of salt.

• Return to the oven for 12 minutes until the whites are just set but the yolks are still runny. Serve immediately with triangles of brown toast.

Potted Beef

SERVES 8

450g (1 lb) good **stewing beef**
  (e.g. chuck steak)
¼ teaspoon freshly ground
  black pepper
¼ teaspoon freshly grated
  nutmeg
1 tablespoon **anchovy
  essence**
110g (4 oz) **unsalted butter**,
  sliced
a little **salt**, if needed

Potted beef is the venerable antecedent of those horrible little jars of meat paste that have ruined so many a sandwich. They taste nothing like the real thing, which is so infinitely superior that it is hard to believe they are related. This particular recipe, one of the finest I've tasted, was given to me by Anne Petch of Heal Farm in Devon. I serve it as a first course, with hot toast and pickled walnuts, or a smear of creamed horseradish.

It will also redeem the meat paste sandwich – spread it thickly over sturdy bread (the Potato, Sunflower Seed and Sage Bread on page 243 or even the Malted Bread on page 117 would go well) and add slices of tomato, and mildly bitter crisp frisée lettuce or sliced chicory.

NB The potted beef will keep for a day or two in the fridge, but if you wish to keep it longer, for up to a week, seal the pots with clarified butter (see page opposite).

• Trim the meat, removing all sinews, and cut into chunks. Place in an ovenproof dish with a tight-fitting lid. Sprinkle over the pepper and nutmeg, then drizzle over the anchovy essence. Lastly, lay the butter over the top. Cover tightly and cook for at least 5 hours at 140°C/275°F/Gas 1, until the meat is extremely tender (you can put it into the oven an hour or two before you go to bed, then retrieve it when you rise in the morning).

• Once it has been in the oven for a couple of hours (or just before you hit the sack), give it a stir, then cover again and leave it be in the oven. Once it is cooked, cool slightly, then process until smooth, pale and light. Taste and add salt only if necessary (the anchovy paste will probably have provided quite enough). Pack into pots, cover with clingfilm and stash in the fridge to solidify.

Butter

You would have thought there wasn't much to be said about butter. After all, it is just cream shaken until the butterfat coagulates to form one solid chunk as the whey separates away. The big question then is merely 'to salt or not to salt' and, Bob's your uncle, a nice pat of butter emerges.

Marvellous, pure simplicity is rarely as simple as it seems on the surface. As with all things there is poor quality, everyday very-nice-thank-you quality, and absolutely outstanding wow-that-is-so-special quality. The good news is that over the past few years it has become increasingly possible to find the latter.

True to my British roots, I have a preference for salted butter on my toast in the morning. I adore the combination of smoky Aga-charred bread with salty, oozing, half-melted butter and the sticky fruit of raspberry jam or quince jelly. My daughter likes unsalted, so to defray argument, I place both on the table.

Less patriotically, I must admit that my favourite salted butter comes from France – the *beurre au sel de Guérande*, studded with crunchy grains of the finest sea salt. I buy it from the supermarket, somewhat reluctantly since in France I can get it from the cheese stall on the market, where there is a choice of three types of butter, piled up in great mountains at the back of the stand. The *patronne* lops off just what you need, wraps it up snugly in waxed paper and places it gently on top of your other purchases.

Here at home, you have to search harder for locally produced butter, but it can be found in farm shops and delis. Look out in particular for whey butter, which is made from the last traces of cream left floating around in the whey drained off the curds that will be turned into cheese. The flavour is different from ordinary sweet cream butter, usually salty, and with a pale pleasing hint of ripeness to give it character.

My local small dairy produces a handsome sunshine yellow butter from the milk of Jersey cows (as well as delectable clotted cream), quite the opposite extreme to the ghostly white goats' butter I've occasionally bought from wholefood shops. It's obvious when you think about it that the individual characteristics of the cream used will affect the colour and taste of the butter, so maybe in the future we'll be given more information to help us distinguish one sort of butter from another.

CLARIFIED BUTTER

Clarified butter is used for sealing jars of potted meat or fish, excluding air so that the contents last longer. It is also superb for frying as the milk solids, which burn so easily in ordinary butter, and some of the water have been removed.

To clarify butter, cut it into cubes (so that it melts quickly and easily) and heat in a heavy-based pan. Bring it gently up to the boil. Draw off the heat and let it settle for a couple of minutes. Strain through a sieve lined with butter muslin, and pour into pots to store in the fridge.

Winter Fish Stew

SERVES 6

700g (1½ lb) **white fish fillets**
 – take what is available and
 looks good

500g (1 lb 2 oz) **mussels** or
 clams

350g (12 oz) cleaned **squid**
 (optional, but an excellent
 addition)

4 **shallots**, thinly sliced

3 cloves **garlic**, chopped

1 tablespoon **coriander seeds**

2 tablespoons **extra virgin
 olive oil**

2 x 400g (14 oz) tins chopped
 tomatoes

2 tablespoons **tomato purée**

1–2 tablespoons **sugar**

3 tablespoons **Pernod**, or
 Noilly Prat

2 strips dried **orange peel**
 (not fresh: see introduction
 on page 209)

1 chunky sprig of **thyme**

300ml (½ pint) **fish stock**

salt and **pepper**

There's no reason why you shouldn't make this in the summer, but it seems particularly appropriate to winter, served up in big, steaming bowlfuls to warm you through. Decide which fish to use at the fish counter and not before so that you can pick whatever looks freshest. One type of fish on its own is fine, or take a mixture of two or three if the choice is there. Mussels improve both look and flavour, but little clams are lovely, too. Squid, though not essential, really lifts the taste way up high, but don't cook it for more than a minute or two, as it will toughen up speedily.

Whatever combination you end up with, the intensely flavoured tomato sauce will hold them together well. The sauce can be made in advance then reheated just before adding the mussels. Serve the finished stew with rice or warm crusty bread.

• Cut the fish fillets into pieces about 4cm (1½ in) across. Scrub the mussels clean, pull away any beard and rinse thoroughly in cold water. Throw out any that have broken shells. Mussels that are gaping wide open should be tapped firmly on the work surface. If they close up they are fine, but if they remain open chuck them in the bin. If using clams, rinse them thoroughly and, again, discard any that do not close when tapped firmly. Slice the squid into rings.

• Now, cook the shallots, garlic and coriander seeds gently in the oil until the shallots are tender and translucent. Add the chopped tomatoes, tomato purée, sugar, Pernod or Noilly Prat, orange peel, thyme and a little salt and pepper and simmer down until thick. Now stir in the fish stock and bring up to the boil. Simmer for 2 minutes, taste and adjust seasoning and your stew base is ready.

• Shortly before you wish to sit down and eat, bring the base back to the boil. Add the mussels, cover and cook for about 3 minutes. Now add the fish and the squid, cover again and simmer gently for a final 2–3 minutes until the mussels have all opened (discard any that stay firmly shut). Serve forthwith.

Buying Fish in Winter

As winter storms set in and fishing supplies become uncertain, you have to be prepared to take what fish you can get. When the seas are topsy-turvy, with mile-high waves and howling winds, the smaller day boats, the ones that bring back the best fish, will be staying snugly tucked up in harbour for the night, well out of harm's way. So, no good us landlubbers going out determined to buy Dover sole and only Dover sole. You might strike lucky, but more than at any other time of year, you might not, and for very good reason. So, as the temperature drops and the winds pick up, stick with recipes that can be adapted to any number of fish, and leave decision making until you are standing right in front of the fishmonger's counter.

Actually, this is sound advice whatever the time of year, as there's no point buying that Dover sole or slab of tuna at vast expense unless it is perfectly, primpingly, glisteningly fresh – it just ain't worth it. Always pass over any fish that looks tired and flabby, with misty, sunken eyes. You would do far better, flavour-wise, to buy a cheaper fish with eyes glittering glassily clear to indicate that it has not long been lifted from the sea. And by the same token, always be wary of special offers, slashed prices, bargain bins or 'reduced for quick sale' labels, whether at the fishmonger's or in a supermarket. Stale fish is no bargain at all unless you are deliberately trying to put the rest of your family or guests off fish for life. I assume that this is not the case.

Farmed fish are more reliable, though there is huge debate about the effects of fish-farming on the environment, as well as some concern about the content of fish feed – if you want to know more, try to get hold of a copy of *Fish*, a book that I co-wrote with William Black, which will give you far more information on this issue than I can offer here. Less controversial (on the whole), and available throughout the winter with a tolerable degree of certainty, are mussels, which as it happens are a great favourite of mine anyway. A big bowlful of blue-black mussels gaping open to expose flashes of orange flesh, swathed in fragrant steam, is a truly joyful sight for anybody with the slightest taste for them. And although you can buy mussels throughout the year these days, they are still at their best in the months with an 'r' in them, in other words, in the autumn and winter, which is exactly when I like to eat them best.

Pot-roast Guinea Fowl

SERVES 4

1 plump **guinea fowl**

1–2 tablespoons **extra virgin olive oil**

3–4 banana **shallots**, or 2 small **onions**, thinly sliced

1 **carrot**, sliced

1 **tomato**, roughly chopped (don't bother to skin or seed)

1 glass **dry white wine**

a small handful of **parsley** sprigs

a little bundle of **dried** or **fresh thyme**, or **marjoram**

salt and **pepper**

This recipe is a basic blueprint for pot-roasting guinea fowl (it works just fine for a chicken or a pheasant or two, as well). I like plenty of onions for their sweetness – a good softener for the acidity of the wine, there for its taste and to get the liquid flowing. Lots of thyme is lovely, but fresh marjoram, or a perky fresh bouquet garni, is a fine replacement. A carrot or two, maybe a stick of celery or a leek, or how about some sliced fennel (definitely to be eaten, not discarded at the end of cooking). A few cloves of garlic wouldn't go amiss, or perhaps some lardons, or slices of smoked pancetta. The variations are endless, so base them on what you have to hand, what's in season.

• In a heavy-based casserole (with a close-fitting lid), brown the guinea fowl as best you can in the oil. When it is well coloured, spoon off or suck up (with a baster) the excess fat, and discard. Tumble the onions, carrot and tomato all around the bird. Pour in the wine, and strew over the herbs, salt and pepper. Turn your bird breast-side down, jumbling up the other ingredients as you do.

• Cover tightly and reduce the heat to low. Leave to burble away nice and gently for about 1½ hours, turning the bird every 20–30 minutes. When the guinea fowl is cooked, lift it out on to a serving dish. Strain the sauce through a sieve, rubbing through some of the softened vegetables to thicken it, if you wish. Serve with the tender-as-bread guinea fowl.

BASTERS

Basters are fabulous kitchen implements, and I wouldn't be without mine. Woe betide the child who borrows it for paintwork or potions and doesn't put it back. But buyer beware. Avoid plastic ones! God alone knows why anyone makes them, as no sooner do you plunge the tip into the sizzling juices below a roast to suck them up for basting, than the plastic softens in the heat, swiftly buckling and sealing the entry hole. No improvement on flavour, and a defunct baster (no good even for infants' art hour) that must be binned. Settle only for a glass tube and nothing less!

Tagine of Chicken, Chickpeas and Apricots

In Morocco a tagine is nothing but food, any food, that has been cooked in a tagine, which is a form of earthenware casserole with a wide shallow base and a witch's hat of a lid. The specific ingredients are neither here nor there. As a cook back here in unexotic Oxfordshire, I use the name loosely to denote a stew flavoured with warm spices and a touch of sweetness. You don't need a tagine proper to make this aromatic stew as any sturdy casserole dish will do. Serve it with rice and stir-fried spinach.

SERVES 4

1 pretty, plump free-range **chicken**, cut into 10 pieces

2 tablespoons **extra virgin olive oil**

1 **onion**, chopped

2.5cm (1 in) **root ginger**, finely chopped

1 teaspoon **ground cinnamon**

½ teaspoon freshly ground **black pepper**

2 teaspoons **cumin seeds**

1 teaspoon **paprika**

110g (4 oz) ready-to-eat **dried apricots**, chopped

2 x 400g (14 oz) tins chopped **tomatoes**

3 tablespoons **honey**

1 x 400g (14 oz) tin of **chickpeas**, drained (or 200g/ 7 oz dried chickpeas, soaked overnight and simmered in fresh water until tender)

a handful of roughly chopped fresh **coriander**

salt

• Pre-heat the oven to 150°C/300°F/Gas 2. Brown the chicken in the oil, then transfer to an ovenproof casserole. Fry the onion and ginger gently in the same fat until tender. Now add all the spices and stir around for some 30 seconds. Tip in the apricots, and stir around for another minute or so. Pour in the tomatoes, honey, 150ml (5 fl oz) water, and season with salt. Bring up to the boil, and simmer for about 3–4 minutes. Stir in the chickpeas, taste and adjust seasoning.

• Pour the sauce over the chicken in the casserole. Cover and transfer to the oven for a further 40 minutes or so, until the chicken is cooked through. Just before serving, perk it up with a scattering of fresh coriander, and dish up with rice.

Roast Goose with Two Stuffings

SERVES 8–12

4–5.5kg (9–12 lb) **goose**

outside-in stuffing (see page 201)

shallot, sage, hazelnut and orange stuffing (see page 200)

salt and **pepper**

If I were you, I wouldn't wait until Christmas to roast a goose, but if you need an excuse to splash out, then Christmas is better than most. Many people imagine that goose is unbearably fatty, but it's not. Much of the fat runs off during cooking, leaving behind a rich, crisp skin and moist, beautifully flavoured, tender flesh that has so much more going for it than turkey. Siphon off the fat every now and then throughout the cooking time and you have a superb medium for sautéing potatoes or squash, or cubes of Jerusalem artichoke, or for making a confit of duck.

Both sage and tart, dried cranberries work well with goose, so for a major blow-out use both stuffings (which, incidentally, will make a relatively small amount of meat stretch around a bigger gathering). For a mere Sunday lunch, you might want to reduce the work by sticking with just one.

• Trim the excess fat from inside the goose. Pack the Outside-in Stuffing into the neck end of the goose, pressing it in firmly and then tucking the flap of skin neatly down around it. Secure firmly underneath with wooden cocktail sticks or a metal skewer. Three-quarters fill the stomach cavity with the Shallot, Sage, Hazelnut and Orange Stuffing.

• Preheat the oven to 190°C/375°F/Gas 5. Prick the skin of the goose all over with a fork. Season with salt and pepper. Lay some of the fat from the cavity over the thighs to keep them moist. Cover with foil and place on a rack in the oven with a tray underneath, so that you can empty out the fat regularly. Roast a 4kg (9 lb) goose for 3 hours, a 4.5–5kg (10–11 lb) goose for 3½ hours, and a 5.5kg (12lb) goose for 4 hours. Remove the foil 30–40 minutes before the end of the cooking time so that the skin can brown and crisp. To test, pierce the fattest part of the thigh with a skewer. If the juices run clear, then the bird is done. Rest for 20–30 minutes, oven turned off, door ajar, before carving.

Two Stuffings for the Christmas Bird

There would be mutiny around our Christmas dinner table if I dared to present a roast turkey or goose without any stuffing. We all adore the stuffing (probably more than the meat itself, if truth be told) and just couldn't do without it. This brace of stuffings works well for either bird – you could just stick with one or, better still, make both, one for the central cavity and one to pat under the neck flap. If you go for the option of both, you will have more than you need, so bake the remainder separately or roll into balls and roast around the bird towards the end of the cooking time.

It is only worth making these stuffings if you start with good quality bread for the crumbs, not white sliced, which turns slimy when cooked. Make sure you season your stuffing emphatically otherwise it will taste bland. Other than that, the making of a top-notch, put-the-bird-to-shame kind of stuffing is as easy as making mud pies – all you really have to do is prepare the ingredients and mix.

Shallot, Sage, Hazelnut and Orange Stuffing

350g (12 oz) **shallots**, thinly sliced

60g (2 oz) **butter**

15g (½ oz) **caster sugar**

finely grated **zest** and **juice** of 1 **orange**

3 heaped tablespoons chopped fresh **sage**

85g (3 oz) roughly chopped roasted, skinned **hazelnuts**

150g (5 oz) fresh **white breadcrumbs**

½ –1 beaten **egg**

salt and **pepper**

This bread-based stuffing is ideal roasted in the centre of the bird, as it contains no meat. If you would rather roll it into balls, use a whole egg, so that it holds together better.

• Fry the shallots gently in the butter until golden, then add the sugar and orange juice. Simmer merrily until the liquid has virtually all evaporated leaving a delicious jammy mass of shallots.

• Pour boiling water over the sage, leave for 1 minute, then drain and squeeze dry. Add to the shallots, together with all the remaining ingredients. Fry a small knob of stuffing in a little extra butter to check the seasoning, and then adjust accordingly.

Outside-in Stuffing: Chestnut, Bacon and Dried Cranberry

110g (4 oz) **dried cranberries**

60ml (2 fl oz) **ruby port**

1 small **onion**, chopped

2 rashers **green back bacon**, cut into strips

45g (1½ oz) **butter**

2 cloves **garlic**, chopped

450g (1 lb) **sausagemeat**

85g (3 oz) fresh **white** or **brown breadcrumbs**

2 tablespoons chopped fresh **parsley**

½ teaspoon chopped fresh **thyme leaves**

150g (5 oz) peeled, cooked **chestnut**s, roughly chopped

1 **egg**, lightly beaten

salt and **pepper**

This stuffing brings together 'all the trimmings' in one gorgeous mass. It is ideal for packing under the neck flap of the turkey or goose, where it will cook through properly. In fact, as long as you are using a fresh bird that has not been frozen, and you make sure that it is properly cooked, it is quite safe to cook a meat-based stuffing in the central cavity and deeply unlikely to induce food poisoning that way.

Use the plainest high-quality sausagemeat you can lay your hands on, preferably made with free-range pork and only the minimum of seasonings and herbs. If you can't find any dried cranberries, use diced dried apricots instead.

• Soak the cranberries in the port for an hour.

• Fry the onion and bacon gently in the butter until the onion is tender and the bacon cooked. Add the garlic and fry for another minute or so. Cool slightly, then mix with all the remaining ingredients, including the cranberries and port, adding enough egg to bind. Fry a knob to test seasoning, and adjust accordingly. Now it's ready to use.

FREE-STANDING STUFFINGS

• If you don't want to push the stuffing into your turkey or goose in the traditional way, it can be baked in a dish, or rolled into balls that will be crisp on the outside and moist inside.

• **To bake**, press the stuffing into an ovenproof dish in a layer that is around 4cm (1½ in) thick. Bake at 200°C/400°F/Gas 6 for about 30 minutes, until browned, and in the case of a sausagemeat stuffing, cooked right through.

• **Or roll into balls** of about 4cm (1½ in) in diameter. Roast in hot fat (they can be tucked around the bird) for 25–30 minutes, turning twice, until crisp and browned on the outside.

Roast Turkey with Two Stuffings

1 free-range **turkey**

shallot, sage, hazelnut and orange stuffing (see page 200)

outside-in stuffing (see page 201)

175g (6 oz) **lightly salted butter**

salt and **pepper**

you will also need a large piece of **butter muslin** (sold cheaply in any fabric shop), approximately 1 metre square

If we are going to have turkey for Christmas lunch, rather than, say, a goose, I cook it just the way my mum did, although adding my own stuffings. The basic method is the same, and has stood the test of two generations of cooks. Method is not all, mind you. If you are going to cook a whole turkey, then make sure it is a good one to begin with. It must be free-range, and it must be fresh, and if it comes from a relatively small flock, raised locally, so much the better. Best varieties are reckoned to be Kelly Bronze and Norfolk Blacks.

The turkey can be stuffed and cloaked in its buttery muslin on Christmas Eve, then kept in a cool place, covered with foil, until Christmas morning.

• Begin by checking that you have not left the plastic bag of giblets lurking inside the bird. Roast plastic does no favours to the taste. Save the liver to make a little turkey liver pâté, and use the rest of the giblets for stock. Fill the cavity of the turkey about three-quarters full with the Shallot, Sage, Hazelnut and Orange Stuffing. Lift the large neck flap, and pack as much of the Outside-in Stuffing under it as you can, then cover with the flap and secure with wooden cocktail sticks or a metal skewer. Now weigh the bird (use the bathroom scales) and calculate the cooking time (see chart on page opposite).

• Put the turkey in a large, deep roasting tin. Season the bird generously with salt and pepper. Melt the butter. Fold the muslin in four and lower it into the melted butter, pushing it in so that it soaks up virtually all the butter. Lift out the folded muslin and lay it over the turkey, making sure that it covers the breast and upper thighs completely.

• Pre-heat the oven to 190°C/375°F/Gas 5. Just before you slide the bird into the oven, pour about 300ml (½ pint) water around it. Baste the bird every half hour, more or less, with the pan juices.

• Test that the turkey is properly cooked though in just the same way as you would a chicken. In other words, pierce the thickest part of the thigh with a skewer. If the juices run clear then the turkey is done. If they are pink, slide it straight back into the oven for a further half hour or so before testing again.

• Once it is done, transfer the turkey to its serving dish, discard the muslin, and leave in a warm place to rest for at least half an hour. This gives you time to finish the gravy (use the juices left in the roasting tin as well as the giblet stock), and get the vegetables and all the trimmings sorted and ready to go. Finally, it's time to present the magnificent bird in full glory. Cheers!

QUANTITIES AND TIMING

This chart gives you a rough idea of how big a turkey you will need and how long it will take to cook. The size you need depends a great deal on what else you are serving and how many courses there are, not to mention individual appetites, so treat this as a loose guide, not gospel.

And while we're on the get-out clauses, ovens vary considerably and over the lengthy cooking time demanded by such a big bird, 3 or 4 degrees one way or the other will make a noticeable difference. So check regularly and aim to have your turkey cooked an hour before you intend to eat, which leaves plenty of extra cooking time if needed, as well as time for resting the meat.

A turkey weighing	Feeds	Cooking Time
4–5kg/9–11 lb	8–10 people	2–2½ hours
5–6kg/11–14 lb	10–12 people	2½–3 hours
6–7kg/14–16 lb	12–16 people	3–3¾ hours
7–8kg/16–18 lb	16–20 people	3¾–4¼ hours

Chestnuts

The cooked-chestnut vendor, with his sweet-smelling brazier, is a cheering sight on a winter's day. There aren't too many of them about any more, so whenever I see one I insist on buying a couple of bags of roast chestnuts in a small attempt to ensure that they don't disappear altogether. This is hardly a burden. The chestnuts warm your hands as you stride on, and each nugget of warm, mealy tender flesh provides a morsel of pleasure. This is the one time when I don't mind peeling chestnuts.

Back at home peeling chestnuts is probably the kitchen task I loathe most. There is no getting round the fact that it is fiddly and tedious and that you always get one small shard of chestnut skin stuck painfully under your nail. I do it once a year, and no more, for the Christmas stuffing. Vacuum-packed cooked chestnuts are nearly as good, though comparatively expensive (you're paying for somebody else's suffering), but they do have an over-waxy texture. If you can stand the peeling process, you and your fellow diners will end up with a superior result. Console yourself with the fact that you can undertake the task several weeks in advance and freeze them until needed. This is how to go about it. First of all buy at least twice the weight of cooked chestnuts stipulated in the recipe, to allow for the weight of the skins and the occasional black or wormy nut. Cut a deep cross in the outer skin of each chestnut, then bring up to the boil. Simmer for 1 minute, then draw off the heat. Pick out the chestnuts one or two at a time, and pull off the outer and inner skin while they are still so hot that you can hardly bear to handle them. As they cool, the inner skin in particular becomes very hard to remove. You may need to bring the pan of nuts back to the boil once or twice before they are all done. Now, simmer the skinned chestnuts in fresh water for a few more minutes until tender, then drain well.

Slow Roast Leg of Lamb with Anchovies, Garlic and Ginger Beer

SERVES 6–8

1 **leg of lamb**, weighing around 2.5–3kg (5–7 lb)

6 **anchovy fillets**, cut in half lengthways

4 cloves **garlic**, cut into slivers

1cm (½ in) length of **root ginger**, cut into matchsticks

a little **olive oil**

2 large **onions**, cut into eighths

400ml (14 fl oz) **ginger beer**

200ml (7 fl oz) **lamb** or **chicken stock**

salt and **pepper**

I can hear what you're thinking. Could it be something like, 'What a ghastly collection of ingredients!'? Well, hold on a moment before you turn the page. It's not really so weird. After all, ginger works well with meat, the anchovies will dissolve into the flesh as it cooks leaving just a subtle saltiness, and you just have to have garlic with a leg of lamb. The sweetness of the ginger beer gets concentrated down with stock and meat juices to produce a delicious light gravy with a touch of sweetness. A great partner for the meltingly tender lamb, cooked so long that it just falls from the bone.

• Pre-heat the oven to 220°C/425°F/Gas 7. Make slits all over the lamb and push in strips of anchovy, slivers of garlic and half the sticks of ginger. Rub a little olive oil over the skin (but don't douse it with oil – there should be plenty of fat in there already if the lamb is half-way decent), then season with salt and pepper. Make a bed of the onion wedges in a roasting tin or dish that is big enough to take the lamb comfortably, and sprinkle over the remaining ginger.

• Lay the lamb on top. Pour the ginger beer and stock around the lamb and place the whole lot in the oven. Roast for 20 minutes, then reduce the heat to a soft and gentle 150°C/300°F/Gas 2. Baste the meat with the ginger beer, and cook for another 4 hours or even a little longer, basting frequently. By the end of the cooking time, the lamb should be so tender that it comes away easily from the bone with a prod of a fork.

• Transfer the lamb to a warm serving dish and rest in a warm place for 20–30 minutes. Skim as much fat as you can from the juices in the roasting tin, then boil down until reduced by about half. Strain then taste and adjust seasoning. Pour into a gravy boat and serve with the lamb.

Pot-roast Pork with Star Anise, Ginger, Tamarind and Port

SERVES 6

1.25–1.5kg (3–3½ lb) boned, rolled **loin of pork**

2 tablespoons **sunflower oil**

1 **onion**, sliced

6 cloves **garlic**, whole but not peeled

2cm (¾ in) length of **root ginger**, finely chopped

1 good-sized sprig of **rosemary**

1 whole **star anise**

85ml (3 fl oz) **ruby port**

3 tablespoons **dark soy sauce**

1 tablespoon **tamarind purée**, or **lemon juice**

2 tablespoons **light muscovado sugar**

plenty of **pepper**

No deliberate fusion of east and west here, just one of those kitchen coincidences of life – a bit of this and a bit of that – and a vague yen for something a little more aromatic than a straight European pot-roast. Nonetheless, the blend of soy sauce, sour tamarind and ginger with ruby port and a touch of rosemary was good enough to repeat, so I did.

I must admit to a distinct fondness for pot-roasts and braised meats. There is something so satisfying about the slow, lengthy cooking period, melting down the muscles in the meat until it is tender enough to cut with a spoon, juices dripping down into a modicum of intensely flavoured gravy. Serve it western style with potatoes and spinach, or with rice and stir-fried ribbons of vegetables.

By the way, you can find ready-made tamarind purée in the spice racks in good supermarkets, though the flavour is not nearly as fine as that you make yourself from a block of tamarind purchased in an Indian supermarket. For information on what to do with such a tamarind block, turn to page 91.

• Wipe the pork dry with kitchen paper. Brown all over in the oil in a heat- and ovenproof casserole. Transfer to a plate for a few minutes while you fry the onion in the same fat – not too fast at first, raising the heat slightly as it becomes tender to brown here and there. Pour off excess fat, leaving the onion behind in the dish. Now return the meat to the pan and add all the remaining ingredients. Bring up to the boil, then cover and either turn the heat down very low, or transfer to the oven, pre-heated to 140°C/275°F/Gas 1.

• Braise gently, turning the meat occasionally, for about 3 hours, until the meat is very tender. Skim as much fat as you can from the juices, then taste and adjust seasoning. Strain and reheat if necessary. Slice the pork thickly, and drizzle with a little of the cooking juices. Serve immediately.

Perfect Pork

There is no mystery about roasting the perfect joint of pork with absurdly crisp crackling. It comes down to just two things. The first is the pork itself, and the second is making sure that the rind is absolutely bone dry as it goes into the oven. Get those two right, and your crackling will crackle crisply, snapping with a dry, clean crack in a most satisfying way.

Getting the pork right is probably the trickiest of the two essentials. The first thing you do is to ignore mass-produced lean meat with a healthily negligible scraping of fat beneath the skin. Fewer calories, less cholesterol, less taste, less crackle. Remind yourself that much of the fat in a joint of pork runs off in the oven, and then set off to find a supplier of real pork.

What you are looking for is something that is becoming increasingly easy to find. Hip hip hurrah! The critical vocabulary you will need to employ begins with the words 'free-range'. A pig needs to roam around and lead a happy life if it is to make us happy as we gather round the table for Sunday lunch. The difference in flavour between an intensively raised pig and a free-range pig is quite remarkable.

Next big word is breed. Look for old-fashioned breeds like Berkshire, Gloucester Old Spot, or, in my neck of the woods, the very cute Oxford Sandy and Black. These are creatures that have not had the fat bred out of them, the ones that will guarantee crisp crackling. Finally, I reckon you need one more phrase to get you what you want, and that's 'old-fashioned butcher' or possibly 'farm-shop with in-house butcher'. Anyway, the point is that you need to be able to depend on someone who knows good meat when she or he sees it, and hasn't been bamboozled by the modern fat-is-bad lobby. Those sad people can't understand that it might be better and just as healthy to eat pork a little less often, but to really enjoy it at its tastiest and most crisply crackling when we do.

A daube is a southern French stew, traditionally cooked for hours in a daubière, an earthenware dish. Anything can be turned into a daube, but the most famous of all is Boeuf en Daube, simmered with red wine and bunches of herbs, often seeded with olives. The parsnips, however, are not French. In France they feed them to the cattle and virtually never dish them up for human consumption. They don't know what they're missing.

Daube of Beef with Parsnips and Red Wine

Three notes: the first is that it is no good substituting fresh orange zest for dried – it provides a rather different, less agreeable flavour. To dry your own, just leave a few strips of zest (with as little of the bitter white pith as possible) on a wire rack for several days – or string on to thread and hang them up – until dry and leathery, then store in an airtight jar. Secondly, you should use the kind of wine that you would be happy to drink – cheap wine of dubious quality will still taste cheap even after hours of cooking. Thirdly, this stew tastes good when it is first made, but even better reheated the next day.

SERVES 6

1.5kg (3½ lb) **shin of beef** or **chuck steak**

60g (2 oz) seasoned **flour**

3 tablespoons **extra virgin olive oil**

220g (8 oz) **lardons of bacon** or **pancetta**

1 **onion**, sliced

1 large **carrot**, diced

1 stick **celery**, sliced

3 cloves **garlic**, chopped

1 **cinnamon stick**

1 generous **bouquet garni** consisting of a large sprig of thyme, several stalks of parsley, 2 bay leaves, a sprig of rosemary and 2 strips of dried orange peel – Seville if possible

3 tablespoons **tomato purée**

1 bottle good **red wine**

900g (2 lb) **parsnips**

a little chopped fresh **parsley**, to serve

salt and **pepper**

• Cut the beef into chunks about 7.5cm (3 in) across. Toss in seasoned flour and shake off the excess. Brown the meat in batches in 2 tablespoons of the oil. Transfer to a casserole dish. Check the pan – dark brown residues in it are great, burnt flour is not. If there is burn to be seen, best rinse the pan out or undertake the next stage in a new pan.

• Pre-heat the oven to 150°C/300°F/Gas 2. Add the remaining oil to the pan, and fry the lardons, onion, carrot and celery in it until beginning to colour – this may take some time, but don't try to hurry it along. Now add the garlic and cook for a minute or two longer. Scrape the whole lot out into the casserole, and while you are at it, tuck in the cinnamon stick and bouquet garni, then season with salt and pepper. Spoon in the tomato purée.

• Pour the red wine into the pan and bring up to the boil. Scrape in all the brown residues from frying, then pour over the meat and vegetables. Cover and transfer to the oven, and leave to cook for a good 2 hours until the meat is very tender. Stir occasionally.

• When your 2 hours are nearly up, prepare the parsnips. Peel and cut into 5cm (2 in) lengths. Quarter the larger pieces and cut out the core. Stir the parsnips into the casserole when the meat is tender. Return the casserole to the oven, uncovered, to cook for another 40–50 minutes until the parsnips are soft. Remove the bouquet garni, taste and adjust seasoning, sprinkle with parsley and serve.

Chicory, Beetroot and Walnut Salad, with a Moroccan Dressing

SERVES 4

2 medium to large **beetroot**, cooked, skinned and diced

2 heads **chicory**, sliced into rings

60g (2 oz) shelled **walnut halves**

FOR THE DRESSING:

thinly shredded **zest** of ½ **orange**

juice of 1 **orange**

juice of ½ **lemon**

1 tablespoon **honey**

1 tablespoon **caster sugar**

1 tablespoon **orange flower water**

¼ teaspoon **ground cinnamon**

salt and **pepper**

Real winter salad vegetables are few and far between. Of course, you can buy any amount of imported rocket and other tender salad leaves, but if you are searching for home-grown saladery the choice is relatively thin. Grated carrots are a possible option, watercress I love, but chicory has to be the best of all with its special sweet-bitter flavour and juicy crispness. Married with roasted beetroot and new season walnuts, it makes a particularly fine winter salad. *But*, to get it at its best, hold back on the mixing of the two main ingredients until the very last moment, so that the purple-red juices of the beetroot wreak minimal damage.

The oil-free dressing is based on Moroccan salad dressings, so is very different to European ones, though every bit as good, and often better. Sugar softens the acidity instead of oil, and soft spices play a surprisingly gentle role.

• To make the dressing, begin by blanching the orange zest in a little boiling water for 2 minutes. Drain and reserve. Put the orange juice, lemon juice, honey and sugar into a pan, and boil until reduced by half. Stir in the orange flower water, cinnamon, salt and pepper.

• Toss the beetroot in half the dressing, the chicory in the remainder. Arrange on a plate, then scatter with walnuts and the blanched orange zest. Serve at room temperature, before the beetroot bleeds too messily all over the chicory.

Beetroot

I've said it before and I'll say it again, beetroot is the most wonderful of vegetables, but it gets a downright rotten deal in this country. And if you dare say that you hate beetroot, then please, please, please, try it again. But this time, make sure you start with fresh raw beets, and cook them yourself, slowly and gently. Just see what a difference it makes. Most people who hate beetroot have had to battle with over-vinegared, badly cooked beetroot, probably at school or in other institutional settings. Or they've been confronted with needle-sharp, mouth-puckeringly acid pickled beetroot drowned in malt vinegar, which is just as bad.

Handled with a modicum of care, beetroot becomes something of a joy. In an ideal world, your beetroot will be small, say a mere brace of inches (for you youngsters, that's around 5cm) across at the most, and just yanked from the moist earth of the vegetable patch down the bottom of the garden. Then you are in for something incredibly special, but I suppose if you are growing your own, you will already be quite aware of that. Non-gardeners should make straight for the vegetable stall at their nearest farmers' market, or to the local greengrocer's (or yes, even to the supermarket) and grab whatever they can. To be fair, baby beetroot are not a winter fixture – they come earlier in the year – but even when the days are shortest, it is still worth picking out the smaller roots rather than the almighty grand and glorious cannonballs.

Now take them home and deal with them as soon as possible. Here's what you do. Trim off any leaves, leaving about 2.5cm (1 in) of stem still attached to the beetroot. Rinse and scrub it, but do not attempt to peel (unless you want raw grated beetroot). Leave roots alone. The less damage you do to the naked root, the less it will bleed, and the better and juicier it will taste. Wrap each beetroot in foil, place in a roasting dish and bake at a low temperature – 150°C/300°F/Gas 2 is ideal, but if you want to speed things up, crank up the temperature a notch or two – for an hour or two or even three, until the skin scrapes easily away from the flesh. Unwrap and peel the beetroot while hot if you wish to serve them straight away, though it is easier on the fingers to leave them until just warm. Pull away the skin and *voila*! Your beetroot is ready to consume in whatever manner you wish.

Try it cold, diced and dressed with a mustardy vinaigrette and thinly sliced spring onions, or hot with slices of fried apple and dollops of crème fraîche. Or grate cooked beetroot and mix it with mashed potato to make the most glorious technicolour pink mash. Wild!

Brussels Sprouts

The choicest sprouts are small and tightly packed, still clinging to their stalk, which, one hopes, has not long been slashed from its root. A quick glance at the cut end will give you a vague idea of how long it is since they were gathered – the more grizzled and brown it is, the less you should feel inclined to purchase. Sprouts on the stalk keep their sweet freshness longer than ones that have been stripped off, so when you are intending to store them for a few days before cooking, it pays to buy them this way. Besides, they look so pretty and enticing, how could you pass them by?

No doubt supermarkets will eventually catch on to the attractiveness of selling them like this, but for the time being hunt them down in smaller greengrocers' (I used to buy them on the stalk from an exemplary Cypriot greengrocer on the Seven Sisters Road in north London), and in farm shops and farmers' markets. Or better still, grow your own, and cut them no more than an hour or two before cooking to discover what a fabulous vegetable the sprout really is. Taking the sprouts off the stalk is a quick enough job once you are armed with a sharp-bladed, small knife. After trimming off any damaged outer leaves, do not start cutting small crosses in the base of each sprout. It is a total waste of time, and may even lead to

soggy sprouts, which are, frankly, only fit for the bin. Heaven knows why this habit started, but it certainly serves no good purpose now.

Steamed or boiled, make sure that sprouts are not overcooked. The ideal is that they should be tender with just a slight resistance to the bite at the very centre. More than that and they begin to develop those nasty over-boiled cabbage flavours that only the masochistic take pleasure in. You can also stir-fry or sauté sprouts (and cabbage too). You'll need to quarter or slice them first, then toss in hot oil for a few minutes until browned at the edges, tender inside – add thinly sliced bacon or Parma ham, finely grated lemon zest, capers, garlic, or a crumble of hot dried chillies, and your humble sprouts are given a new lease of life.

Gratin of Brussels Sprouts with Lardons, Cream and Almonds

This is the luxury end of the Brussels sprout spectrum, and how they love that cream. A special dish, that turns sprouts into gorgeous starlets.

• Pre-heat the oven to 200°C/400°F/Gas 6. Simmer the sprouts in salted water until almost but not quite cooked (around 4 minutes). Drain thoroughly, and cut in half.

• Sauté the lardons and almonds in the butter and oil in a wide frying pan until lightly browned. Add the sprouts and cook for a further 2–3 minutes, stirring almost constantly. Add the cream, bring up to the boil, and let it bubble away merrily for some 2–4 minutes until reduced to a rich sauce. Season with a touch of salt and plenty of pepper.

• Draw off the heat, stir in the lemon juice, then spoon into a gratin dish. Mix the breadcrumbs and Parmesan, and scatter evenly over the sprouts. Bake for about 20 minutes until the top is golden brown, with the cream bubbling though seductively here and there. Serve when the cream has quietened down a little.

SERVES 4–6

700g (1½ lb) **Brussels sprouts**, trimmed

100g (3½ oz) **lardons**, or **back bacon** cut into strips

15g (½ oz) **flaked almonds**

15g (½ oz) **butter**

1 tablespoon **sunflower oil**

300ml (½ pint) **double cream**

dash of **lemon juice**

4 tablespoons fresh **breadcrumbs**

3 tablespoons freshly grated **Parmesan**

salt and freshly ground **pepper**

Gratin of White Cabbage and Lentils

I'm wary of vegetarian 'bakes' – they take me back to student days, trying to convince myself that the hefty brown sludges dished up at the PC health-food shop down the road were worth eating – but here is a gratin that tastes twenty times better than its main ingredients might suggest.

Use high-quality lentils and take care not to overcook them (that way leads to sludge), and likewise make sure that the cabbage is just *al dente* before mixing it in. Season the sauce energetically to balance the starch of the lentils. Getting these elements right disperses any lingering memories of dismal worthy bakes.

Just to make absolutely sure, serve the gratin with a lively green salad, with plenty of watercress in it and a sprightly dressing.

SERVES 4–6

⅓ **white cabbage**, shredded

150g (5 oz) **brown** or **green lentils** (Puy lentils are extra good)

30g (1 oz) **brown** or **white breadcrumbs**

30g (1 oz) freshly grated **Parmesan**

a drizzle of **extra virgin olive oil**

FOR THE TOMATO SAUCE:

1 **red onion**, chopped

2 cloves **garlic**, chopped

1 **red pepper**, deseeded and cut into postage stamp-sized squares

3 tablespoons **extra virgin olive oil**

1 teaspoon coarsely **ground coriander**

2 generous sprigs of **thyme**

2 x 400g (14 oz) tins chopped **tomatoes**

1 tablespoon **tomato purée**

1 teaspoon **caster sugar**

leaves of a small handful of **basil**, roughly torn up

salt and **pepper**

• Pre-heat the oven to 200°C/400°F/Gas 6. To make the tomato sauce, fry the onion, garlic and red pepper in the olive oil until soft. Add the coriander and thyme, and stir for 30 seconds or so. Now tip in the tomatoes, tomato purée and sugar and season with salt and pepper. Leave to simmer down to a thick sauce, stirring occasionally – about 15–20 minutes. Taste and adjust seasoning and stir in the basil.

• Blanch the cabbage in boiling salted water for about 3–4 minutes, until just tender. Drain and run under the cold tap, then drain again, thoroughly. Cook the lentils in boiling unsalted water for about 20–30 minutes until just tender, then drain. Mix the cabbage and lentils with the tomato sauce, and spoon into a shallow ovenproof gratin dish – it should end up filled to a depth of around 2.5cm (1 in).

• Mix the breadcrumbs and cheese, and scatter over the mixture in an even layer. Drizzle with a little extra virgin olive oil. Bake for about 20–30 minutes until sizzling and patched appetisingly with brown. Serve hot.

Sweet and Sour Red Cabbage

SERVES 6

1 **red cabbage**

1 large **cooking apple**, peeled, cored and cut into chunks

1 **onion**, sliced

30g (1 oz) **caster sugar**

60g (2 oz) **light muscovado sugar**

4 **allspice berries**

1 **cinnamon stick**

½ tablespoon **caraway seeds**

30g (1 oz) **butter**

1 big glass **red wine**

2 tablespoons **red wine vinegar**

salt and **pepper**

There *are* other ways of cooking red cabbage (it's very nice stir-fried, for instance), but in the end this is the king and reigns supreme. The idea is, I believe, originally from Germany, but it's been naturalised here, something of a winter classic to serve with casseroles and game, alongside a big mound of buttery mash.

There are endless variations on the basic method – you can replace wine with port or orange juice, replace some of the sugar with honey, increase the caraway seeds and reduce the other spices, use goose fat or fatty bacon instead of butter, and so on and so forth. Take this as a model, and adapt it to what lingers in your cupboards.

• Quarter the cabbage and cut out the tough core. Shred the rest thinly. Now layer in a heatproof casserole with the apple, onion, sugars, spices, salt and pepper. Dot with the butter then pour over the wine and vinegar. Cover tightly and cook gently over a low heat, stirring occasionally, for about 1½–2 hours until the cabbage is meltingly soft and most of the liquid has been absorbed. Taste and adjust seasoning and serve, or better still, leave to get cold, and then reheat to serve next day.

• If you prefer, you can cook it in the oven, set to around 150°C/300°F/Gas 2, for around the same length of time.

Celery, Orange and Roasted Chilli Salad

SERVES 3–4

2 fresh **red chillies** (see recipe introduction)

1 large **orange**

2 sticks of **celery**, thinly sliced

FOR THE DRESSING:

½ tablespoon **white wine vinegar**

2 tablespoons **extra virgin olive oil**

salt and **pepper**

A particularly refreshing salad, with a mild kick to it. You will need to choose chillies that have relatively thick walls of flesh. In practice this means the 'fresno' type chillies that are commonly sold in every supermarket and greengrocer's. These are the cone-shaped chillies, wide at the stalk end tapering down to a stubby point, usually around 5cm (2 in) long. They also happen to be fairly mild on the whole, and as roasting emphasises the sweetness of ripe red ones, the impact that two of them make should not be unbearable. Even so, it might be worth nibbling a strip just before adding them to the salad, in case you've fallen on an unusually fiery batch.

• Pre-heat the grill. Spear the chillies, tip to stem, on a skewer, and grill close to the heat until the skin is blackened and blistered all over. Turn them frequently so that they are as evenly cooked as possible. Slide off the skewer and drop into a plastic bag. Knot the bag loosely, then leave the chillies until cool enough to handle. Pull off the skins, deseed and cut into thin strips.

• Use a sharp knife to slice off the top and base of the orange and then cut off the skin, slicing down from top to bottom to expose the orange flesh. Cut the orange into thin slices, then cut each slice into eighths. Mix with the celery and chilli.

• To make the dressing, whisk the salt and pepper into the vinegar, then whisk in the oil gradually. Toss the orange, celery and chilli in the dressing, and serve.

Pommes Anna

SERVES 4–6

45g (1½ oz) **butter**

around 1kg (2 lb 4 oz) **main
crop potatoes** (I particularly
like a slightly waxy one, such
as Cara, but King Edwards,
or Estima, or Desiree will do
almost as well)

3 cloves **garlic**, sliced

approximately 450ml (¾ pint)
chicken, **lamb** or **vegetable
stock**

salt and **pepper**

**It's Sunday. You've slept in. Nonetheless, lunch
beckons. You have pondered over the wonders of
pommes dauphinoise, with its oodles of voluptuous
cream. But there is no cream. What to put with the
leg of lamb? Well, one thing I do usually have in my
freezer is a small stash of stock – made with
chicken bones left from another lunch, or good
vegetable trimmings, or a lamb bone or two, or
even a mix (not orthodox but the ingredients of
a decent stock are not writ in stone). So, pommes
Anna it is, and so much lighter, anyway, than
dauphinoise. Not that it is exactly a healthy option
for it still demands a generous hand with the
butter. Hardly any point making it otherwise. Still,
the melting slow-cooked potatoes sozzled with
stock and butter are a sterling accompaniment to
a roast of any kind.**

• Pre-heat the oven to 150°C/300°F/Gas 2. Smear a 27 x 21cm
(11 x 8½ in) – or something thereabouts – ovenproof dish thickly
with some of the butter. Peel and slice the first potato thinly, then
arrange slices to cover the bottom of the dish. Season with salt and
pepper, strew with some of the garlic, and dot with butter. Repeat
with the remaining potatoes, garlic and butter, finishing with a top
layer of potatoes. Season again, dot with a final sexy amount of
butter, and pour the stock in around the sides of the dish, allowing
a little to bathe the centre.

• Cover with foil and bake for 45 minutes. Remove foil and return
to the oven for another 45 minutes or so, until the potatoes are
very tender when pierced with a skewer, and lightly browned on
top. Serve hot or warm.

A Very Good Cauliflower Cheese

The idea is simple and familiar – cauliflower baked in a cheese sauce – but it is the execution that counts. Casual inattention is the death knell. Vigilance and respect are the passwords to success. This is a fabulous dish, worthy of main course status when it is cooked well.

Most important thing of all is that the cauliflower should a) be fresh and b) not be one iota overcooked initially; there's nothing worse than water-logged, greying, overdone elderly cauli. Secondly, the sauce must be robustly flavoured and properly cooked through, otherwise the whole dish becomes insipid. So... nothing to it, really.

SERVES 4

1 beautiful, creamy white **cauliflower**, trimmed and broken into florets

1 **shallot**, sliced

30g (1 oz) **butter**, plus a little extra to finish

6 tinned **anchovy fillets**, chopped

30g (1 oz) **plain flour**

600ml (1 pint) **milk**

60g (2 oz) mature **Cheddar cheese**, grated

2 tablespoons **crème fraîche** (optional, but a mighty improvement)

squeeze of **lemon juice**

30g (1 oz) fine **breadcrumbs**

30g (1 oz) freshly grated **Parmesan**

salt and **pepper**

• Pre-heat the oven to 200°C/400°F/Gas 6. Cook the cauliflower in salted water until just tender, but not a minim more. Mind you, don't underdo it either – crunchy *al dente* cauliflower is not appropriate. Drain thoroughly. Use a little extra butter to grease the sides and edges of an ovenproof dish large enough to take the cauliflower in a closely packed layer, then tip in the cauliflower.

• To make the sauce, soften the shallot in the butter. When it is almost tender, add the anchovy and stir, mashing down the pieces until they have more or less dissolved into the butter. Now sprinkle over the flour and stir for about 1 minute without allowing it to brown. Draw off the heat and gradually beat in the milk, a few spoonfuls at a time at first, increasing the flow as the sauce thins. Return to the heat and simmer gently for at least 5 minutes and probably nearer 10 until the sauce is thick and creamy. Stir frequently to prevent catching on the base. Take off the heat and stir in the Cheddar, cream, salt and pepper and a squeeze of lemon juice. Taste and adjust seasoning, making sure that it is fairly punchy. Pour over the cauliflower.

• Mix the breadcrumbs and Parmesan, and sprinkle evenly over the surface of the cauliflower cheese. Dot with a little extra butter. Bake for about 20–30 minutes, until browned and bubbling. Serve immediately.

Lebanese Deep-fried Cauliflower with Lemon, Mint and Garlic Dressing

This is so simple, but transforms cauliflower into a total treat. Serve as a side dish or a starter, hot from the pan, warm or at room temperature, within an hour or two of frying at most. When it comes to the eating, I think fingers are best here – just pick up a piece of fried cauliflower, dip it into the vivid green dressing and pop straight into your mouth. Fabulous.

- To make the dressing, put the garlic, mint, lemon juice, salt and pepper in a liquidiser. Set the blades whirling, and trickle in the olive oil. Taste and adjust seasoning.

- Cook the cauliflower florets in boiling salted water for about 5 minutes until almost cooked but still very slightly *al dente*. Drain well, then pat dry on a clean tea towel or kitchen paper.

- Heat the oil to 180°C/350°F. To test that it has reached the right temperature, lower a piece of cauliflower into the fat – it should sizzle and bubble merrily. Deep-fry the cauliflower in several small batches until golden brown – just a matter of a minute or two. Lift out and drain on kitchen paper. Season with salt.

- Serve with the lemon, mint and garlic dressing.

SERVES 4–6

1 **cauliflower**, broken into small florets

sunflower or **vegetable oil** for deep-frying

salt

FOR THE DRESSING:

1 large or 2 small cloves **garlic**, roughly chopped

about 30g (1 oz) fresh **mint leaves** (no thick stalks)

juice of 1 **lemon**

150ml (5 fl oz) **extra virgin olive oil**

salt and **pepper**

Real Baked Beans

SERVES 8

450g (1 lb) **dried haricot beans**

1 **onion**, quartered

1 **bay leaf**

1 large sprig of **thyme**

150g (5 oz) **slab of smoked bacon**, cut into lardons, or thick-cut smoked bacon, cut into wide strips

200ml (7 fl oz) **maple syrup**

1 tablespoon **Dijon mustard**

300ml (½ pint) **passata**

2 teaspoons **salt**

plenty of **pepper**

I had such a passion for tinned baked beans as a child (preferably with those little pappy sausages in them) that I insisted on eating them every morning before school, and my mother happily obliged. Indeed, she used to joke that I would turn into a baked bean if I ate many more.

I still enjoy them, but on the rare occasions that I cook real baked beans, I like them even better. Yes, they do take an awfully long time to cook, but they require only the minimum of attention once they are in the oven. The end result is so delicious that I reckon it's worth it at least once or twice every winter. Besides, what doesn't get eaten at their first serving tastes even better when reheated next day, and the rest freezes well.

If you have to cut down on time, then you could substitute 900g (2 lb) tinned haricot beans, well rinsed, for the dried.

• Soak the beans overnight, then drain and pile into a saucepan. Cover generously with water, bring up to the boil and simmer until tender. Allow a good 40 minutes to 1½ hours for this – timing will depend on the age of the beans. Drain well.

• Preheat the oven to 150°C/300°F/Gas 2. Find a decent-sized casserole or ovenproof dish. Lay the onion in the base, tip in the beans, and then bury the herbs in among them. Scatter bacon over the top. Mix the maple syrup, mustard, passata, salt and pepper and pour over, then add enough water just to barely cover the beans. Cover and bake for 5 hours, or even longer. Check the crock occasionally, give it a stir, and add a little more water if you think the beans are in danger of drying out. Remove the cover for the last hour so that the sauce reduces a little to coat the beans thickly. Taste and adjust seasoning. Serve straight away, or leave to cool and reheat when needed – they will taste even better. You will probably have to add a cup or so of water to keep them moist.

Dried Beans

Dried beans are made to keep, and all too often that's precisely what they do. They keep and keep and keep, gathering dust somewhere in the back of my big store cupboard. Lurking are the finest Spanish chickpeas, small and utterly delicious black-eyed beans, big creamy butter beans, speckled botlotti, pale green delicate flageolots, and some mysterious stangers form Italy that have lost thier label. Why, I wonder, don't I cook dried beans and pulses more often? They work so beautifully in stews, eking out meat and sopping up juices, in big peasant soups that line the stomach and stave off icy chills, in roughly mashed purées with herbs and garlic and olive oil, in curries saturated with spices, or just as a side helping, perhaps in a little tomato sauce, replacing potatoes or rice.

Plain white haricot beans, cannellini beans and navy beans are all very similar, and are the ones that I find most useful of all – they make their way in and out of my cupboard with realtive speed, lovely not only for real baked beans, but also for salads, especially Italian style, mixed with tuna, finely diced shallot and tomato, parsley, olive oil and lemon or white wine vinegar.

Most varieties of bean benefit from being soaked overnight (black-eyed beans and lentils cook quickly enough without). Change the water before cooking, and don't add salt or anything acidic, which will prevent the beans from softening. Herbs, cloves of garlic, quartered onions or carrots can all be thrown in the pan to boost flavour, but no tomatoes, because of their sharpness. Bring up to the boil, and then simmer until tender, which may take anything from half an hour to two hours, when beans are either very old or particularly large.

In the past, you were always advised to boil dried pulses, especially kidney beans, for ten minutes before reducing the heat to a simmer to eliminate toxins. Most modern varieties have had these toxins bred out of them, but if you are using beans from obscure corners of the world, it is a good idea to boil them hard for ten minutes, just in case.

Once the beans are just tender but before they start to go mushy, drain and run under the cold tap to halt the cooking process. Now is the time to introduce salt and sharp-tasting ingredients such as vinegar, lemon juice and tomato. With those in the pan, you can carry on cooking the beans for virtually as long as you want to, as the acid-content delays further softening.

Stuffed Roast Potatoes with Feta and Sun-dried Tomatoes

A family supper dish, not haute cuisine. It takes very little to transform a baked potato into a worthy main item on the dinner plate, and one that will fill both vegetarians and omnivores.

• Bake the potato in the usual way until tender. Raise the heat of the oven to 220°C/425°F/Gas 7. Halve the potato and scoop most of the flesh out, leaving two fairly sturdy potato shells. Place these in a lightly greased, shallow ovenproof dish. Mash the potato flesh with the feta and sun-dried tomato, then beat in the melted butter, the egg yolk and enough milk to make a thick but creamy mixture. Season well with pepper and a little salt if it needs it. Whisk the egg white until it forms stiff peaks, then fold into the potato, feta and sun-dried tomato. Pile it into and over the potato shells – you'll have more than enough to fill them, so don't worry when it spills over the sides. Whip them straight into the oven and bake for 20–25 minutes, until handsomely browned on top. Serve hot.

PER PERSON

1 **baking potato**

20g (⅔ oz) **feta cheese**, crumbled

1 piece **sun-dried tomato**, chopped

2 teaspoons melted **butter**

1 **egg**, separated

a splash of **milk**

salt and **pepper**

Queen of Puddings

SERVES 5–6

60g (2 oz) **soft white breadcrumbs**

45g (1½ oz) **butter**

600ml (1 pint) **full-cream milk**

finely grated **zest** of 1 **lemon**

30g (1 oz) **vanilla sugar**, or **caster sugar** with ½ teaspoon **vanilla extract**

4 large **eggs**, separated

2–3 tablespoons **raspberry** or **apricot jam**, warmed

110g (4 oz) **caster sugar** (for the meringue)

Mrs Beeton called it Queen of Bread Puddings, while her latter-day equivalent Prue Leith refers to it as Queen's Pudding. For me, Queen of Puddings is the best and most apt of titles, as this is one of the choicest of our British puddings, with its light airy meringue separated from the golden barely sweetened custard by a thin layer of jam. Simple homely ingredients transformed into something royal and elegant.

Though raspberry jam has become the modern essential, older recipes give apricot as an alternative. Not quite so good, I think, but the tartness is welcome. Brown bread crumbs can be used, but give a somewhat murky tinge to the custard.

• Pre-heat the oven to 180°C/350°F/Gas 4. Place the breadcrumbs in a mixing bowl. Bring the butter, milk, lemon zest and vanilla sugar gently up to the boil. Pour over the breadcrumbs, stir and leave until tepid.

• Beat in the egg yolks and pour into a buttered 1.5-litre (2½-pint) pie dish. Bake for about 25–30 minutes, until the custard mixture is just set, but no more; the exact timing will depend on the size of your dish, so check it towards the end of the cooking period. Let it cool a little. Spread the warmed jam thinly over the surface.

• Set aside a teaspoonful of the caster sugar. Whisk the egg whites until stiff. Sprinkle over half the remaining caster sugar, then whisk again until the sugar dissolves into the mixture to give a glossy soft meringue. Now fold in the remaining caster sugar. Dollop the meringue over the jam, spreading it roughly so that it is heaped up but covers the jam and custard completely. Sprinkle over the reserved caster sugar. Bake for a further 10 minutes or so, until the meringue is honey-brown. Serve hot, warm, or at room temperature, with cream.

Elizabeth Raffald's Orange Custards

SERVES 8–10

zest of ½ **Seville orange**,
  pared off in wide strips
1 tablespoon **brandy** or **Grand
  Marnier**
juice of 1 **Seville orange**
110g (4 oz) **granulated** or
  caster sugar
6 large **egg yolks**
600ml (1 pint) **whipping cream**
candied orange peel

Elizabeth Raffald published her cookery book *The Experienced English Housekeeper* in 1769. During her life, she worked as a housekeeper at Arley Hall in Cheshire, ran several cooked-food shops, a domestic servants' employment agency and two posting-houses in Manchester, and put together the first street and trade directory in Manchester, as well as raising a large family. Quite a woman.

My mother used to make these gorgeous baked orange custards every January, when the Sevilles hit the shops, having adapted the recipe from Elizabeth Raffald's original. Obviously, Mrs Raffald did not have access to a blender, but it's far easier than pounding the zest to a fine paste. What she would have owned was a handsome set of glass custard cups. They are quite easy to find in antique shops, but small ramekins work perfectly well instead.

Out of season, you can substitute a mixture of sweet orange and lemon juice and rind, but it is never quite so good. And really, why would you, for part of the charm of these custards is that you can enjoy them only for a few short weeks of the year.

• Pre-heat the oven to 160°C/325°F/Gas 3. Simmer the orange zest in water for 2 minutes, then drain. Liquidise with the brandy or Grand Marnier, orange juice, sugar and egg yolks. Bring the cream up to the boil, then stir into the liquidised mixture. Have a quick sip, and add more orange juice or sugar if you think it will need it.

• Pour the mixture into 8 or 10 custard cups or small ramekins. Stand them in a pan of hot water and slide into the oven. Cook for 30 minutes or so, until just set. Serve warm, or lightly chilled (the best, I think), with a decorative piece of candied orange peel in the centre of each one.

Seville Oranges

I love making marmalade, but have given up. The trouble is that we almost never eat enough of it. For a couple of years, I would expend a good deal of effort in giving away jars of marmalade in late November and early December, trying to clear out the old stuff ready for the arrival of the new season's Seville oranges in January. Eventually I realised that this was a pointless exercise, but I still look forward to the few brief weeks when sour oranges are back on the market. That's because I've learnt to use them in other ways, entrapping their highly aromatic scent without all the boiling and bubbling of a marmalade session.

So, come January, I begin to look out for them, searching out their rough exterior, often paler in colour than sweet oranges. The skin appears less glossy, too, but this is largely a cosmetic trick – most sweet oranges are buffed up with a coating of wax to make them look more appealing.

The sour, scented juice can be used like lemon juice in many instances – to make a buttery curd (see page 236), or in marinades,

particularly for fish and chicken. Or just cut wedges and squeeze them over a swiftly fried fillet of plaice or sole, or a kebab of grilled prawns, or cubes of monkfish. There's also a clear affinity with leafy vegetables – I like a hint of Seville juice in stir-fried spinach, added right at the end when the leaves are wilting down, and it makes a good dressing for green salad, sourness softened with a touch of honey, or sugar, and plenty of fruity olive oil.

Coeurs à la Crème with Pineapple Compote

Coeurs à la crème are divinely delicate mounds of ivory richness that demand to be served with juicy, sweet fresh fruit, like pineapple or mango in winter, raspberries or strawberries in the summer. They take their name from the heart-shape porcelain moulds they are traditionally made in. You can buy these moulds (perforated so the whey can drip out) from smart kitchen shops, but failing that, you can use clean yoghurt pots, holes pierced in the bottom with a hot skewer.

Note that the coeurs à la crème must be started the day before eating, so that they have time to drain properly. As for the butter muslin, it is cheaper to buy from a fabric shop than from a cookware shop.

SERVES 4

FOR THE COEURS À LA CRÈME:

175g (6 oz) **cream cheese**
150g (5 oz) **crème fraîche**
110g (4 oz) **Greek yoghurt**
30g (1 oz) **caster sugar**
½ teaspoon **vanilla extract**
2 **egg whites**

FOR THE PINEAPPLE COMPOTE:

1 small **pineapple**
2 large **passion fruit**
icing sugar

• Line 4 coeur à la crème moulds, or 1 larger pierced mould, with a layer of butter muslin (or, at a pinch, a new J-cloth that has been rinsed out several times in boiling water). Beat the cream cheese with the crème fraîche and yoghurt until smooth. Beat in the sugar and vanilla extract. Whisk the egg whites until they form stiff peaks, and then fold into the cream mixture. Divide the mixture between the moulds and smooth down lightly. Flip the dangling edges of the muslin over the mixture, then sit them on a rack in a shallow dish and transfer to the fridge. Leave overnight.

• Next day, not too long before you sit down to eat, peel the pineapple and remove the core. Slice thinly, and place in a bowl, with the pulp from the passion fruit (break it up a bit so that it doesn't sit in large unglamorous clumps) and a dusting of icing sugar. Turn gently to mix, then leave to macerate until ready to eat.

• When you are ready for pudding, take the coeurs à la crème out of the fridge, uncover and turn out on to plates, removing the muslin. Spoon some of the pineapple and passion fruit and the juices around the coeurs, and enjoy.

Coconut Meringues with Lemon Curd

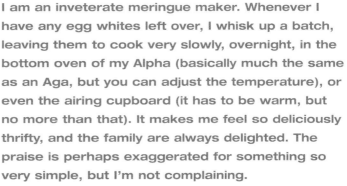

MAKE 8–9

2 **egg whites**

85g (3 oz) **caster sugar**

30g (1 oz) **light muscovado sugar**

45g (1½ oz) unsweetened **desiccated coconut**

3 tablespoons **lemon curd** (see page 236)

2–3 tablespoons **clotted** or **whipped cream** (optional)

I am an inveterate meringue maker. Whenever I have any egg whites left over, I whisk up a batch, leaving them to cook very slowly, overnight, in the bottom oven of my Alpha (basically much the same as an Aga, but you can adjust the temperature), or even the airing cupboard (it has to be warm, but no more than that). It makes me feel so deliciously thrifty, and the family are always delighted. The praise is perhaps exaggerated for something so very simple, but I'm not complaining.

Every now and then I play with the basic recipe, and these coconut meringues have proved something of a success. Coconut and lemon curd (as long as it is real lemon curd, not some ghastly commercial fake) go very well together. I like a touch of cream in there too, but some might consider this overindulgent.

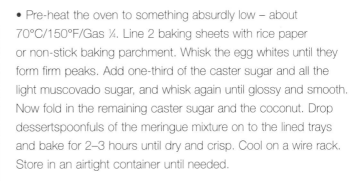

• Pre-heat the oven to something absurdly low – about 70°C/150°F/Gas ¼. Line 2 baking sheets with rice paper or non-stick baking parchment. Whisk the egg whites until they form firm peaks. Add one-third of the caster sugar and all the light muscovado sugar, and whisk again until glossy and smooth. Now fold in the remaining caster sugar and the coconut. Drop dessertspoonfuls of the meringue mixture on to the lined trays and bake for 2–3 hours until dry and crisp. Cool on a wire rack. Store in an airtight container until needed.

• To serve, spread the flat side of half the meringues with the lemon curd, the other with the cream, then sandwich together. Eat fairly soon after, before the meringues soften.

Steamed Apple, Orange and Ginger Suet Pudding

I still haven't decided whether this pudding is better made with cooking apples or eating apples – I probably need to try it out both ways a few more times before I can be sure... Either way, it is the long, slow, moist cooking that melds the flavours together in an utterly heavenly manner, ready to ooze out as the suet crust is cut into.

SERVES 4–6

FOR THE SUET CRUST:
220g (8 oz) **self-raising flour**
pinch of **salt**
110g (4 oz) **suet**
about 150–250ml (5–8 fl oz)
   milk and **water** mixed
a little **butter** for greasing the
   bowl

FOR THE FILLING:
about 675g (1 lb 7 oz) **eating** or
   cooking apples, peeled,
   cored and cut into chunks
finely grated **juice** and **zest** of
   1 **orange**
1 knob **preserved stem
   ginger**, finely chopped
175–220g (6–8 oz) **caster** or
   demerara sugar

• To make the crust, sift the flour with the salt and mix with the suet. Add enough milk and water to make a soft but not sticky dough. Grease the inside of a 1.5-litre (2½-pint) pudding basin.

• Roll the pastry out on a floured work surface to give a circle large enough to line the basin. Cut out about a quarter of it and set aside to make the lid. Lower the rest of the pastry into the basin, pinch the cut sides together, and press the pastry gently into place so that the basin is completely lined.

• Mix the filling ingredients together, then pile into the lined basin. Roll out the remaining pastry to form a circle large enough to cover the basin. Lay it over the top and pinch the edges together all round to seal the filling right in.

• Take a sheet of foil and make a pleat down the centre. Lay it over the basin and tie firmly into place with a long piece of string. Take one of the trailing ends over the top of the dish, slide it under the string on the other side of the bowl from the knot, and then tie the two ends together loosely so that you have a handle.

• Stand the pudding in a close-fitting saucepan, and pour in enough boiling water to come about halfway up the sides. Place on the heat and adjust the temperature so that it boils gently. Cover with the lid (or if necessary a dome of foil), and leave to bubble away happily for some 2 hours or so. Check regularly and top up the water level with more boiling water, as needed.

• To serve, remove string and foil and carefully run a knife around the edge to loosen, then invert on to a shallow serving dish. Serve at once, with cream or custard. Mmmm…

Steamed suet puddings are among Britain's most important contributions to world harmony. I make them occasionally for French friends who all laugh heartily at the concept, until they come to the actual tasting. Only then do they begin to understand what an amazingly wonderful creation the steamed pud is.

Preserved Stem Ginger

The ginger jar lived on a high shelf at the back of the larder. I can see it still. Curving up from a base just wide enough to keep it stable, white china, swirled with lines of blue in intricate Chinese patterns, covered with an upturned cup of a lid. It was not exactly off limits, but it was something special, to be brought out on Occasions – when friends came to stay, birthdays, a new book contract for my mother or father, perhaps. On these special days, the dumb waiter would be placed in the centre of the table, weighed down with small bowls of choice sweetmeats to be picked at for a lazy pudding. The sticky spheres of ginger in a puddle of gingery syrup would be among them, decanted into a small bowl.

The ginger jar came out of the larder again whenever my mother made Grasmere gingerbread, more of a biscuit than a cake. The preserved stem ginger from the jar went into the best bit of all, the ginger butter icing that she made to sandwich the two slabs of gingerbread together. It featured again in the ginger ice cream that she made – another memorable pudding that takes me instantly back to the round table we ate at every day.

I have no idea what became of that ginger jar. I would have liked to claim it, to perpetuate the small island of homely pleasure. Perhaps it broke sometime after I left home, but I never thought to ask until it was too late. But if I can't have the jar, I can still have the ginger itself, and that, for me, is something special. Excellent in all manner of sweet dishes, the ginger syrup also has its uses in savoury foods. It works wonders in marinades, for instance, adding a sticky, whiskery slurp of ginger, or as a glaze on gammon. I've used it, too, with stir-fried prawns, where it is a more surprising ally, as long as it is used in restrained quantity.

It is the round knobs of ginger themselves, though, that are the real stars. In memory of my mother, I might stir them, chopped, into three-quarters frozen vanilla ice cream, or add them to fruit crumbles and pies. In Sticky Gingerbread (see page 234) they introduce a nugget of a new texture, or try mixing them into shortbread dough for crumbly ginger shortbread. I like them, too, sliced thinly, in moderation, in fruit salads, with a little of their syrup added to ginger things up. At this time of year, which is when the warmth of ginger comes into its own, I partner ginger with thinly sliced orange, or with imported exotics such as mango or lychees.

One final practical tip, which you may well have worked out for yourselves if you are partial to preserved stem ginger. Hoick the spheres of ginger out of their glass jar with a fork. To chop them, spear each knob on the tines of the fork. Begin by slicing the ginger through the gaps between the tines, and follow by slicing across at right angles, so that the whole lot falls into strips without you ever getting your hands sticky. Then all you need is a few rough cuts across the mass to reduce it to small cubes.

Rhubarb and Apple Crumble

The bright pink of forced rhubarb is irresistible, and livens up the last of the cooking apples that have survived ramshackle storage in our garage. Together they make a good filling for a crumble.

SERVES 6 (UNLESS YOU ARE ALL VERY GREEDY)

450g (1 lb) **forced rhubarb**, or later on, **garden rhubarb**, shorn of leaves, trimmed and cut into 2.5cm (1 in) lengths

450g (1 lb) **cooking apples**, peeled, cored and cut into chunks

150g (5 oz) **light muscovado sugar**

1 teaspoon **ground cinnamon**

FOR THE CRUMBLE:

60g (2 oz) **rolled oats**

175g (6 oz) **plain flour**

110g (4 oz) **unsalted butter**

110g (4 oz) **demerara sugar**

• Pre-heat the oven to 200°C/400°F/Gas 6. To make the crumble topping, mix the oats and flour, and rub in the butter until you have a pile of small crumbs. Stir in the sugar.

• Mix the rhubarb and apples in a pie dish and dredge with the light muscovado sugar, then sprinkle with cinnamon. Sprinkle the crumble mixture evenly and thickly over the top. Bake for about 30 minutes, or a little longer if necessary, until the top is golden brown, with the juice bubbling up a little round the sides. Serve hot or warm, with cream or custard or even some gorgeous white chocolate ice cream to melt and ooze into the hot juices.

Vanilla Pain Perdu with Quince Jelly

SERVES 4

4 thick slices of stale **bread**, crusts removed

2 **eggs**

300ml (½ pint) **milk**

1 tablespoon **caster sugar**

½ teaspoon **vanilla extract**

butter and **oil** for frying

quince jelly, to serve

Pain perdu is another name for sweetened French toast, a quick and economic kitchen pudding that can be made at the drop of a hat as long as you have some old bread, eggs, sugar and milk. What makes it so very good is the sexy combination of crisp golden exterior with the almost jellied, soft interior. I like to add a shot of vanilla extract to the soaking mixture, and crown the toast with a dollop of quince jelly.

The one thing to watch is that you soak the bread long enough to moisten it well, but not so long that it collapses. The staler the bread, the longer it will need in its milk and egg bath. Sliced white commercial bread does not make good pain perdu – far too slimy.

• Cut the slices of bread in half. Whisk the eggs with the milk, caster sugar and vanilla extract in a shallow dish. Heat a knob of butter and a splash of oil (to reduce the chance of burning the butter) until the butter foams. Meanwhile, soak the first piece of bread in the egg mixture, turning it over and lifting it out when it is well soaked, but before it becomes soggy enough to fall apart. Fry over a moderate heat until golden brown on both sides. Do the same with the rest of the bread, without ever overcrowding the pan.

• Lift the cooked pain perdu on to warm plates and top each piece with a spoonful of quince jelly.

Sticky Gingerbread

MAKES ENOUGH FOR AROUND 8–10 PEOPLE

280g (10 oz) **plain flour**

1 teaspoon **bicarbonate of soda**

1 tablespoon **ground ginger**

1 teaspoon **ground cinnamon**

¼ teaspoon **salt**

170g (6 oz) **unsalted butter**, softened

90g (3 oz) **light muscovado sugar**

220g (8 oz) **golden syrup**

1 **egg**

200ml (7 fl oz) **milk**

4 knobs **preserved stem ginger**, chopped

A strange longing came over me recently – I yearned for a square of gingerbread, moist and sticky and tingling with real ginger. I've tried out several recipes, but this is the best yet, with its underlying hint of cinnamon, and lots of small nuggets of preserved stem ginger (the sort that comes in syrup) studded through it.

It comes out of the oven with a fluffy texture that is very appealing, especially while it is still slightly warm, but for a seriously sticky gingerbread, wrap the slab in greaseproof paper and foil, and stash away in an airtight tin for a couple of days to mature. Either way, it is particularly nice eaten with a slice of Caerphilly or Lancashire cheese, or spread with salted butter.

• Pre-heat the oven to 180°C/350°F/Gas 4. Line the base of a 20-cm (8-in) square cake tin with non-stick baking parchment, and butter the sides. Sift the flour with the bicarbonate of soda, ginger, cinnamon and salt. Cream the butter with the sugar until light and fluffy. Now beat in the golden syrup, then a heaped tablespoonful of the flour mixture followed by the egg. Beat in the remaining flour, followed by the milk to form a smooth batter. Stir in the stem ginger and scrape into the prepared tin. Bake for about 40–45 minutes until firm to the touch. Test by inserting a skewer deep into the centre. If it comes out clean then it is done. Let the gingerbread cool in the tin for 5–10 minutes, then turn out on to a wire rack and leave to cool.

Murrambidgee Cake

**MAKES 1 CAKE,
ENOUGH FOR
12 PEOPLE**

200g (7 oz) whole shelled
  Brazil nuts

150g (5 oz) **walnut halves**

250g (9 oz) stoned, halved
  dates

175g (6 oz) **glacé cherries**

100g (3½ oz) **seedless raisins**

100g (3½ oz) chopped **candied
  peel**

finely grated **zest** of 1 **lemon**

100g (3½ oz) **flour**

½ teaspoon each **baking
  powder** and **salt**

150g (5 oz) **caster sugar**

3 large **eggs**

1 teaspoon pure **vanilla extract**

to finish: **brandy**, **rum** or other
  spirit or liqueur

I don't care for Christmas cake. I don't hate it either, but I really wouldn't mind if I never tasted one again. As a result I've never cooked one, either. Instead, we make this Murrambidgee cake, which is nothing more than a big mass of mixed whole glacé fruits and nuts, glued together with the minimum of batter. Far nicer, if you ask me.

Some years I've made it well in advance, feeding it with brandy every few days for a month or more, but we have now all decided that we prefer to eat it relatively freshly baked, say within a week or two, with only the one initial benediction with booze.

It's not the kind of cake that will take kindly to icing, so forget marzipan, snowmen and reindeer. If you want to doll it up, then glue on more whole candied fruit and nuts to cover the top, with a boiled apricot-jam glaze.

• Line a 450-g (1-lb) loaf tin with non-stick baking parchment or buttered greaseproof paper. Pre-heat the oven to 150°C/300°F/ Gas 2.

• Mix the nuts, fruit, candied peel and zest. Sift the dry ingredients together and add to the fruit and nuts. Beat the eggs and vanilla together and stir thoroughly into the rest of the ingredients. Put into the tin, smoothing the top down.

• Bake for 1½–2 hours, protecting the top with paper if it browns too fast. Test with a skewer – if it comes out dry, then the cake is done. Leave to cool for 10 minutes in the tin, then turn on to a clean cloth. Pierce several holes in the cake and pour in the alcohol of your choice. Wrap in greaseproof paper, then enclose in clingfilm or foil and store in an airtight tin.

• Either start slicing and eating it straight away, or feed with a little more alcohol and rewrap every three or four days for up to 2 months.

Lemon or Seville Orange Curd

MAKES AROUND 1.3KG (3 LB)

9–12 large **lemons** or **Seville oranges**

550g (1¼ lb) **caster sugar**

220g (8 oz) **unsalted butter**, diced

5 large **eggs**

You can buy real lemon curd, made with nothing more than lemon, sugar, butter and eggs, but you have to tread carefully. All too often, jars of fake, third-rate, so-called lemon curd are dressed up with labels carefully designed to make you think you are buying some lovely bit of old-fashioned reality, when what you are actually purchasing is a horrible mixture of margarine, lemon oil, flavourings, stabilisers and thickeners.

Making your own lemon curd is one way to guarantee that you can spread this heavenly manna in its full glory on your morning toast, or between the layers of a light, home-baked Victoria sponge.

Seville oranges, with their unique aromatic tartness, also make a good curd with a pleasing hint of bitterness that cuts the richness.

• Grate the zest of half the lemons or oranges. One at a time, squeeze the juice and strain it into a measuring jug until you have 300ml (½ pint). Pour into a heatproof bowl and add the finely grated zest, the sugar and butter. Set over a pan of gently simmering water, making sure that the base of the bowl doesn't dip right down into the water. Stir until the butter has melted and the sugar has dissolved.

• Beat the eggs together, then strain through a sieve into the warm juice, sugar and butter mixture. Stir constantly, still over the pan of water, until the mixture has thickened enough to coat the back of a spoon. Allow plenty of time for this (say 20–25 minutes) and make sure that the curds never heat up to anything approaching boiling point. If the water in the saucepan is boiling too fast, this could happen, so double-check that it is just simmering quietly.

• Once the mixture has thickened, lift the bowl out of the pan, and pour the curd into warm sterilised jars. Seal tightly, label and leave to cool. Store in the fridge.

Look out for unwaxed lemons, or be sure to scrub them under warm water before grating. Seville oranges are rarely waxed, so just rinse briefly before using. To extract the maximum quantity of juice from each fruit, pop it in the microwave for 20–30 seconds, and/or roll it around on the work surface, pressing down firmly with the palm of your hand.

Orangines

MAKES AROUND 40

60g (2 oz) blanched **whole almonds**

60g (2 oz) **candied orange peel**, roughly chopped

finely grated **zest** of 1 **orange**

45g (1½ oz) **flour**

60g (2 oz) unsalted or lightly salted **butter**

60g (2 oz) **caster sugar**

1 tablespoon **milk**

Over the years, these crisp scented biscuits have made their way into the handful of biscuit recipes that I make on a regular basis, mostly to go with puddings, or to give as presents. I first came across the recipe back in the late 1980s, when I worked with chef Joyce Molyneux on a book of her recipes from the Carved Angel Restaurant in Dartmouth. The recipe goes back at least another thirty years, to the Constance Spry's *Cookery Book*, first published in 1956. Joyce added the orange zest to the original and did away with the carmine colouring, and I can't remember now whether it was she or I who decided you could do practically all the work in the processor.

The end result is a biscuit that is spectacularly easy to make, considering how very special it is. What does make a difference, though, is using high-quality candied orange peel. The chilled 'log' of biscuit dough will keep in the fridge for five or more days, which is very handy over holiday periods, as you can slice off what you need at a moment's notice.

• Process the almonds and the peel together until finely chopped. Add the remaining ingredients and pulse-process to a smooth dough. Roll into a log about 2.5–4cm (1–1½ in) wide, wrap in clingfilm or silver foil and chill for at least 30 minutes.

• Pre-heat the oven to 160°C/325°F/Gas 3. Line several baking trays with non-stick baking parchment. Slice the log of dough as thinly as you can, giving it a quarter turn after each slice, so that it doesn't squish out of shape. Arrange the slices on the baking trays, leaving a decent gap between them as they will spread a little. Bake for 10–15 minutes, checking occasionally, until lightly browned around the edges. Leave them on the tray for a couple of minutes to set, then transfer to a wire rack to cool.

Candied Peel

The very best candied peel I've ever tasted came from Amalfi just below Naples. I'll be even more specific – it came from the Pasticceria Pansa, close by the steps that lead from the main piazza up to the cathedral. They make it themselves, from the skin of oranges and lemons form the orchards that line the terraced hills all along the coast. The peel comes straight from the tree to the shop, to begin the slow process of candying, which takes days of boiling up in sugar syrup and then leaving it to cool. It is not something to be hurried, or at least, not if you want to end up with candied peel to die for. What eventually emerges from these vats of sugar are supple pieces of sugar-crusted, sugar-sodden peel, with all the heavenly aromatic zest of the fresh fruit, ripened in the warm autumnal sun of the south of Italy. Perfection.

I'm not suggesting that you should trek all the way to Amalfi every time you need 60g of candied peel for a recipe, but you don't have to resort to those nasty little tubs of ready-chopped candied peel that are sold in every supermarket either. The little cubes inside don't come close to the real thing, lacking all the genuine citrus flavour that good candied peel should have. Instead, take yourself off to a good deli, especially an Italian one, and ask if they sell whole candied peel. If they don't, berate them kindly and ask them to order some in – after all, it keeps for ages. That's half the point.

Back at home, sharpen your best knife and chop your peel yourself. Assuming it has been stored well, it will be supple but not soft, demanding a mite of pressure from the blade, but not a heavy-handed approach. Any that you don't use immediately should be wrapped tightly in clingfilm and kept in an airtight box in the cupboard until next needed.

If your airtight box should prove not to be entirely airtight, then your peel will harden. Try spraying it lightly with water, then wrapping in clingfilm again and microwaving for a few seconds on medium power. That should soften it up again…

Christmas Tree Biscuits

I find it easiest to make and bake the biscuits myself, then put them, with all the decorative bits and bobs, on the table so that the children can let rip their creative talents.

MAKES A LOT

150g (5 oz) **golden syrup**

110g (4 oz) **golden caster sugar**

1 teaspoon **ground cinnamon**

1 teaspoon **vanilla extract**

¼ teaspoon **bicarbonate of soda**

110g (4 oz) softened **unsalted butter**

1 large **egg**

450g (1 lb) **plain flour**

TO DECORATE:

royal icing (see below)

icing writing pens

silver balls and other **edible decorations**

• Pre-heat the oven to 150°C/300°F/Gas 2. Put the syrup, sugar, cinnamon and vanilla into a heavy saucepan. Stir over a low heat until the sugar has completely dissolved, then bring up to the boil. Now stir in the bicarbonate of soda. It will become foamy and very thick – draw the pan off the heat.

• Immediately pour the mixture on to the butter in a large bowl and stir until it has all dissolved. Now beat in the egg, and then add the flour in four or five batches, beating it in well each time, until you have a thick soft dough. Chill for at least an hour before using. Roll the dough out on a well floured surface to a thickness of a £1 coin, and then stamp out stars, diamonds, reindeers, or whatever other shapes you fancy. Pierce a hole in each one to take the ribbon or thread, making it a little larger than you need, as the dough will spread slightly as it cooks. Bake on baking sheets lined with non-stick baking parchment for about 20 minutes until dry as a bone.

• Cool on wire racks, then decorate with royal icing if you fancy, or just simply with icing writing pens and colourful baubles. Leave to dry, then thread ribbon or thread or wool through the hole and knot so that the biscuits can be hung from the tree.

TO MAKE ROYAL ICING Beat 1 egg white lightly, then add enough icing sugar (roughly 220g/8 oz) to make a thick icing.

Yeast

Given the choice, I'd rather use fresh yeast for baking bread, but it is becoming increasingly difficult to buy. It works swiftly and satisfyingly, and produces a lighter crumb, with a less intrusive yeasty taste. Independent bakers may sell it, but many are understandably reluctant to part with yeast when they would far rather you bought their bread. Some delis stock it with lesser qualms, and at least one of the big supermarkets used to sell it from their bakery section, but only to those who asked, since it was rarely displayed on the shelves.

You might have thought that the proliferation of bread-making machines would encourage retailers to promote the sales of fresh yeast, but no. Bread-makers are all about convenience and speed of use. Fresh yeast? No, no – far too much fiddling about before you add it to the other ingredients, and then it starts to work straight away! The point of the bread-maker is minimal involvement – tip the ingredients in, set the dial, and then, lo and behold, you have hot bread whenever you want it. Good in theory, but I've yet to taste bread from a bread-maker that can compare with real home-made bread.

When I can't get fresh yeast easily, I make do with instant yeast, often sold as easy-bake or easy-blend yeast, which makes life easy without doing away with genuine involvement. This is just dried yeast, with extra-small granules that dissolve virtually the second they meet water, ready to start working right away. They are mixed straight into the flour, and come alive with cold water, rather than begging for warmth. Since I suspect that most people are in the same position, I use this in my recipes for bread, rather than fresh yeast.

However, if you do have access to a ready supply of fresh yeast, this is how to use it:

Replace each sachet of easy-bake yeast with 15g (½ oz) fresh yeast. Take a cupful of warm water, add a tablespoonful of sugar or honey, and crumble in the yeast. Stir until most of it has dissolved, then leave the bowl in a warm place for about 10 minutes until the surface is all of a froth. Just for fun, hold the palm of your hand just above the surface to feel the spray of droplets of liquid as the yeast gets to work. Now mix this in with the warmed flour, salt and any other ingredients, adding just enough water to make a soft but not sticky dough. And then carry on just as you would with dried yeast.

Incidentally, it is worth buying more fresh yeast than you can use immediately, as yeast freezes well for a couple of months. Cut it into suitably sized pieces, wrap well in clingfilm and freeze in a bag, ready to be used as needed.

Potato, Sunflower Seed and Sage Bread

You wouldn't instantly know that there was potato in this bread – you can't see it or taste it – but it gives the loaf a particularly addictive texture and moistness. Use potatoes that have been baked or microwaved in their skins, so that they are not sodden with water.

The waft of sage means that the bread is excellent with any hard British cheese, but for a change you could try replacing it with finely chopped fresh rosemary, thyme or dill.

MAKES 1 ENTICING LOAF

150g (5 oz) **cooked potato** (after discarding skin)

2 tablespoons **extra virgin olive oil**

400g (14 oz) **strong white flour**

100g (3½ oz) **strong wholemeal flour**

1 sachet (7g) **easy-blend yeast**

2 teaspoons **salt**

2 tablespoons chopped fresh **sage**

60g (2 oz) **sunflower seeds**

• Mash the potato with the oil in a large bowl. Add the flours, yeast, salt and sage. Work in enough water to make a soft but not sticky dough. Now knead the dough, flouring occasionally with extra flour if necessary, until smooth as a baby's bottom and just as bouncy. Shape into a ball.

• Oil a bowl with a little extra olive oil, and turn the dough into it. Roll it around so that it is coated in oil, then cover with a damp tea towel and leave in a warm place to rise until doubled in size.

• Knock back the dough, knead again briefly, working in the sunflower seeds. Shape into a handsome round loaf. Place on a baking sheet generously dusted with flour. Leave for another hour or so, until doubled in size. Pre-heat the oven to 220°C/425°F/Gas 7 and place a baking tray in it to heat through. Now place the baking sheet with the loaf on it directly on the hot one in the oven. Quickly splash a quarter of a glass of water on the floor of the oven to create a blast of steam. Close the door and leave for 10 minutes, before reducing the heat to 190°C/375°F/Gas 5. Bake for a further 30 minutes, until beautifully browned. It is done when the loaf sounds hollow when it is tapped on its base.

• Cool on a wire rack, before slicing.